JOHN MOSCHOS' *SPIRIT*

John Moschos' perennially popular Spiritual Meadow *has received a worthy and thorough examination in this excellent study written by Brenda Llewellyn Ihssen. She has taken up the daunting task of cutting a path through Moschos' rich text, inviting readers to pause and reflect on some of the great themes that sprout up along the way: poverty and almsgiving, health and sickness, death and dignified dying. Especially noteworthy are her insights on how Moschos elaborates the reality of spiritual authority and where it resides. While the* Spiritual Meadow *has long been valued for its information about early Christian monasticism, Llewellyn Ihssen draws attention to the broader social context reflected in its numerous anecdotes and offers practical guidance on how to read those anecdotes for spiritual profit and delight.*
    T. Allan Smith, Pontifical Institute of Mediaeval Studies, Canada

Wandering with John Moschos and Sophronios through the cultural and religious landscapes of Eastern Christian monasticism at the end of antiquity, Llewellyn Ihssen uncovers a monastic author who both documents and comments on his world. Ascetic discipline provides not only knowledge of the self but a vantage point from which to observe and to critique inequality and poverty, illness and health care, and to interpret the mortality that defines the human condition. Moschos emerges as much a social critic as a hagiographer.
    Derek Krueger, University of North Carolina at Greensboro, USA

John Moschos' *Spiritual Meadow* is one of the most important sources for late sixth-early seventh century Palestinian, Syrian and Egyptian monasticism. This undisputedly invaluable collection of beneficial tales provides contemporary society with a fuller picture of an imperfect social history of this period: it is a rich source for understanding not only the piety of the monk but also the poor farmer. Brenda Llewellyn Ihssen fills a lacuna in classical monastic secondary literature by highlighting Moschos' unique contribution to the way in which a fertile Christian theology informed the ethics of not only those serving at the altar but also those being served.

Introducing appropriate historical and theological background to the tales, Llewellyn Ihssen demonstrates how Moschos' tales addresses issues of the autonomy of individual ascetics and lay persons in relationship with authority figures. Economic practices, health care, death and burials of lay persons and ascetics are examined for the theology and history that they obscure and reveal. Whilst teaching us about the complicated relationships between personal agency and divine intercession, Moschos' tales can also be seen to reveal liminal boundaries we know existed between the secular and the religious.

John Moschos' *Spiritual Meadow*
Authority and Autonomy at the End of the Antique World

BRENDA LLEWELLYN IHSSEN
Pacific Lutheran University, Washington, USA

LONDON AND NEW YORK

First published 2014 by Ashgate Publishing

Published 2016 by Routledge
2 Park Square, Milton Park, Abingdon, Oxon OX14 4RN
605 Third Avenue, New York, NY 10017

First issued in paperback 2021

Routledge is an imprint of the Taylor & Francis Group, an informa business

Copyright © 2014 Brenda Llewellyn Ihssen

Brenda Llewellyn Ihssen has asserted her right under the Copyright, Designs and Patents Act, 1988, to be identified as the author of this work.

All rights reserved. No part of this book may be reprinted or reproduced or utilised in any form or by any electronic, mechanical, or other means, now known or hereafter invented, including photocopying and recording, or in any information storage or retrieval system, without permission in writing from the publishers.

Notice:
Product or corporate names may be trademarks or registered trademarks, and are used only for identification and explanation without intent to infringe.

Publisher's Note
The publisher has gone to great lengths to ensure the quality of this reprint but points out that some imperfections in the original copies may be apparent.

British Library Cataloguing in Publication Data
A catalogue record for this book is available from the British Library

The Library of Congress has cataloged the printed edition as follows:
Ihssen, Brenda Llewellyn.
 John Moschos' spiritual meadow / by Brenda Llewellyn Ihssen.
    pages cm
 Includes bibliographical references and index.
 ISBN 978-1-4094-3516-7 (hardcover)
1. Moschus, John, approximately 550-619. Pratum spirituale. 2. Monastic and religious life–History–Early church, ca. 30-600. 3. Asceticism–Orthodox Eastern Church. I. Title.
 BX385.A1I447 2014
 271.009'021–dc23

2013021095

ISBN 13: 978-1-03-209902-6 (pbk)
ISBN 13: 978-1-4094-3516-7 (hbk)

Contents

Foreword   *vii*
Preface   *ix*
Acknowledgements   *xi*
List of Abbreviations   *xiii*

Introduction   1

1   Monks in *The Meadow*: Proving and Improving the Ascetic Program   19
     Introduction   19
     "In every sphere, foreign": Proving the Ascetic Program   24
     "God's servants, working together": Improving the Ascetic Program   35

2   Money in *The Meadow*: Coin, Cost and Conversion   45
     Introduction   45
     Christ in the Suffering Poor   47
     Poverty for the Sake of Salvation   55
     Almsgiving: Who Gets to Give?   62

3   Medical Management in *The Meadow*: Curing, Enduring and Identity Formation   71
     Introduction   71
     A Theology of Health and Healing   73
     Medical Management in Early Medieval Byzantium: Curing   84
     Medical Management in Early Medieval Byzantium: Enduring   97

4   Mortality in *The Meadow*: Dying, Death and Predetermination   105
     Introduction   105
     Predetermination: Forewarned is Forearmed   107
     Conflict and the Corpse   117
     A "Middle Way" in *The Meadow*: Night of the Living Dead   124

Conclusion   137

Bibliography   *145*
Index   *175*

Foreword

John Moschos' *Spiritual Meadow* (*PS*) is probably the best known and the most neglected of the major documents describing the early centuries of Christian monachism. The large quantity of surviving manuscripts and the number of modern translations attest to its popularity; the rather slender secondary literature and the absence of anything resembling a definitive text to its neglect. And not all those who have paid any attention to it have taken Moschos' collection of monastic lore seriously, at least not so seriously as they do the other two *fin de siècle* collections: the tales associated with Anastasius the Sinaïte and the *Lives* of Cyril of Scythopolis. This is partly because the proportion of tales to sayings in *PS* is far higher than in other collections of monastic lore, a fact that no doubt accounts for the popularity of the work every bit as much as it provides ammunition for its detractors. On the other hand it is precisely the anecdotal element that provides such a happy hunting ground for those seeking that rarest of commodities: the wherewithal to write a social history at the end of the antique world. Unfortunately such writers do not always remember that John was writing to *inspire*, not to record; hence the words he used can bear no more weight than do, say, the words of Jesus in the parables.

The words John actually wrote remain a grave problem as nobody has yet succeeded in identifying a reliable text in the mass of surviving manuscript material; and maybe nobody ever will. It may be the fate of the *Urtext* of works that entered the public domain almost at birth and then had to take their chances on the by no means tranquil sea of simultaneous oral and written transmission to be lost forever. In such cases the best one can do is to produce an edition of what appears to the best recension. Professor Bernard Flusin and Mme Marina Flusin are now embarking on such a project; their intention is to make an edition of what is known as Recension φ of *PS*, generally agreed to be the best recension, the one known to us through the invaluable Latin translation (printed in *PG* 86) by "Fra Ambrogio," the Italian humanist Ambrogio Traversari, *ca* 1386–1439.

This of course is very good news for all who concern themselves with John's sweet *Meadow* but even better news is that although there is still no definitive text on which to proceed, Dr Llewellyn Ihssen has undertaken a serious study of what John had to say and, more to the point, why he felt compelled to say (or, more correctly, to write) it. One is always a little puzzled as to *why* John Moschos and the mysterious sophist Sophronius (possibly the future patriarch of Jerusalem) were travelling around, so far and for so many years. They were (on the one hand) seriously in default since the burden of monastic teaching was clearly that the monk should stay in his cell and never go far from it. On the other hand they can hardly be said to have been *perigrini* in the sense of subjecting themselves to voluntary exile [*xeniteia*] because they stayed long periods at various places and seem generally to have been well received. We may never know exactly how they fitted into the complex pattern of early monachism, but we can and must be grateful for their travels and for John's ability to recognize a good story when he heard one. Now too we can be grateful to Dr Llewellyn Ihssen for her careful, insightful and very rewarding study of what he probably wrote. Let me say of her chapters what John says of meadows in spring: "They display to the beholder a rich diversity of flowers which arrests him with its charm, for it brings delight to the eyes and perfume to the nostrils." That may be a little over-stated, but the reader's delight in and profit from this book are guaranteed.

John Wortley

Preface

In 1993, late in the spring, I was dropped off at the Graduate Theological Union bookstore in Berkeley, California. I had taken the 4:10 pm "Martin Looper" bus down from the Pacific Lutheran Theological Seminary where I was a student, and I was dawdling before I walked down to the transit station. From there I would take the train to Fremont, and then drive the remainder of the way to San Jose, where I lived. It was a long process that I did not enjoy, and I paused in the bookstore, browsing the stacks. I was always drawn in the bookstore to a small shelf that never held more than 15 books and was affixed with a label that constantly peeled up at the sides: "Eastern Christianity." All of the books on this shelf had cover art that usually included an icon of some sort, or a picture of the desert. My religious background was Lutheran and I grew up in the Pacific Northwest corner of the United States; both religious art and deserts were foreign to me, so naturally I was drawn to learn about each of them. Further, each book on the shelf—but one—employed dark hues in the cover art, no doubt to reflect the seriousness of the theology contained within. But that day I focused on the one book whose cover sported neither icon nor desert, or the reliable dark hue. The pretty pastel colors along the spine of John Wortley's translation of Moschos' *Spiritual Meadow* stood in sharp contrast to the official dark tones. I pulled it from the shelf, flipped it open and read the following:

> When we came to the Thebaïd one of the elders told us that there was an elder of great repute living outside the city of Antinoë, one who had kept his cell for about seventy years. He had ten disciples but one of them was very careless so far as his own soul was concerned. The elder often besought and entreated him, saying: "Brother, pay attention to your own soul, for death awaits you and the road to punishment." The brother always disregarded the elder, refusing to accept what was said by him. Well, after a time, death carried the brother off and the elder was deeply troubled on his account, knowing that he had left this world sadly lacking in faith and devotion. The elder fell to his prayers and said: "Lord Jesus Christ, our true God, reveal to me the state of the brother's soul." He went into a trance and saw a river of fire with a multitude [of people] in the fire itself. Right in the middle was the brother, submerged up to his neck. The elder said to him: "Was it not because of this retribution that I called on you to look after your own soul my child?" The brother answered and said to the elder: "I thank God, father, that there is relief for my head. Thanks to your prayers I am standing on the head of a bishop."

At first I thought I had read it wrong. I cannot possibly be reading something funny, I thought, not from this shelf. So I read that last line again, and then threw back my head and laughed out loud, disrupting the peace and solemnity of a theology bookstore. To be clear, John Moschos' *Pratum Spirituale*, or *Spiritual Meadow*, is not a collection of monastic comedy. But humor embedded within a deeply Chalcedonian monastic text was a fascinating discovery to me, and speaking as someone who has far too many times been irreverent when gravity was more appropriate, finding this tale was like discovering a gold-bearing vein.

Would it not be wonderful if, 20 years later, I had a more dignified motive for wanting to write this book beyond the fact that I truly enjoy reading it? Beyond pure enjoyment, however, the academic rationale for this manuscript is evident: in tales that depict life at the end of the antique world one gains insight not only into theologies and philosophies that permeated Palestine and Sinai, but also the economies, behaviors, motivations, diseases, fears and, yes, even the wit of early Byzantine monastics and laity. Were not all these other factors present, though, could we not agree that wit is enough?

Brenda Llewellyn Ihssen
Tacoma, Washington

Acknowledgements

I would like to thank the following people for support, guidance, instruction, advice and friendship during the life of this project. I would like first to thank Dr John Wortley, whose translation of the *Pratum Spirituale* made beneficial tales accessible to me in the first place, and whose encouragement and gentle spirit through our phone and email conversations has made this project all the more fulfilling and accurate. I wish to thank Dr Richard Steele for his careful reading and discerning eye, both of which will save me much embarrassment. I thank also my editor, Sarah Lloyd, for her graciousness and kindness in the face of my often glaring ignorance about the process.

I wish to thank the 2011 Religion Department Acting-Chair Dr Samuel Torvend, the Humanities Chairs Council and Humanities Dean Dr James Albrecht for support of my application for the Regency Award, and the Pacific Lutheran University Office of the Provost for their gracious gift of the Regency Advancement Award. This award funded my presentation of foundational research on this project at the 16th International Patristics Conference in Oxford.

I wish to thank friends and colleagues in the academic community who encouraged me at various stages of this project: Dr Derek Krueger, Dr Philip Rousseau, Dr Pauline Allen, Dr Susan Holman, Dr Charlie Scalise, Dr Georgia Frank, Dr T. Allan Smith, Dr James Skedros, Dr Vasiliki Liberis, Dr Brian Matz, Dr Paul K. Piff and Dr Philip Booth, who kindly let me read his beautifully written forthcoming work titled *Moschus, Sophronius, Maximus: Asceticism, Sacrament and Dissent at the End of Empire* (University of California Press).

I have benefited tremendously throughout this process from the support of many people on the PLU campus, all of whom have helped me in some way, either by acquiring research materials, scanning documents, by being kind or by telling me to go home and rest. I would like to thank members of the PLU Religion Department for patiently reading portions of this over the years during our monthly colloquium, and Religion Department Chair Dr Marit Trelstad for encouraging me to ask for what I wanted. I would like especially to acknowledge the hard work and good humor of librarians Sue Golden, Pam Dearinger, Kathy Hornsburger, Diane Harris, Ann Dodge, Iwona Bonieka-Hicker; Humanities Division student workers Chelsea Paulsen, Anna Rasmussen, Emma Da Foe, Brianna Walling; and Humanities Administrative Assistant Cynthia Parkman and Assistant to the Dean of Humanities Tracy Williamson.

I wish to also thank my friends and family for their patience and kindness, for keeping me grounded in the twenty-first century even though my brain is often centuries away: Susan Greenleaf, Laura and Jeff Grealish, Dr Heracles Panagiotides and Dr Pauline Kaurin. And to my dear friends Father Tryphon, Father Paul and Father Moses of the All-Merciful Savior Russian Orthodox Monastery, thank you for silence, laughter, good food, coffee and vodka in equal proportions. I wish to thank also my friend Theodore Charles, with whom I have spent many hours discussing the "finer things," a category that includes our friendship.

And to my family, thank you for being willing to share my attention. Thanks to my parents Paul and Mary Llewellyn, my sister Livia Llewellyn, and the most immediate members of the household, Hector, Victor, Little Jimmy, Maeve and Tim. I would like to end this section of gratitude by especially noting thanks to my husband Tim and our daughter Maeve, both of whom have cheerfully and very unselfishly granted me time to bury myself in this project for several years. I am so fortunate to live with individuals who do not hold me hostage to particular types of domestic models that I do not fit, and who neither begrudge me my academic pleasures nor suffer jealousy over my affection for a seventh-century monk.

List of Abbreviations

Acta XIII CIAC	*Acta XIII Congressus internationalis archaeologiae christianae*
ACW	*Ancient Christian Writers*
AFP	*American Family Physician*
AnBoll	*Analecta Bollandiana*
Apalph	*Apophthegmata Patrum, collectio alphabetica*
APanon	*Anonymous Apophthegmata*
APsys	*Apophthegmata Patrum, collectio systematica*
ASCH	*American Society of Church History*
ATR	*Anglican Theological Review*
BA	*Biblical Archaeologist*
BHG	*Bibliotheca Hagiographica Graeca*, 3rd edn, ed. F. Halkin (Brussels, 1957)
BHM	*Bulletin of the History of Medicine*
BMGS	*Byzantine and Modern Greek Studies*
ΒΘ	*Βυζαντινά Θεσσαλονίκη*
BZ	*Byzantinische Zeitschrift*
CPG	*Clavis partum latinorum*
CS	*Civilisations et Sociétés*
CSCO	*Corpus Scriptorum Christianorum Orientalium*
CSEL	*Corpus scriptorium ecclesiasticorum latinorum*
Differences	*Differences: A Journal of Feminist Cultural Studies*
Doc Ophthalmol	*Documenta ophthalmologica. Advances in ophthalmology*
DOP	*Dumbarton Oaks Papers*
DOS	*Dumbarton Oaks Studies*
ECR	*Eastern Churches Review*
EHR	*The English Historical Review*
EO	*Echos d'Orient*
Eth.Coll.	*Ethiopian Collection*
FC	*Fathers of the Church*
GNO	*Gregorii Nysseni Opera*
GOTR	*Greek Orthodox Theological Review*
GRS	*Greece and Rome Studies*
HE	*Ecclesiastical History of Sozomen, Comprising a History of the Church*
HF	*Human Fertility*
Hist.eccl.	*Historia ecclesiastica, The Ecclesiastical History of Evagrius Scholasticus*

Hist.Laus.	Palladius, *Historia Lausiaca, Lausiac History*
HM	*History & Memory*
HME	*Historia monachorum in Æepypto*
HR	*Historia Religiosa*
HSPh	*Harvard Studies in Classical Philology*
HTR	*Harvard Theological Review*
IMJ	*Illinois Medical Journal*
Int. Congr. Ser.	*International Congress Series*
Isr J Zool	*Israel Journal of Zoology*
JAAR	*Journal of the American Academy of Religion*
JAC	*Jahrbuch für Antike und Christentum*
JECS	*Journal of Early Christian Studies Studies*
JHS	*Journal of the History of Sexuality*
JIH	*Journal of Interdisciplinary History*
JMEMS	*Journal of Medieval and Early Modern Studies*
JPN	*Journal of Psychosocial Nursing & Mental Health Services*
JPSP	*Journal of Personality and Social Psychology*
JR	*Journal of Religion*
JRA	*Journal of Roman Archaeology*
JRAS	*Journal of the Royal Asiatic Society*
JRH	*Journal of Religion and Health*
JRS	*Journal of Roman Studies*
JSNT	*Journal for the Study of the New Testament Supplement Series*
JTS	*Journal of Theological Studies*
LCL	*Loeb Classical Library*
MA	*Mediterranean Archaeology*
MMM	*Medicine in the Medieval Mediterranean*
NWH	*Nursing for Women's Health*
OC	*Oriens Christianus*
OCP	*Orientalia Christiana Periodica*
OECS	*Oxford Early Christian Studies*
OECT	*Oxford Early Christian Texts*
OLA	*Orientalia Lovaniensia Analecta*
OSB	*Oxford Studies in Byzantium*
OSHT	*Oxford Studies in Historical Theology*
PG	*Patrologia cursus completus: Series graeca*
Pharm Hist	*Pharmacy in History*
PL	*Patrologia cursus completus: Series latina*
PO	*Patrologia orientalis*
Prat. sp.	*Pratum spirituale*
RHR	*Revue de l'histoire des religions*
ROC	*Revue de l'Orient Chrétien*
RSBN	*Rivista di studi bizantini e neoellenici*
SAS	*Sciences of Antiquity Series*

SC	*Sources chrétiennes*
SCH	*Studies in Church History*
SCO	*Studi classici e orientali*
StP	*Studia Patristica*
SubsHag	*Subsidia Hagiographica*
TCH	*Transformation of the Classical Heritage*
TS	*Theological Studies*
ZAC	*Zeitschrift für Antikes Christentum*

Introduction

What little we know of John Moschos comes from three sources. Some details are found in an anonymous biography that was omitted from the Migne edition[1] and later re-edited. Second, we find sparse details in a description of *The Meadow* contained in Patriarch Photios' *Bibliotecha*.[2] Finally, even as Moschos seemed to write something about every monk he encountered but himself, nevertheless *The Meadow* provides the discerning reader with hints about Moschos' life, his travels, his theology and his monastic "kin."

Evidence suggests that John came from Damascus and that he was likely born during the reign of Emperor Justinian I (527–65),[3] which provides us with a rather large time frame. Further, it is not known definitively when—or even where—John died, although the general consensus is that he died in Rome at the beginning of the eighth Indiction—which is dated to either 619 or 634, depending on how one interprets its dating[4]—and that his remains were brought by Sophronios to Jerusalem, by John's request. John was surnamed "Εὐκρατᾶς,"[5] a surname about which there is lively academic discussion. Scholars note that this Byzantine surname intentionally identifies John's loyalty to and affinity with Chalcedonian Christianity, which we know from *Meadow* tales to be a discussion of great importance. John began his monastic career sometime in the mid-sixth century at a large and well-organized Judean monastery located about five miles west of Bethlehem. Founded in 478 by St Theodosius—whose first cell was believed to be the site where the Magi rested on their way home when

---

[1] H. Usener (ed.), *Der heilige Tychon* (Leipzig, 1907): 91–3.
[2] *Bibliotheca veterum partum*, cod. 199 (Paris, 1624) t. 2: 1050–55; PL 74: 119–244; Wortley, "Translator's Note," xvi. See also N.G. Wilson, trans., *Photius: The Bibliotheca. A selection translated with notes* (London: Duckworth, 1994): 182–3; Warren T. Treadgold, *The Nature of The Bibliotheca of Photius* (Washington, DC: Dumbarton Oaks, 1980): 60.
[3] S. Vailhe, "Jean Mosch," EO, Vol. 5 (1901): 108.
[4] Michael F. Hendy, *Studies in Byzantine Monetary Economy, c. 300–1450* (Cambridge University Press, 1985): 160. Anthony Bryer, "Chronology and Dating," in Elizabeth Jeffreys, John Haldon and Robin Cormack (eds), *The Oxford Handbook of Byzantine Studies* (Oxford University Press, 2008): 33.
[5] Henry Chadwick, "John Moschus and His Friend Sophronius the Sophist", JTS, Vol. 25 (1974): 59 and n. 1; and Pauline Allen and Bronwen Neil (eds), *Maximus the Confessor and His Companions: Documents from Exile*, OECT (Oxford University Press, 2002): 178f., n. 30; Christoph von Schönborn, *Sophrone de Jérusalem: vie monastique et confession dogmatique* (Paris: Beauchesne, 1972): 56–7, n. 13.

they were directed to take an alternative route by the angel[6]—this prestigious monastery housed hundreds of monks, had several churches and workshops, and was known for its hospitality and provision of services for the physically and mentally ill, the aged and the poor.[7] After a period of ascetic withdrawl in the more remote Paran Monastery at the now-abandoned monastery of St Chariton as well as time spent in the Great Lavra of St Sabas,[8] John was joined by that time by his disciple, fellow pilgrim, friend and future patriarch of Jerusalem, Sophronios.[9] Outstanding analysis on the nature of their relationship within the greater context of monastic companionship has been done by Derek Krueger, who notes that their deeply committed partnership is cast in various ways within the texts.[10] However they defined their relationship, this monastic couple embarked on the practice of a form of ascesis known as "*xeniteia*,"[11] a voluntary rootless existence that forces the monastic figure to be dependent entirely on the hospitality of others. John and Sophronios did not practice the extreme form of "*xeniteia*" that drove ascetics into the wilderness and sometimes to starvation; rather, their ascetic peregrinations—coupled with a literary task that Moschos clearly understood as a form of monastic

---

[6] Matthew 2.12. *Life of St. Theodosius*, in *Cyril of Scythopolis: The Lives of the Monks of Palestine*, trans. R.M. Price (Kalamazoo, MI: Cistercian Publications, 1991): 262–8. Wortley, "Translator's Note," xviii; *Life of Theodosius* (H. Usener (ed.), *Der heilige Theodosius, Schriften des Theodoros und Kyrillos* (Leipzig: Teubner, 1890): 3–101; Vailhe, "Jean Mosch," 108.

[7] Wortley, "Translator's Note," xviii. Hirschfeld notes the influence of the social welfare of Basil's *Rules* on Theodosius: Yizhar Hirschfeld, *The Judean Desert Monasteries in the Byzantine Period* (Yale University Press, 1992): 15; Susan R. Holman, "Rich and Poor in the *Miracles of Saints Cyrus and John*," in Holman (ed.), *Wealth and Poverty in Early Church and Society* (Ada, MI: Baker Academic): 105–6, n. 13; H. Usener (ed.), *Vita S. Theodosii a Cyrillo Scythopolitano Scripta* (Bonne: Typis C. Gergi University, 1890): 35.

[8] Wortley, "Translator's Note," xviii; Chadwick, "Moschus and his friend Sophronios," 49–55.

[9] Derek Krueger, "Between Monks: Tales of Monastic Companionship in Early Byzantium," JHS, Vol. 20, No. 1 (2011): 30.

[10] Beginning with a dedication to his "sacred and faithful child Sophronios" ("ἱερὸν καὶ πιστὸν τέκνον," PG 87.2852), Moschos refers to Sophronios variously as "companion" ("ὁ ἑταῖρός μου," PG 87.2976), "partner" or "colleague" ("ἑταῖρον," PG 87.2977), "brother" ("ἀδελφῷ," PG 87.2949; 2960; 2997), "Lord" or "my Lord" ("κύρις" or "κύριος," PG 87.2920; 2929; 2973).

[11] Daniel Caner, *Wandering, Begging Monks: Spiritual Authority and the Promotion of Monasticism in Late Antiquity* (University of California Press, 2002); "Monastic Rules and Wandering Monks," in Maribel Dietz, *Wandering Monks, Virgins and Pilgrims: Ascetic Travel in the Mediterranean World, A.D. 300–800* (Pennsylvania State University Press, 2005): 69–105. Joseph Patrich, *Sabas, Leader of Palestinian Monasticism: A Comparative Study in Eastern Monasticism, Fourth to Seventh Centuries* (Washington, DC: Dumbarton Oaks, 1995): 43.

ascesis[12]—kept them closer to communities that could provide hospitality as well as tales for the collection. Herrin writes that they personify a particularly "Chalcedonian diaspora of monks, forced to move from one centre to another, welcomed in their travels by communities respectful of their ascetic experiences, learning, and monastic faith."[13]

It is not known precisely when John and Sophronios first headed south, but it is suggested that they did so during the reign of Emperor Tiberius II Constantius, whose short reign was from 578 to 582. Between approximately 578 and 602/603[14] they traveled first to Egypt, then Mount Sinai, where, by John's own account, they spent a decade at the Lavra of the Æliotes.[15] They returned to Palestine to visit various communities, all the while collecting the traditional wisdom and folklore of monastic life. In 603 or 604, however, they left Palestine for a second and final time, a move likely prompted initially by the murder of Emperor Maurice and the subsequent Persian invasion into the Byzantine Empire under the pretext of defending the empire from the tyrant usurper Phocas.[16] John and Sophronios first headed north to Antioch, a city that was, at that time, a very dangerous place for Chalcedonian Christians due to the welcome given to the Persians by Monophysite Christians in areas such as Antioch.[17] From Antioch they sailed to Alexandria, where they remained in the employ of the patriarch of Alexandria, John the Almsgiver, tending to the needs of the thousands of refugees who headed south after the capture of Jerusalem in 614.[18] When the Persians arrived in Egypt in 618, John and Sophronios departed for Rome on the Tiber or "New Rome"

---

[12] Derek Krueger, *Writing and Holiness: The Practice of Authorship in the Early Christian East* (University of Pennsylvania Press, 2004): 95; Derek Krueger, "Literary Composition and Monastic Practice in Early Byzantium: On Genre and Discipline," in *Monastères, images, pouvoirs et société à Byzance* (Paris: Publications de la Sorbonne, 2006): 43–8; Derek Krueger, "Early Byzantine Hagiography and Hagiography as Different Modes of Christian Practice," in Arietta Papaconstantinou (ed.), *Writing 'True Stories': Historians and Hagiographers in the Late Antique and Medieval Near East* (Belgium: Brepols, 2010): 13–20.

[13] Judith Herrin, *The Formation of Christendom* (Princeton University Press, 1987): 210.

[14] Vailhe, "Jean Mosch," 109–12; James Howard-Johnston, *Witnesses to a World Crisis: Historians and Histories of the Middle East in the Seventh Century* (Oxford University Press, 2012): 171–2.

[15] *Prat sp.* 67 (PG 87.2917). Chadwick dates this period from 580/81 to 590/91; Chadwick, "Moschus and his friend Sophronios," 57.

[16] Wortley, "Translator's Note," xix; see also Herrin, n. 16.

[17] Herrin, *Formation of Christendom*, 205.

[18] Wortley, "Translator's Note," xix; von Schönborn, *Sophrone de Jérusalem*, 69. Bishop Sophronius and John Moschos, *The Life of Our holy Father, John the Almsgiver*, and see also Bishop Leontius, *A Supplement to the Life of John the Almsgiver, our saintly father and Archbishop of Alexandria, written by Leontius, Bishop of Neapolis in the Island of Cyprus* and *The Life of St. Theodore of Sykeon* for information on the effects of the Persian raids, in *Three Byzantine Saints: Contemporary Biographies of St. Daniel the*

(Constantinople), where John, after finishing his *Meadow*, passed from this life.[19] The debate about where and when he passed is lively. According to Vailhe, "il est impossible de placer la mort de Jean Mosch après l'année 619."[20] Christoph von Schönborn writes touchingly on the return of John's body to "the same monastery": "towards the end of 619, they arrived at St. Theodosius, the starting point of the two inseparable friends long wandering, voluntary and forced."[21]

Wortley notes Enrica Follieri's suggestion that John died not in Rome on the Tiber in 619, but in Constantinople and after 620, but Wortley points out that "learned opinion" accepts the earlier date of 619.[22] Andrew Louth challenges Follieri's claim regarding John's death, which is dependent on understanding "ἡ τῶν Ῥωμαίων μεγάλη πόλις"[23] as referring to Constantinople ("New Rome") rather than Rome on the Tiber. Ultimately, Louth concludes, "Follieri may possibly be right ... But her conclusion that John died in Constantinople can hardly be regarded as 'conclusively demonstrated.'"[24] Walter Kaegi, noting both sides of the discussion, writes that Sophronios returned the remains to Palestine in 634.[25] Most recently, Philip Booth, also noting the discussion, relies on very convincing internal evidence within *The Meadow* as well as external evidence to conclude that Moschos' death can be attributed to the later date.[26] Regardless of when John died, the indisputable fact remains that he did. Sophronios, unable to return with the body to Sinai as the way was blocked by Arab tribes,[27] buried his friend in the rubble of the St Theodosios' monastery; it had been burned to the ground in 614 by the Persians. The details of John's life and manuscript that remain are very much like that rubble, for they do not fit together tightly and thus a great deal is uncertain.

Stylite, St. Theodore of Sykeon and St. John the Almsgiver, trans. Elizabeth Dawes and Norman H. Baynes (Crestwood, NY: St Vladimir's Seminary Press, 1996): 199–62.

[19] Wortley, "Translator's Note," xix. See note 4 for the debate on where and when John died.

[20] Vailhe, "Jean Mosch," 114.

[21] "*ce même monastère* " : "*On est alors vers la fin de l'an 619 quand ils arrivent à Saint-Théodose, le point de départ de la longue errance, volontaire et forcée, des deax amis imséparables.*" Schönborn, *Sophrone de Jérusalem*, 70.

[22] Wortley, "Translator's Note," xix–xx.

[23] Enrica Follieri, "Dove e quando mori Giovanni Mosco?" RSBN, Vol. 25 (1988): 6.

[24] Andrew Louth, "Did John Moschos Really Die in Constantinople?" JTS, Vol. 49, No. 1 (1998): 149–54.

[25] Walter E. Kaegi, *Heraclius, Emperor of Byzantium* (Cambridge University Press, 2007): 270, n. 13. Howard-Johnston, *Witnesses to a World Crisis*, 172.

[26] Phil Booth, *Moschus, Sophronius, Maximus: Asceticism, Sacrament and Dissent at the End of Empire*, Transformation of the Classical Heritage (Berkeley, CA: University of California Press, 2013): 174, see n. 162. I am grateful to Dr Booth for reading this introduction and providing some helpful corrections.

[27] PL 74.121; Alexander A. Vasiliev, "Notes on Some Episodes concerning the Relations between the Arabs and the Byzantine Empire from the Fourth to the Sixth Century," DOP, Vol. 9/10 (1956): 315–16; Hagith Sivan, *Palestine in Late Antiquity* (Oxford University Press, 2008): 77.

What remains quite certain is that the tales in John's *Meadow* were collected and composed against the backdrop of multiple and constantly shifting boundaries, including geographic, political, economic, theological and literary. Regarding Byzantine boundaries, historians write: "The eastern borderlands of Byzantium were not static ... We must speak of a permeable frontier zone, with cities forming the primary nodes of political control, the vertebrae of the Byzantine backbone."[28] Because of the relevance of these boundaries for best understanding the milieu of the tales, it is worthwhile to offer a few words on historical context, even as the boundaries cannot be completely disentangled from one another.

War in the sixth century between the Byzantines and Persians over Iberia, Armenia, Cappadocia and Syria[29] had a significant impact on and for the empire. These territories, especially Syria, suffered in addition not only from invasions but also from a series of disasters including earthquake and plague. In addition to the loss and destruction of local populations not carried away by the outbreak of plague in 541–2,[30] capture of terrain and an estimated 100,000 *solidi* of gold and silver, (not to mention costly financial deals meant to secure peace), significant portions of the inhabitants allowed to live were deported to Persian territory.[31] Although the reign of Justinian began in prosperity and left behind a fixed legacy of legal, artistic, architectural achievements and a revival of trade from east to west, still, his hard-won frontiers ultimately collapsed under the weight of Visigoths, Berbers, Lombards and Persians, who challenged Emperor Maurice externally while civil

---

[28] Michael Decker, "Frontier Settlement and Economy in the Byzantine East," DOP, Vol. 61 (2007): 217–20. Olster writes, "Yet, beneath the outward manifestation of power, the Empire's hold on its borders was precarious, its fiscal condition near collapse, its subjects restive, and its army undermanned and poorly fed." David Michael Olster, *The Politics of Usurpation in the Seventh Century: Rhetoric and Revolution in Byzantium* (Amsterdam: Adolf M. Hakkert, 1993): 23; see also Walter E. Kaegi, "Reconceptualizing Byzantium's Eastern Frontiers in the Seventh Century," in Ralph W. Mathisen and Hagith S. Sivan (eds), *Shifting Frontiers in Late Antiquity* (Aldershot: Variorum, Ashgate, 1996): 82–92.

[29] Andreas N. Stratos, *Byzantium in the Seventh Century, I: 602–634*, trans. Marc Ogilvie-Grant (Amsterdam: Adolf M. Hakkert, 1968); Clive Foss, "Syria in Transition, A.D., 550–750: An Archaeological Approach," DOP, Vol. 51 (1997): 189–269. Decker, "Frontier Settlement and Economy," 234; see also Foss, "Syria in Transition," 189.

[30] Allen notes that the lack of demographic data makes mortality estimations difficult. Pauline Allen, "The 'Justinianic' Plague," *Byzantion* 49 (1979): 5–20; Lawrence I. Conrad, "Epidemic Disease in Central Syria in the Late Sixth Century: Some New Insights from the Verse of Hassán ibn Thábit," BMGS 18 (1994): 12–58; B. Grmek, "Les conséquences de la peste de Justinien dans l'Illyricum," *Acta XIII CIAC*, 3 vols (Vatican City ; Split, 1998), 2: 787–94.

[31] Procopius, *History of the Wars*, trans. H.B. Dewing, Vol. 1 (Harvard University Press, 1914): 2.9.14–18; A.D. Lee, *War in Late Antiquity: A Social History* (Wiley-Blackwell, 2007): 102; 111–12; 123–46.

unrest in major cities challenged him internally.[32] In the latter half of the sixth century cities in the empire varied in prosperity, from the near impoverishment of Rome[33] to the new prosperity of North African and coastal Greek cities; villas declined as villages—barely differentiated from small cities—arose, clustered most often around ecclesiastical structures. Costly defenses against foreign attacks had been coupled with urban reconstruction in the wake of natural disasters, such as the 526 and 528 earthquakes in Antioch and—as mentioned above—the plague, the implications of which were lack of manpower and, subsequently, shortages of wheat and wine.[34]

In 591, a decade-long peace treaty was concluded between Emperor Maurice and Persian King Chosroes II.[35] Peaceable relations only continued, however, until the day Chosroes was informed that the emperor and his male children were dead,[36] their bodies thrown into the harbor and their heads displayed for citizen viewing.[37] Posturing as the avenging son, Chosroes II took the opportunity to fight not against the empire, but against the usurper Phocas who had—with the support of the army—mutinied against Maurice.[38] Confusion in primary sources notwithstanding,[39] Persians appeared in Mesopotamia and Byzantine Armenia in 603 or 604,[40] invaded the Byzantine portion of Armenia, devastated Cappadocia up to the city of Chalcedon and retreated. This early activity resulted in a loss of Armenia, Mesopotamia and parts of Syria, the destruction of villages

---

[32] Angeliki E. Laiou, "Political History: An Outline," in Angeliki E. Laiou (ed.), *The Economic History of Byzantium: From the Seventh Through the Fifteenth Century*, Vol. 1 (Washington, DC: Dumbarton Oaks, 2002): 12–13.

[33] Morrisson and Sodini, "The Sixth Century Economy," in Laiou, *Economic History of Byzantium*, 172 and 189; S. Barnish, "The Transformation of Classical Cities and the Pirenne Debate," JRA, Vol. 2 (1989): 385–400.

[34] Morrisson and Sodini, "The Sixth Century Economy," 173–94.

[35] Mark Whittow, *The Making of Byzantium, 600–1025* (University of California Press, 1996): 48; Stratos, *Byzantium in the Seventh Century*, 14–23.

[36] Whittow, *The Making of Byzantium*, 72; Stratos, *Byzantium in the Seventh Century*, 52; Theophylactos Simocattes, *The History of Theophylact Simocatta: An English Translation with Introduction*, trans. Michael and Mary Whitby (Oxford University Press, 1986): viii.3, n. 62; Theophanes the Confessor, *The Chronicle of Theophanes: Anni mundi 6095–6305 (A.D. 602–813)*, Harry Turtledove, trans. (University of Pennsylvania Press, 1982): 291.1; Michael Whitby, "Greek Historical Writing After Procopius: Variety and Vitality," in Averil Cameron, Lawrence I. Conrad and John Haldon (eds), *The Byzantine East and Early Islamic Near East I: Problems in the Literary Source Material* (Princeton, NJ: Darwin Press, 1992): 47.

[37] Stratos, *Byzantium in the Seventh Century*, 52–3.

[38] Whittow, *The Making of Byzantium*, 69.

[39] Stratos, *Byzantium in the Seventh Century*, 61. Theophanes, *Chronicle*, 292.2; Sebeos, *The Armenian History Attributed to Sebeos*, Part I, trans. R.W. Thompson (Liverpool University Press, 1999): 56–7.

[40] Kaegi, "Byzantium's Eastern Frontiers," 84.

and subsequent economic decay,[41] and the emptying and loss of Chalcedonian (Orthodox) monasteries and churches.[42] Syria, a territory of fundamental importance for the Byzantines,[43] deteriorated as more than 700 villages were emptied, land suffered from frequent invasions,[44] trade routes were blocked and populations shifted.[45] Hard winters in 608 and 609 affecting not only production of food but transportation so stretched the social fabric of the Empire that insults shouted at Phocas in the Hippodrome produced a violent backlash against dissidents; this led not to silence, but to open revolt.[46]

This lamentable situation culminated in the usurpation in 610 of the Byzantine throne by Heraclius the younger, son of the respectable exarch of Africa, Heraclius the elder, who sent his son by sea to Constantinople. Heraclius the younger was crowned before he even reached the city.[47] After Phocas was overthrown, humiliated, chopped into pieces, dragged through the city and burnt, Heraclius reigned for 31 years over an empire besieged by Persians in the east and Turkic Avars in the west, urban unrest, violent religious conflict and a financial situation that was appalling: the treasury was empty, the gold supply was in the control of the Persians, huge tracts of land were empty and uncultivated, and the populations had either been killed or fled to cities or monasteries.[48] While Heraclius turned his attention to the Avars, Persians reentered Cappadocia and also Antioch, and the way was clear to acquire the remainder of Syria, Palestine and Egypt.[49] They destroyed the Church of the Holy Sepulchre and carried off to Ctesiphon the relic of the alleged True Cross.[50] While Persian invasion did not result in a complete casting-off of traces of an imported Roman culture, initial events of stunning brutality—destruction of architecture, enslavement of portions of the population, disruption of trade

---

[41] Sebeos, *Armenian History*, 59–62.

[42] Stratos, *Byzantium in the Seventh Century*, 61–6; Bernard Flusin, *Saint Anastase le Perse: et l'Histoire de la Palestine au Début du VIIe Siècle* (Paris: Editions du Centre National de la Recherche Scientifique, 1992): 70–83.

[43] Decker, "Frontier Settlement and Economy," 234; Foss, "Syria in Transition," 189.

[44] Decker, "Frontier Settlement and Economy," 235.

[45] Kaegi, "Byzantium's Eastern Frontiers," 87.

[46] Stratos, *Byzantium in the Seventh Century*, 78–9; Kaegi, *Heraclius*, 39.

[47] Kaegi writes on the multiple reasons for revolt—the illegitimacy of Phocas' rule, tyrannical methods—but encourages cautious reading. Kaegi, *Heraclius*, 37–8.

[48] Ibid.; 55; Stratos, *Byzantium in the Seventh Century*, 124.

[49] Sources vary on these dates: Theophanes reports 611 for the attack on Syria; Syrian chronicler Dionysius claims the first year of Heraclius' reign (610–11). According to Clive Foss, numismatic evidence supports an earlier date. Clive Foss, "The Persians in the Roman near East (602–630 AD)," JRAS, Vol. 13, No. 2 (2003): 152.

[50] Ibid., 153–4; Kaegi, *Heraclius*, 78; John Haldon, "The Reign of Heraclius. A Context for Change?" in Gerrit J. Reinik and Bernard H. Stolte (eds), *The Reign of Heraclius (610–641): Crisis and Confrontation* (Leuven: Peeters, 2002): 2–4; A.A. Vasiliev, *History of the Byzantine Empire*, Vol. 1 (University of Wisconsin Press, 1980): 194–6; Whittow, *The Making of Byzantium*, 75–6.

and agriculture[51]—were followed by the reestablishment of relative stability by a people more than capable of and known for the organization of a massive empire.[52]

Of no less consequence for Eastern Christians than war, theological dissension that troubled Byzantine Christianity in the sixth century must also be taken into account when considering Moschos' text, as theological claims were intimately connected with issues of cultural and ethnic identity and loyalty, as well as salvation.[53] At the Fourth Ecumenical Council in Chalcedon in 451, these boundaries of theological identity were further formed when it was resolved that Jesus was known in two natures "[which exist] without confusion, without change, without division, without separation ... the properties of each being preserved, and [both] concurring into one Person."[54] Affirmed in the *Tome* of Leo,[55] this doctrinal formula—it was hoped—would end the discussion on the natures of Christ, marking in a permanent way the boundaries of doctrine as well as the relationship between God and Jesus, and Jesus and humanity. This was largely the doctrinal position of the Patriarchate of Constantinople and, after 518,[56] that of the emperor as well. Adherents to this Chalcedonian doctrinal formula in time became known as "Melkites"[57] or "Chalcedonians." But the affirmation of Chalcedonian theology, though accepted at the council, did not end the discussion at all, nor did Justinian's renewed efforts through the Fifth Ecumenical Council in 553, which only intensified division. In brief, various theological formulas at that time were represented by the Chalcedonians (largely the patriarchates of Rome, Constantinople, Antioch and Jerusalem, as well as Christians in parts of Palestine and western Syria), who understood Jesus to be one hypostasis in two natures (divine and human); the smaller party of dissent represented by the Nestorians (Christians in Mesopotamia and Persian Christians), who understood Jesus to be two hypostases in two natures; and the larger party of opposing theology

---

[51] A.A. Vasiliev, *History of the Byzantine Empire*, Vol. 1 (The University of Wisconsin Press, 1980): 193; Leslie MacCoull, "Coptic Egypt During the Persian Occupation." SCO, Vol. 36 (1986): 307–13; Foss, "Persians in the Near East," 169–70.

[52] Foss, "Persians in the Near East," 167. Foss writes that "[e]vidence from the occupied provinces—from Armenia to Egypt—reveals a consistent pattern: stability, continuity and tolerance followed an initial period of violence." Ibid., 168.

[53] Averil Cameron, "New Themes and Styles in Greek Literature: Seventh–Eighth Centuries," *The Byzantine East and Early Islamic Near East I*, 85, 88. See also Philip Wood, *"We have no king but Christ": Christian Political Thought in Greater Syria on the Eve of the Arab Conquest* (Oxford University Press, 2010): 12–16.

[54] A. Grillmeier, S.J. and H. Bacht, S.J. (eds), *Das Konzil von Chalkedon: Geschichte und Gegenwart*, 3 vols (1951–4): 1.390. John Meyendorff, *Imperial Unity and Christian Division: The Church 460–680 A.D.*, The Church in History, Vol. III (Crestwood, NY: St Vladimir's Seminary Press, 1989): 165–206.

[55] Meyendorff, *Imperial Unity and Christian Division*, 173.

[56] Emperor Anastasios, the last Monophysite emperor, died in 518. Whittow, *The Making of Byzantium*, 43.

[57] From the Semitic "" (*mélekh*) for "king." Whittow, *The Making of Byzantium*, 43.

represented by the Monophysites (occasionally the Patriarchate of Alexandria, and Christians in Egypt, eastern Syria and Persian Armenia), who understood Jesus to be one hypostasis in one nature. To some degree—and due, in part, to violent methods by which allegiance was demanded—by the time of John Moschos, doctrinal statements on the person of Jesus had become nationalist movements as well as methods of resistance and competition between patriarchal sees, with all parties considering themselves "orthodox" and others heretical. This was particularly important in the sixth and seventh centuries and these distinctions do matter for reading *The Meadow*. John's position was strictly Chalcedonian; thus individuals in *The Meadow* who hold theologies other than Chalcedonian factor into his text only as heretics, and therefore Monophysites and Nestorians—some of whom aided the Persians in emptying cities, Chalcedonian churches and monasteries—are not simply wrong Christians, but traitors to the empire. As well, these theological distinctions become important elements in the construction of identity in the empire. Cameron writes: "Indeed, one of the most important problems for Byzantines in the pre-Islamic period was precisely, I would say, this question of identity— to what society did a monk of Sinai or Jerusalem, or an official in Alexandria actually owe his allegiance?"[58]

But while divisions among Christians can account for some of the difficulties that the empire faced at the time, it is no longer fashionable to blame these divisions for the loss of eastern territory to the empire and, despite these divisions, Christianity was a major unifying factor in the eastern Roman world.[59] But in Moschos' text one will not find theological reflection on doctrinal positions so much as theological consequences; the righteous were known as much by the activities in which they engaged as by a theology to which they held fast.

The military and political activity of the sixth century produced widespread social unrest and changes in urban society on the eve of Arab military successes in land most recently wrested by the Byzantines from the Persians. Literary culture—as well as agriculture, government, military—experienced change as well, and the subsequent decline in the seventh century in the production of particular types of writing has led scholars of various disciplines to label this era as that of a "Dark Age" in which few literary works were produced.[60] This

---

[58] Cameron, "New Themes and Styles in Greek Literature," 85, 88. See also Wood, *We have no king but Christ*, 12–16.

[59] Whittow, *The Making of Byzantium*, 44–6.

[60] Cyril Mango, *Byzantium: The Empire of New Rome* (New York: Charles Scribner's Sons, 1980): 69.

trend is slowly reversing;[61] it has been recently and successfully argued in the work of Cameron, Conrad and Whitby that although the production of history and historiography did experience a lull at this point in time,[62] nevertheless various types of theological writing produced in this era "can be equally revealing about their historical and social context,"[63] provided historians are willing to look in other directions.[64] The primary "other direction" historians must face is in the direction of literature produced by the religious community, into which Moschos' *Meadow* falls.

Moschos' *Spiritual Meadow* is most appropriately described as a collection of "spiritually beneficial tales" ("διηγήσεις ψυχωφελεῖς"), of which it is one of several collections of *gerontika* composed and collected between the fifth and eight centuries.[65] Identified as an important "relique de Byzance,"[66] beneficial tales

---

[61] John Wortley, *A Répertoire of Byzantine Beneficial Tales*, http://home.cc.umanitoba. ca/~wortley; A.P. Kazhdan and Ann Wharton Epstein, *Change in Byzantine Culture in the Eleventh and Twelfth Centuries* (University of California Press, 1985): 4; Barnish, "The Transformation of Classical Cities and the Pirenne Debate," 385–400. Hugh Kennedy, "From Polis to Medina: Urban Change in Late Antique and Early Islamic Syria," *Past and Present*, Vol. 106 (1985) 3–27; Cameron and Conrad, "Introduction," *The Byzantine East and Early Islamic Near East I*, 11.

[62] Whitby, "Greek Historical Writing After Procopius," 70–74.

[63] Cameron and Conrad, "Introduction," *Byzantine East and Early Islamic Near East I*, 11.

[64] James Russell, "Transformations in Early Byzantine Urban Life: the Contribution and Limitations of Archaeological Evidence," *17th International Byzantine Congress, Major Papers* (New Rochelle, NY: Aristide D. Caratzas, 1986): 138; Cameron, "New Themes and Styles in Greek Literature," 85, 88.

[65] *Historia monachorum in Æepypto* (HME), ed. A.J. Festugiere, SubsHag, Vol. 53 (Brussels, 1971); N. Russell, *The Lives of the Desert Fathers* (Kalamazoo, MI: Cistercian Publications, 1981); Palladius of Hellenopolis, *Historia Lausiaca* (*Hist. Laus.*), ed. Cuthbert Butler, *The Lausiac History of Palladius* (Cambridge, 1904); Robert T. Meyer, ACW, Vol. 36 (Westminster, MD: 1965); *Apophthegmata Patrum, collectio alphabetica*, J.B. Cotelier (ed.), PG 65.71–440; Benedicta Ward, *The Sayings of the Desert Fathers* (Kalamazoo, MI: Cistercian Publications, 1975); *Apophthegmata Patrum, collectio systematica*, ed. F. Nau, "Histoires des solitaires égyptiens," ROC, Vol. 12–18 (1907–13); John Wortley, *The Book of the Elders: The Systematic Collection* (Collegeville, MN: Liturgical Press, 2012); various *Vie et récits* of Daniel of Scêtê, in L. Clugnet (ed.), ROC, Vol. 5 (1900) and in Wortley, trans. *The Book of the Elders*; John Moschos' *Pratum spirituale*, PG 87.2851–3112; M.J. Rouët de Journel, *Le Pré spiritual*, SC, Vol. 12 (Paris, 1946); R. Maisano, *Giovanni Mosco, Il Proto* (Naples, 1982); John Wortley, *The Spiritual Meadow* (Kalamazoo, MI: Cistercian Publications, 1992); Theodoret of Cyrrhus, *Historia Religiosa*, trans. R.M. Price, *A History of the Monks of Syria* (Kalamazoo, MI: Cistercian Publications, 1985); Anastasios the Sinaite, ed. F. Nau, "Le texte grec du récit du moine Anastase sur les saints pères du Sinaï," 1–40, OC, Vol. 2 (1902); John of Ephesus, *Lives of the Eastern Saints*, ed. and trans. E.W. Brooks, PO, Vol. 17, No. 1 (1923), Vol. 18, No. 4 (1924) and Vol. 19, No. 3 (1926).

[66] Wortley, *A Répertoire of Byzantine Beneficial Tales*, http://home.cc.umanitoba. ca/~wortley.

and their later version, the "late stories,"[67] are difficult to classify both as a genre and in terms of individual collections (most especially the Moschos' manuscript, as will be addressed below). Depending on how one defines "beneficial tale," it is possible to number individual tales at close to 1,000.[68] Scholars have defined them and their purpose variously, including Delehaye's claim that they were designed to illuminate a particular religious doctrine,[69] and Halkin's claim that while they can include fictitious persons who exist in anonymity of both time and place,[70] the subjects are not always imaginary.[71] But despite difficulty in defining the term, this does not mean that one cannot clearly identify elements about beneficial tales that remain fairly consistent. Less of a "Life" and more of a "Day in the Life," beneficial tales are anecdotal, are often repeated, appear in various forms in other accounts or contribute to the development of other accounts.[72] For example, Leontius references Moschos and Sophronios in his prologue to his *Life* of John the Almsgiver, which he clearly understands as a supplement to the work of "others, who before us wrote about this wonderful man and high priest."[73] Beneficial tales have roots in the Egyptian, Syrian and Palestinian desert literature of the early Christian era[74] and likely began in an oral monastic environment, a milieu within which words—or *apothegmata*—were chosen carefully and thus charged with great significance.[75] And while it is tempting to conclude that they began with a "word" ["λόγος" or "ῥῆμα"] and seamlessly made the transition from oral to written, from *apophthegm* to *vita*,[76] this suggests a natural shift that is complicated

---

[67] "récits tardifs," Wortley, *A Répertoire of Byzantine Beneficial Tales*, http://home.cc.umanitoba.ca/~wortley; Wortley, *Spiritually Beneficial Tales of Paul, Bishop of Monembasia* (Kalamazoo, MI: Cistercian Publications, 1996): 44.

[68] Wortley, *Spiritually Beneficial Tales*, 29.

[69] "à mettre en lumière une doctrine religieuse," H. Delehaye, *Un groupe de récits "utiles à l'âme,"* in *Mélanges Bidez* (Bruxelles, 1934): 257.

[70] "les personages fictifs," "un anonymat," and "pays ni aucune époque." F. Halkin, "La vision de Kaioumos et le sort éternal de Philentolos Olympiou," AnBoll, Vol. 63 (1945): 56.

[71] "dont les héros ne sont pas toujours imaginaires." F. Halkin, *Recherches et documents d'hagiographie Byzantine*, SubsHag, Vol. 51 (Brussels, 1971): 261.

[72] Compare *Prat. sp.* 91 PG 87.2947–50 with "On Patermuthius," HME 10.9; 1997b. See also J. Palmer, 'John Moschus as a Source for the Lives of St. Symeon and St. Andrew the Fools,' *SP* 32: 366–70.

[73] Leontius, *A Supplement to the Life of John the Almsgiver, our saintly father and Archbishop of Alexandria*, in Dawes and Baynes, 207.

[74] Wortley, *A Répertoire of Byzantine Beneficial Tales*, http://home.cc.umanitoba.ca/~wortley.

[75] Douglas Burton-Christie, *The Word in the Desert: Scripture and the Quest for Holiness in Early Christian Monasticism* (Oxford University Press, 1993): 76–81 and 134–77; see also William Harmless, *Desert Christians: An Introduction to the Literature of Early Monasticism* (Oxford University Press, 2004): 171–3.

[76] François Halkin, BHG, Vol. 3 (Brussels, 1957): 175–214.

by the free borrowing of themes from author to author. A textual evolution of beneficial tales is also complicated by the fact that the considerable degree of variation existing within the content of multiple manuscripts has led Wortley to note the "extraordinary degree of license"[77] scribes took with the material to the extent that copies of the text were not so much copies as their own "editions" of the tales, enhanced with their own individual memories of how the tales had been told to them;[78] further, the skeletal structure of the majority of beneficial tales has prompted Wortley to query if they were not intended to function as prompts in an oral transmission. The oral factor would contribute to the paucity of content of literature originally intended for a monastic audience,[79] people who appreciate how the right word, so carefully placed, can make the silence in between all the more beautiful and alluring.

Unlike highbrow hagiography cousins, beneficial tales remained primarily within the monastic milieu—even as secular elements most certainly were present in the tales themselves. Consistent also in the history of beneficial tales is an understanding that the content is shared knowledge among folks, and thus a type of folklore of sorts, or "monk-lore," if one insists. Sadly, literature of such a type as the beneficial tales is often disparaged when placed against other types of literary output that are considered "high," such as homilies, exegetical works and the theology of learned bishops. Patriarch Photios notes that the rhetorical style—by comparison—"tends to a lower and less educated level," but even the "intelligent and pious reader" can profit from the subject matter and should offer no complaint.[80] But beneficial tales in general, and Moschos' tales in particular, each have a simple, significant message to offer the devout monk, the lay person and the scholar, even if they inspire little confidence in the latter in the way of profound theology, accurate history or eloquent narrative. And yet despite the lack of—at times—all three of these desired qualities, scholars consistently praise the value of Moschos' *Meadow* for what it does provide. Norman H. Baynes wrote that it was a surprise that *The Meadow* gathered little attention, primarily because—in his view—the text is rich with potential, for it "can be dated with precision: it reflects the conditions within the Empire in the sixth and early years of the seventh century ... unlike much hagiographical writing, it is free from tortured rhetoric."[81] Baynes explores several categories of stories in *The Meadow* to demonstrate the way in which the text reveals much of the social history of the early Byzantine Empire, including attitudes towards the sacraments, ethics, piety, economics and the role of

---

[77] John Wortley, "The genre of the Spiritually Beneficial Tale," *Scripta & Escripta*, Vol. 8–9, Institute of Literature, Sofia, Bulgaria, 2010, 16.

[78] Ibid., 21.

[79] Ibid., 22.

[80] *Photius: The Bibliotheca*, CPG 7376, 199; Wilson, *Photius: The Bibliotheca*, 182.

[81] Norman H. Baynes, "The Pratum Spirituale," in *Byzantine Studies and Other Essays* (University of London: The Athlone Press, 1955): 261; originally published in OCP, Vol. 13 (1947): 404–14.

the holy person and monastic in Byzantine society. Although, like Baynes, Philip Pattendem would likely disagree about the accuracy of the dating of the text in its entirety to the late sixth–early seventh century, he believes that Moschos' text is rich in "vernacular language as much as its content in theological and social views."[82] J.S. Palmer addresses several ways in which Moschos' work contributes to our understanding of the eastern monastic life and material culture of the era and geography;[83] John Wortley, who has written extensively on beneficial tales as a genre, both cautions against blind acceptance of what is said as evidence of "popular" mentality but also affirms that "the value of the tales rests in the light they can shed on the social, intellectual and spiritual condition of the mass of the people who are so little known."[84] Most recently Yizhar Hirschfeld regards *The Meadow* as one of the most important sources of Palestinian, Syrian and Egyptian monasticism, second only to Cyril of Scythopolis' *History of the Monks of Palestine*.[85]

Christian literature of all genres has long been concerned with methods, forms and expressions of truth-telling, and the legitimacy of the claim is enhanced by convincing the audience that what is being transmitted comes from a reliable source. We find in many of John's tales an acknowledgement of this need for authenticity, as he often reveals not only the source of the tale, but the source's source, as well as where various characters in the tale were living—or dying—when they received the information, all for the purpose of validating the "truth" and accuracy of the account for John's audience. For the faithful of Moschos' day, the veracity of any account in his "copious and accurate collection"[86] lies not within a systematic series of names of those adherents of the Chalcedonian faith; the names are verification that they will direct the faithful to that which is "true" in a far more important and deeper way. Distinct from this, however, is what the historian hopes to find, even as

---

[82] Philip Pattenden, "The Text of the Pratum Spirituale," JTS NS, Vol. 26 (1975): 38. Elsewhere, he writes: "Very many of the stories of the Patrum are embellished with factual information. Often we are told the provenances of people, the exact location of monasteries and churches, the prices of items. These indications are, for the secular reader, the chief use of the work, for they provide details for the social history of the East in the period immediately before the Arab conquest in a way few other works do." Pattenden, *Prolegomena to a New Edition of the Pratum Spirituale of John Moschus with a Specimen of the Edition* (PhD diss., University of Oxford, 1979): 22.

[83] José Simón Palmer, "Materielle Kultur im Pratum spirituale vom Johannes Moschos," in *XVIIth International Congress of Byzantine Studies. Summaries of communications*, Vol. 2 (1991): 1068–70; José Simón Palmer, *El monacato oriental en el Pratum spirituale de Juan Mosco* (Madrid, 1993).

[84] Wortley, *Spiritually Beneficial Tales of Paul*, 48. It is worth noting that he is writing about a selection of tales. Regardless, the same sentiment applies to beneficial tales as a genre.

[85] Yizhar Hirschfeld, *The Judean Desert Monasteries in the Byzantine Period* (Yale University Press, 1992).

[86] PG 87.2852; Wortley, *The Spiritual Meadow*, 4.

she might look to those same details for an altogether distinct type of truth. Elizabeth Clark's study of women in hagiographic accounts provides excellent examples of these distinctions, reminding us that holy "lives" do not necessarily reflect life at all, but the ideal image of what a holy life should be.[87] Consequently, Averil Cameron notes, a historian of our era, presented with the significant challenges that she faces when looking for history in texts that did not intend to function as such, should recognize that she "cannot apply the same criteria to these works as we would to formal history; but … we cannot afford to not take them seriously either as indicative of contemporary attitudes or, in many cases, as sources of historical information."[88] This is a more generous attitude concerning the possibility that theological claims might aid historical understanding than that expressed by Frederick Conybeare, who writes in the introduction to his translation of Antiochus Stategos' eyewitness account of the 614 sack of Jerusalem that "I have much reduced its bulk by omitting pious ejaculations and other passages devoid of historical interest."[89] It is well to keep that level of cynicism in check when reading John's *Meadow*, with his wide-ranging collection of anecdotes for wisdom, amusement or education. That said, verification of occasional practices and activities that emerge in other texts reveals to us glimmers of the social history of their era, evidence of what Clark notes, that "historians of late antiquity see these tales as rich mines for the construction of social history, even when they turn a skeptical eye on the reports of miracles and demons."[90]

This would all be considerably simpler if the manuscript as we have it today were exactly what John wrote. The manuscript tradition clearly suggests, however, that the text that remains is not as John composed it.[91] Surviving manuscripts of *The Meadow* vary in content and location,[92] the former of which is most often blamed on the enthusiastic copyist, who likely altered written forms of *The Meadow* when the text in front of him did not match what he knew in his memory to be true about the accounts he was being asked to preserve.[93] Thus, over time, an informal editing of *The Meadow* emerged naturally as society moved away from oral tradition, producing, Wortley claims, "as many *Meadows* as there were 'copies,' which in truth are *versions* in many cases, rather than copies."[94] Pattenden notes this as well, affirming that the production of versions emerged early on: "Since

---

[87] Elizabeth Clark, "Holy Women, Holy Words: Early Christian Women, Social History and the 'Linguistic Turn,'" JECS, Vol. 6 (1998): 413–30.

[88] Cameron, "New Themes and Styles in Greek Literature," 92.

[89] Frederick C. Conybeare, "Notes and Documents: Antiochus Strategos' Account of the Sack of Jerusalem in A.D. 614," EHR, Vol. 25, No. 99 (1910): 502.

[90] Clark, "Holy Women, Holy Words," 418–19.

[91] Pattenden, "The Text of the Pratum Spirituale," 38

[92] Pattenden notes that the Great Lavra on Mount Athos has at least ten manuscripts that date to the tenth century, but as he had not found anyone willing to cooperate in providing access to them, he could not make a judgment. Pattenden, *Prolegomena*, 33 and 41.

[93] Wortley notes, in conversation, that the tale begins with the outline, the details of which are provided either by a scribe or the teller of the tale.

[94] Wortley, "Translator's Note," xiii.

no single surviving manuscript contains all tales attributed to Moschus, it follows that the tradition of the text became divided at an early period and that various copies were made of various parts of it."[95] This presents a significant challenge, for it is inaccurate to suggest that something that was *not* written in the seventh century reflects the social history of the seventh century, and ideally a historian makes every attempt to be precise in their understanding of the past; however, it is accurate to suggest that tales that were added or altered over the years clearly drew on the model that Moschos provided, and to that extent Moschos most certainly set a standard for a type of writing that could reasonably bloom and flourish if transplanted into *The Meadow*.

In light of manuscript variables, I am glad that Pattenden asked the questions that he asked of the editions (specifically "Did John write this or not?"), but that is not my question. Rather, questions I bring to the text reflect my training as a historian of theological and hagiographical texts largely within the Byzantine/ Eastern Christian realm; consequently, my concern is how a particular edifying and beneficial tale reveals to us what mattered for the author and audience roughly contemporary with the text. Authorship, while important, is not my affair. And thus these various contexts and "shifting boundaries"—geographic, theological, economic, political and literary—matter for reading this text precisely because this present study is concerned with the way in which *The Meadow* allows us to construct something of the social history of a turbulent early medieval Byzantine Empire, including attitudes towards ethics, piety and sacraments,[96] poverty,[97] demons[98] and miracles, orthodoxy and heresy,[99] the role of the ascetic,[100] organizations and relationships,[101] and—specific to this project—how relationships among laity and the professional religious, issues of wealth and poverty, health and healing, death and dying were addressed among early Byzantine religious and secular society. Consequently, Moschos' *Meadow*, despite what few facts we have about authorship and dates of composition, remains valuable for it provides our

---

[95] Pattenden, *Prolegomena*, 33.

[96] Booth, *Moschus, Sophronius, Maximus*, 8–35; 70–106.

[97] Évelyne Patlagean, *Pauvreté économique et pauvreté sociale à Byzance, 4e–7e siècles*, Civilisations et Sociétés 48 (Paris: De Gruyter Mouton, 1977). See Chapter 2 of this volume for specific references.

[98] José Simón Palmer, "Demonología en el Pratum spirituale de Juan Mosco," in *Actas del VIII Congreso Español de Estudios Clásicos*, Vol. 3 (Madrid, 1994): 304–8; see also Palmer, *El monacato oriental en el Pratum spirituale*, 357–70.

[99] José Simón Palmer, "Juan Mosco y la defensa del dogma de Calcedón," in M. Morfakidis and M. Alganza (eds), *La religión en el mundo griego. De la Antigüedad a la Grecia moderna* (Granada, 1997): 289–97; Palmer, *El monacato oriental en el Pratum spirituale*, 371–91.

[100] Palmer, *El monacato oriental en el Pratum spirituale*; see ch. 6.

[101] Palmer, *El monacato oriental en el Pratum spirituale*; see chs 2, 3, 7 and 10; Harry J. Magoulias, "The Lives of the Saints as Sources for Byzantine Agrarian Life in the Sixth and Seventh Centuries," GOTR, Vol. 35, No. 1 (1990): 59–70.

contemporary society with a fuller picture and richer history of an era accessible to us only imperfectly and vaguely. In this way it is an internationally recognized bountiful source for understanding not only the piety of the monk, but that of the poor farmer; it reveals the way in which a fertile Christian theology informed the social ethics of those serving at the altar and those served. And yet I caution that as we consider to what degree these texts might reflect seventh-century social history, I also wish to be clear that they might very well not. Greater minds than mine have concluded already that *The Meadow* is important for understanding this era, and thus I do not feel compelled to apologize for the manuscript as it was composed in the Migne edition (PG 87.2851–3166) alongside the Latin translation by Ambrose Traversari (Fra Ambrogio). Appropriately, it is worth saying something at this point about the Greek text that I used. First, occasional titles to which I refer have been drawn from the titles from Wortley's translation, as I do as well with lengthier Greek passages (as I trust his expert abilities more than my own). As there remains no critical edition of *The Meadow*, the Greek text from which I worked is a PDF of a warped photocopy of the J.P. Migne edition, kindly provided to me by my dear friend Dr Heracles Panagiotides. In addition, I made use of additional tales edited in Elpidio Mioni, "Il Pratum Spirituale de Giovanni Mosco; gli episodi inediti del Cod. Marciano greco II.21," OCP (1951): 61–94 and Theodor Nissen, "Unbekannte Erzählungen aus dem Pratum Spirituale," BZ, Vol. 38 (1938): 351–76. Also worth mentioning are French and Italian translations easily available, and exceedingly helpful: *Le Pré Spirituel*, translated by Paris M.-J. Rouët de Journel (*Sources Chrétiennes* 12, 1946), and *Giovanni Mosco, Il Prato*, translated by Riccardo Maisano (Naples: D'Auria M., 1982).

To return to the context of the text itself, interaction of these aforementioned elements forms the foundation of the four chapters that follow, as each chapter considers how an imperfect sense of history might enable us to understand the theology, and, conversely, how understanding the theology aids us in reconstructing something of the social history. Specifically, I am interested in exploring how these texts address issues of agency and providence, and the autonomy and independence of the individual (ascetic and lay) against the authority figure as they are represented in the literary evidence. The first chapter will take an intimate look at what the texts reveal to us about social relations between ascetics and lay persons, and how these relations might teach us something about how individuals used their relationships to "prove" or "improve" ascetic programs. Because the majority—if not all—of the tales were collected against a backdrop of impoverished circumstances, the second chapter will consider the way in which select tales demonstrate economic practices that were clearly grounded in contemporary patristic theology, specifically concerning the presence of Christ in the suffering poor, poverty for the sake of salvation, and the activity of almsgiving. As well, because Moschos assembled his tales during an age when all levels of society struggled not only with poverty but also with illness, the third chapter will consider the way in which Moschos' text presents a unique picture of complicated relationships between personal agency and divine intercession, a relationship that allows bodies with diseases to be cured or diseases to be endured to contribute to the creation of religious and social identity. Finally, as a proper conclusion to a consideration of illness and in recognition that death remains the sole way in which we are bound intimately to the histories of those in the past, the final chapter considers what Moschos' beneficial tales might teach us about how monks and those who interacted with them faced and interpreted death, as well as how the concept of death shaped their relations with one another. Common to all of these chapters is the theme of autonomy. In a precarious world of shifting boundaries, *The Meadow* tales reveal tensions particular to the seventh century and the twenty-first: between the established institution and the individual, the communal and the solitary, the wealthy and the poor, the male and the female, the novice and the elder, the ill and the healthy, the living and the dead. In this way, we can know that while Moschos' *Meadow* might teach us something of the seventh century, it will certainly teach us something of ourselves at the same time.

Chapter 1

Monks in *The Meadow*:
Proving and Improving the Ascetic Program

Introduction

In 1992, Christopher Johnson McCandless died of starvation in an abandoned bus north of Mt McKinley, Alaska. Two years earlier he had graduated from Emory University and quickly divested himself of his possessions, his money and his relationship with his family. Adventure and travel writer Jon Krakauer reported McCandless' story for *Outside* magazine,[1] which he later expanded into a national bestseller and feature film, both titled *Into the Wild*.[2] McCandless' story was riveting and polarizing, and produced strong commentary that either lauded his romanticism or harshly criticized what people unsympathetically considered a foolish lack of basic survival skills.[3] His story would have been as captivating to monks of Moschos' era, some of whom would claim that one does not seek the angelic life on one's own, while others would claim that survival is not necessarily the point of walking into the wild.

Whether each point were to be argued by a monastic in the sixth century or a lay person in the twenty-first, both positions betray a fundamental misunderstanding about lines drawn between a life dedicated to ascetic ideals and a life that is not, and, further, what physical movement contributes to conversation between the two positions. Scholarship on the movement of monastic figures has successfully uncovered their vibrant lives and has rightly linked them—no matter how transient or isolated—with economic and social structures of the Mediterranean world.[4] John Wortley notes that "it is clear from that material itself that the separation between the wilderness and the world was not by any means absolute,"[5] and religious and

---

[1] Jon Krakauer, "Death of an Innocent: How Christopher McCandless lost his way in the wilds," *Outside Magazine*, January 1993.

[2] Jon Krakauer, *Into the Wild* (New York: Anchor Books, 1996); Jon Krakauer and Sean Penn, *Into the Wild*, directed by Sean Penn (2007; Los Angeles, Paramount Vantage).

[3] Krakauer, *Into the Wild*, 70–72.

[4] Peter Charanis, "The Monk as an Element of Byzantine Society," DOP, Vol. 25 (1971): 61–84.

[5] Wortley, "The Genre of the Spiritually Beneficial Tale," 22; see also Derwas J. Chitty, *The Desert a City: An Introduction to the Study of Egyptian and Palestinian Monasticism Under the Christian Empire* (Crestwood, NY: St Vladimir's Seminary Press, 1995), 46–64; Marilyn Dunn, *The Emergence of Monasticism: From the Desert Fathers to the Early Middle Ages* (Oxford: Blackwell, 2003): 36–45; Susanna Elm, *Virgins of God:*

ethnic dislocation into which Christian monasticism emerged and developed contributed in its own way to the general culture of movement.[6] This, in turn, shaped social relations, self-sufficiency and the development of the landscape, as evident in Moschos' text as in any other of the genre.[7] Several centuries of migrations and invasions into western provinces by various Germanic tribes and into eastern provinces by Slavic, Bulgar and Persian tribes created an atmosphere in which movement of all types of individuals carried with it the potential to be permeated with religious import.[8] In her careful and extensive treatment of religious travel, Maribel Dietz distinguishes between those exiled as a result of conciliar decision, restless individuals, spiritual/monastic wanderings, pilgrimage travel and missionary activity before considering the "worst" or "inferior" types of traveling monks, identified by Jerome and Cassian as "remnouth" and "sarabaites" respectively, and a category of traveling monastics more carefully refined in the *Regula Magistri* as "gyrovagues."[9] Regarding remnouth, Jerome writes that "These men live together in twos and threes, seldom in larger numbers, and live according to their own will and ruling."[10] Curiously, this description fits many figures in *The Meadow*, including the author and his companion. Regarding sarabaites, Cassian writes that they are despised *because* of their separation and concern for their own needs.[11] Although Palladius mentions the gyrovagues also in his *Lausiac History*—confirming that this was not a problem limited to western monastic communities[12]—these flaws do not appear to pertain to Moschos and Sophronios; there are no passages in *The Meadow* to suggest that they are neither welcomed nor treated with proper hospitality, or suspected of being imposters. That

---

The Making of Asceticism in Late Antiquity (Oxford University Press, 1996): 311–30; Caner, *Wandering, Begging Monks*, 47–9; Philip Rousseau, "Christian Asceticism and the Early Monks," in Ian Hazlett (ed.), *Early Christianity: Origins and Evolution to A.D. 600* (London: Abingdon Press, 1991): 117.

[6] Miriam Raub Vivian, "Monastic Mobility and Roman Transformation: The Example of St. Daniel the Stylite," *Studia Patristica*, Vol. 39 (Leuven: Peeters, 2009): 461–2.

[7] José Simón Palmer, "El monje ye la ciudad en el '*Pratum spirituale*' de Juan Mosco," in Χαρις Διδασκαλιας, *Studia In Honorem Ludovici Aegidii Edendi Curam Paraverunt* (Madrid: Editorial Complutense, 1994): 495–504.

[8] Maribel Dietz, *Wandering Monks, Virgins and Pilgrims: Ascetic Travel in the Mediterranean World, A.D. 300–800* (Pennsylvania State University Press, 2005): 2, 23–6.

[9] "deterrimum atque neglectum," in Jerome, *Ep.* 22.34, in *Hieronymus, Epistularum Pars I, Epistulae I–LXX*, ed. Isidorus Hilberg, *Corpus Scriptorum Ecclesiasticorum Latinorum*, Vol. LIV (Wien: VÖAW, 1996): 196–7; *Select Letters of St. Jerome*, trans. F.A. Wright (Harvard University Press, 1963), 136–7.

[10] Jerome, *Ep.* 22.34 (Hilberg, 197); Wright, *Select Letters*, 136–7.

[11] "ils se séparaient des communautés cénobitiques et veillaient eux-mêmes à leurs besoins." John Cassian, 18.4, in Jean Cassien, *Conférences*, XVIII–XXIV, trans. Dom E. Pichery, *Sources Chrétiennes*, No. 64 (Paris: Les Éditions du Cerf, 1959): 17–18.

[12] Palladius, *Historia Lausiaca*, 32.5 (PG 65.1099–100); *Palladius: The Lausiac History*, trans. Robert T. Meyer, ACW, 34 (New York: Paulist Press, 1964): 93.

said, I would not argue that Moschos makes a claim for the spiritual significance of his itinerancy or that of any of the wandering monks in his tales, or at least not an overt one such as that of Fabiola, whose feelings of confinement led her to seek an itinerant life in which she was "in every sphere, foreign."[13] Rather, Moschos' argument is that the virtuous life be focused not only on "studying [what is] divine"[14] but on the composition of the praiseworthy lives of others. Wandering *itself* is not Moschos' goal, even as he does an awful lot of it; wandering occurs because writing about the tales that he gathers is a significant component of his particular ascetic program, an element of his monastic vocation and discipline, and he cannot write tales that have not been gleaned from the meadow. In Moschos' case—like the Scottish-American writer and environmental champion John Muir many centuries later and, dare I add, Chris McCandless—wilderness and movement within it contribute to Moschos' ability to produce thoughtful reflections on his environment, which results in their preservation.

Evidence of positions for and against wandering exist, which present challenges if one hopes for continuity; for example, note the distinction between a brother's complaint to Abba Sisoes that the brothers are mocking him for "making a practice of racing from place to place"[15] with the tale of John the elder, whose injured feet were healed by an angel who ordered him to return to his life of grazing and "wandering from place to place."[16] Likewise, Antony did not always appear to obey the counsel that he is credited with giving, that one should not be too eager to move on.[17] Although the link between asceticism and travel is neither explicitly identified nor denied in eastern monasticism, the link between writing and ascesis has been quite persuasively acknowledged. Recent studies on how the holy life is—and might have been—understood reveal how hagiographers were more than cultural or spiritual voyeurs; in the process of collecting and writing beneficial tales, Moschos himself engaged in more than preservation. Writing allowed him to participate in the virtuous lives of the subjects of the tales, even if he did not emulate their particular ascesis directly. Claudia Rapp observes that author, saint, text and audience are tied

---

[13] "in omni orbe peregrine," Jerome, *Ep.* 77.8, Hilberg, 46; Wright, *Select Letters*.
[14] "θεια μελέτη," *Prat. sp.* PG 87.2851–2.
[15] Eth.Coll. 14.37, trans. Victor Arras, 87, in Caner, *Wandering, Begging Monks*, 22.
[16] HME 13.3–8, in *The Lives of the Desert Fathers*, trans. Norman Russell (Oxford: Cistercian Publications, 1980), 93–4.
[17] *Vita Antonii*, 3 (PG 26.843–6). Caner, in *Wandering, Begging Monks*, 21–2, notes the academic discussion as well as source material, with emphasis on Rousseau and Gould concerning degrees to which one can uncover an original view on monastic mobility; see also Philip Rousseau, *Ascetics, Authority and the Church in the Age of Jerome and Cassian* (University of Notre Dame Press, 2010): 40–49; Graham Gould, "Moving On and Staying Put in the *Apophthegmata Patrum*," *Studia Patristica* 20 (1989): 231–7; Brouria Bitton-Ashkelony, *Encountering the Sacred: The Debate on Christian Pilgrimage in Late Antiquity* (University of California Press, 2005): 140–83; Hans Von Campenhausen, "The Ascetic Idea of Exile in Ancient and Medieval Monasticism," in *Tradition and Life in The Church; Essays and Lectures in Church History* (Philadelphia, PA: Fortress Press, 1968): 231–51.

together in a complex web of relations, as an author is participant, model, witness and "prototype of the saint's clientele."[18] In this way, Krueger notes, authors of ascetic activity and monastic history engaged in a creative spiritual endeavor equally as beneficial as that of the ascetic action in its most pure form,[19] thus providing—not unlike an icon—a vehicle of uncreated grace and blessing in imitation, a material point of contact for those unable to access the body of the ascetic.[20] Cox Miller notes, in fact, that at times Moschos presents a series of conflated visuals, as in the tale of a woman who sees a vision of a man who tells her to lower an icon of a holy person into a well in order to encourage the well to bring forth water.[21]

Moschos was able to access many of these ascetic bodies or, at the very least, those who spoke of them. But despite brief notations of physical endeavors, *The Meadow* is characteristically bereft of Moschos' interior expedition; as befits a beneficial tale he dwells neither on his own travel nor on travel as a mirror of his spiritual journey. Rather, he directs the gaze of the reader or his audience (present and future) to the accounts he offers: various ascetic practices and lives that he records are "roses," "lilies" and "violets,"[22] whose beauty captivates the viewer by their unique offerings. As the Introduction to this study covers reasons for Moschos' and Sophronios' travel within the historical context of late sixth-century Byzantium, I note here that the travel required for this particular asceticism reveals not only the management that Moschos and Sophronios must have had over their own ascetic regime, but that in the process they uncover a great deal of additional monastic movement, ascetic practices and a variety of interactions and relationships with laity. Such a degree of activity points to fluid and creative categories of monastic life in the early Byzantine east and, further, suggests some degree of self-regulation, some degree of "loose" control over and creative approach to one's own spiritual movement. If one cannot point to a clear indication that monastic travel is proper use of a monk's time, Moschos' own defense of his participation in the ascetic life through writing on the diversity and variety of practices offers some clue to his thinking about these various factors.

Self-management is never more apparent than when considering various relationships and personal encounters in *The Meadow*, moments into which

---

[18] Claudia Rapp, "Storytelling as Spiritual Communication in Early Greek Hagiography: The Use of Diegesis," JECS, Vol. 6, No. 3 (1998): 432.

[19] Krueger, *Writing and Holiness*, 94; Derek Krueger, "Writing as Devotion: Hagiographical Composition and the Cult of the Saints in Theodoret of Cyrrhus and Cyril of Scythopolis," ASCH, Vol. 66, No. 4 (1997): 707–19; Derek Krueger, "Hagiography as an Ascetic Practice in the Early Christian East," JR, Vol. 79, No. 2 (1999): 216–32.

[20] Krueger, *Writing and Holiness*, 96.

[21] *Prat. sp.* 81 (PG 87.2939–40); Patricia Cox Miller, *The Corporeal Imagination: Signifying the Holy in Late Antique Christianity* (University of Pennsylvania Press, 2009), 149; Patricia Cox Miller, "Desert Asceticism and the 'The Body from Nowhere,'" JECS, Vol. 2, No. 2 (1994): 144.

[22] "ῥόδων, κρίνοις" and "ἴων," *Prat. sp.* PG 87.2851–2.

ascetics enter as free persons[23] liberated from the distractions of the world. In this way, however, the theory of asceticism is betrayed consistently because even as engagement with others flows logically from ascetic practice, it creates a tension between practice and theory that simply is not solvable. The results of this conflict are as polarizing as opinions towards asceticism itself, and this is not assisted in any way by the general body of hagiographic literature.

Historic stress on the theme of "ἀναχώρησις" in hagiography has made it convenient to understand the term as "isolated from" rather than recognizing that the concept is simply more ambiguous. "In itself," Kallistos Ware writes, "*anachōrēsis* can be either negative or positive, either world-denying or world-affirming."[24] To a certain extent, relationships and interaction among ascetics and others is necessary in order that an ascetic may either prove the level of their ascetic program or improve it in light of individual need, criticism, education or counsel. In this way, the ambiguity that Ware identifies has the opportunity for transformation within the ascetic program of the individual ascetic. Subsequent chapters in this study will consider the way in which ascetics use their bodies as tools of subversion, to seek control over their circumstances, health, ascetic programs, death, relationships with other monks or to express disdain for systems and individuals.[25] But we might begin here by taking into account the way in which their relationships with each other and with those exterior to the monastic life might have shaped an understanding of the ascetic life, a life entirely dependent on the need to continuously prove and improve the spiritual self.

Richard Valantasis—who constructs a theory of asceticism in light of Weber, Foucault and Harpham—claims that asceticism is at its core the practice of refashioning the individual self, recasting all relationships and recreating the environment within which one exists.[26] When one considers asceticism using Valantasis' definition, it can be viewed as a profoundly hopeful practice, as it suggests persistent movement on all planes towards a transformed and perfected self and reality: "Through asceticism, integration into a culture occurs at every level of human existence: consciously and unconsciously; voluntarily and involuntarily; somatic and mental; emotional and intellectual; religious and secular."[27] For Valantasis, asceticism is a constantly tilting lens; the ascetic must struggle to keep in view the new subjectivity towards which they move by actions that create a distinct culture and define and redefine, prove and improve relationships. Precisely on account of ascesis—not in spite of it or in defiance of it—ascetics are able to enter freely into relationships and "prove or

---

[23] Donald A. Lowrie, *Christian Existentialism: A Berdyaev Anthology* (London, 1965): 86–7.

[24] Kallistos Ware, "The Way of the Ascetics: Negative or Affirmative?" in Vincent L. Wimbush (ed.), *Asceticism* (Oxford University Press, 1995): 4.

[25] Chapters 3 and 4.

[26] Richard Valantasis, "A Theory of the Social Function of Asceticism," in Vincent L. Wimbush and Richard Valantasis (eds), *Asceticism* (Oxford University Press, 1995).

[27] Ibid., 547.

improve" themselves because the individual encountered ideally receives the benefit of engagement with one who, not being held captive by their distraction with sin, "is capable of genuine love."[28] To consider what "proving and improving" might look like in Moschos' beneficial tales and, consequently, what this might reveal to us about social relations between ascetics and lay persons, this first chapter will address how (1) relations among ascetic figures contribute towards proving the ascetic life and (2) how relations among and between ascetic figures and laity contribute towards improving the ascetic life.

"In every sphere, foreign"[29]: Proving the Ascetic Program

One day a peasant was working on his land when he was approached by an individual identified in the text as an anchorite.[30] "Out of charity," the anchorite requested, "take your mattock (pick-axe) and spade and come with me."[31] The peasant agreed, and was led up a mountain to the tomb of the anchorite's elder, who had only just recently died and been buried by his disciple. The anchorite directed the peasant to dig up the grave while he stood in prayer, after which he embraced the peasant, went into the grave, lay down on top of the body of his elder and died. The peasant filled the grave, later musing that he should have taken a blessing from them.[32] Try as he might, however, he was unable to find their grave, and thus these anchorites remained as firm in their renunciation of social relations in death as they did in life. That the identities of the anchorites remain as obscure to us as their graves were to the peasant reveals as much about notions of anonymity and identity, the desire to remain "in omni urbe peregrine"[33] in an environment of shifting boundaries as it does about agency. But while we can note that they successfully lived and died beneath the radar of those close to them— the peasant does not indicate that he knows the disciple, the disciple does not greet him by name, and no reference is made to grieving over the death of these two other than lamenting a lost opportunity for a blessing—nevertheless when it became necessary, the disciple undertook a journey into the "*oikoumenê*,"[34] into the inhabited world in order that his specific needs might be met. *The Meadow* features several note-worthy monks and famous individuals whose names we do know: possibly Daniel of Sketis,[35] for example, as well as Abba Gerasimus

---

[28] Ware, "The Way of the Ascetics: Negative or Affirmative?" 12.
[29] "et in omni urbe peregrina." Jerome, *Ep.* 77.8, Hilberg; Wright, *Select Letters*, 46.
[30] *Prat. sp.* 90 (PG 87.2947–8).
[31] "Ποίησον ἀγάπην, καλόγηρε, λάβε ὀρύγιον καὶ ἅμην, καὶ δευρο μετ' ἐμου." Ibid.
[32] "Ὄντως εἶχον λαβειν εὐλογίαν των ἁγίων." Ibid.
[33] See note 29.
[34] "οἰκουμένης," *Prat. sp.* 90 (PG 87.2948).
[35] *Prat. sp.* 114 (PG 87.2977–80); Il Mioni, "Il Pratum Spirituale de Giovanni Mosco," 92–3; Tim Vivian (ed.), *Witness to Holiness: Abba Daniel of Scetis* (Kalamazoo,

with his lion,[36] and even emperors.[37] But other anonymous characters feature prominently, such as our aforementioned nameless anchorite and his elder. The advantage of a collection of unidentified individuals is that it provides historians with different opportunities from those presented in majestic tales of well-known ascetics, whose deeds and saintly authority have taken them much further up the spiritual ladder, but whose activity was previously treated with either too much caution or not enough.[38] In texts such as *The Meadow*, however, we find ourselves closer to the ground of ascetic practice than in tales of holy exemplars;[39] it is particularly ironic that the most perfected form of asceticism would truly leave no traces of its existence at all.

Of *Meadow* anchorites, no category is closer to the ground than "βοσκοί" or "grazers," and tales highlight this particular method of proving one's ascetic program either because it holds a particular fascination for Moschos personally or because of its considerable popularity among anchorites.[40] The category of anchorites—a term that suggests commentary on spatial withdrawal ("ἀναχώρησις")—is vague. "βοσκός" ("*bruteur*," Ltn/Fr.)—a term that suggests commentary on their tendency to graze ("βόσκω") on grasses, wild roots, berries, nuts, fruits and vegetables[41]— is not vague at all; it is quite precise. One might be an anchorite for one's entire monastic career, but grazing was a *form* of "ἀναχώρησις" that might be merely a temporary state. "Ἀναχώρησις" can be loosely connected to every single monk, and, if one is being literal, to every person at one point or another in their lifetime; grazing less so, for since the development of agricultural methods, considerably fewer people have intentionally survived by grazing, unless one is a Bedouin[42] or unless starvation was the alternative. Problems connected with this practice in

---

MI: Cistercian Publications, 2008): 90–91; Chitty, *The Desert a City*, 145–7; Britt Dahlman, *Saint Daniel of Sketis: A Group of Hagiographic Texts*, Studia Byzantina Upsaliensia (Uppsala Universitet, 2007): 55–6.

[36] *Prat. sp.* 107 (PG 87.2965–70).

[37] *Prat. sp.* 175 (PG 87.3043–4), *Prat. sp.* 186 (PG 87.3061–4); 12 Mioni, "Il Pratum Spirituale de Giovanni Mosco," 93–4.

[38] Patricia Cox Miller, "Strategies of Representation in Collective Biography," in Tomas Hägg, Christian Høgel and Philip Rousseau (eds), *Greek Biography and Panegyric in Late Antiquity* (University of California Press, 2000): 209–54; Patlagean, "Ancient Byzantine Hagiography and Social History," in Stephen Wilson (ed.), *Saints and Their Cults: Studies in Religious Sociology, Folklore and History* (University of Cambridge, 1993): 101–2.

[39] Averil Cameron, *Christianity and the Rhetoric of Empire: The Development of Christian Discourse* (University of California Press, 1991): 123.

[40] Palmer, *El monacato oriental en el Pratum spirituale*, 239–41.

[41] Yizar Hirschfeld, "Edible Wild Plants: The Secret Diet of Monks in the Judean Desert," *Israel: Land and Nature*, 16 (1990): 27; Hirschfeld, *Judean Desert Monasteries*, 82–91; 215. John Binns, *Ascetics and Ambassadors of Christ: The Monasteries of Palestine 314–631*, OECS (Oxford University Press, 1996): 108. Sozomen, *HE*, 6.33.2 (PG 67.1393–4).

[42] Andrew Jotischky, *A Hermit's Cookbook: Monks, Food and Fasting in the Middle Ages* (London: Continuum International, 2011): 41.

urban areas appeared to emerge as individuals moved from satisfying only their needs to snacking or shopping in the fields of others.[43]

This particular type of asceticism was quite popular in the early centuries of Christianity, particularly in Egypt, Syria and Palestine, and might be connected in practice and philosophy to those identified in Syriac as a particular type of "*avilo*" (anchorite) who identified themselves as "mourners."[44] And as anchorites withdrew for the purpose of becoming the very scripture they recited in the *synaxis*,[45] "βοσκοί" become the very *terra firma* they renounced. No example speaks more clearly to the accuracy of this than Ephraem's observation that "[t]here are many of them who, while they were kneeling in prayer, quietly attained their rest before the Lord."[46] Recall our story at the beginning of the chapter; had the anchorite been unable to find someone to assist him in burial he would surely have returned to the grave of his elder and pressed himself to the earth. As the earth nourished these determined idealists in perhaps the most organic form of "natural asceticism,"[47] "βοσκοί" reaped in abundance the very renunciation they sought.

Although it is tempting to claim them as such, "βοσκοί" are not emotionally unstable, mentally ill or purposely foolish individuals, though a propensity for nudity, cultivation of excessive body hair and an intentionally challenging diet might lead the uninformed to that opinion.[48] They are also neither beggars—as they ask for nothing from no one—nor transients, although their specialized diets mean that they might spend a great deal of time foraging, which requires them, like grazing animals, to cover a certain amount of ground. Further, their isolation does not mean that they are social misfits or misanthropes; they do not shun human relationships as many times they traveled in pairs or groups, or were attended to by disciples, as we may have seen in the example above, and as we will certainly learn in the second part of this chapter. In his study of Judaean desert "βοσκοί," Wortley notes that Moschos includes more tales of "βοσκοί" in his *Meadow* combined then in all hagiography exterior to this text,[49] with 11 passages referencing at least 15

---

[43] Gildas Hamel, *Poverty and charity in Roman Palestine, first three centuries C.E.* (University of California Press, 1990): 17–18. See: Augustine, *De opera monachorum* 23.28. See also the account of Zeno, a desert father who was tempted to nick a cucumber. *APalph*, Zeno 6 (PG 65.177–8); *The Sayings of the Desert Fathers*, trans. Benedicta Ward, 66–7.

[44] Andrew Palmer, *Monk and Mason on the Tigris Frontier: The Early History of Tur 'Abdin* (Cambridge University Press, 1990): 85.

[45] Burton-Christie, *The Word in the Desert*, 117–29.

[46] Chapter 107 in John Wortley, "Grazers (ΒΟΣΚΟΙ) in the Judaean Desert," in Joseph Patrich (ed.), *The Sabaite Heritage in the Orthodox Church from the Fifth Century to the Present* (Leuven: Peeters, 2001): 47 and earlier.

[47] Ware, "The Way of the Ascetics: Negative or Affirmative?" 8–12.

[48] Sergey A. Ivanov, *Holy Fools in Byzantium and Beyond*, OSB (Oxford University Press, 2006); Derek Krueger, *Symeon the Holy Fool: Leontius's Life and the Late Antique City*, TCH (University of California Press, 1996).

[49] Wortley, "Grazers," 39–41.

grazers;[50] this suggests to Wortley a familiarity that makes it a "well defined"[51] tradition in Moschos' context.[52] In addition to being well defined, *The Meadow* affirms that grazing is well practiced in anchoritic life. Despite fairly consistent anonymity of "βοσκοί," encounters with others provide them with opportunity to "prove" or defend commitment to this ascetic program. It would be uncharitable and inaccurate to suggest that ascetics engaged in self-analysis solely or primarily for self-promotion; and yet, when one's entire life is organized around analysis of the *self*, as Maud Gleason points out, "status negotiation and behavioral regulation"[53] are dependent on actions and the words of others, the collection of which we have determined was at least some component of Moschos' ascetic practice.

The first tale to consider is an account of Abba Elijah.[54] After helping a thirsty female grazer[55] the abba is overcome by lustful thoughts and sets out to satisfy what "ὁ διάβολος" placed there,[56] a convenient—and not abnormal—deflection of sinful thoughts. He passes out and in a trance sees the open earth filled with decayed, rotting corpses; he is informed that he might do to the male and female corpses whatever he wants, but to be mindful of how much he is destroying for so little pleasure.[57] Although it is tempting to get lost in the sexual drama of what the abba sees and smells in the "*apertam terram*"—not to mention that he is shown many bodies and told to do whatever his passion dictates[58]—still, I wish to highlight two points: first, that abba is narrating this account of his ascetic triumph to Moschos and Sophronios[59] *at all*. Were he to not describe these events, how would anyone be able to profit by his struggle and—lest we forget—how else might he prove to what heights his ascetic program has led him? The woman whom he assists fails to appear again in the tale; she drinks and departs. Without her, there are no witnesses to his defeat of temptation. The telling of the tale is an imperative, for his status will not be recognized without transmission of the account; in this, Moschos is an essential component of the aforementioned "status negotiation and behavioral regulation"[60] of this particular society for he provides the opportunity for the tale to be told, remembered, written down, preserved. A second point worth noting is that the tale concerns a time in the ascetic's life when he was "not in communion"

---

[50] Wortley, "Grazers," 38. Wortley lists the following *Meadow* accounts: 19, 21, 84, 86, 92, 115, 129, 154, 159 and 167. To this list I would add 179, to be discussed below.

[51] Wortley, "Grazers," 38.

[52] Ibid.; Hirschfeld, *Judean Monasteries*, 214.

[53] Maud Gleason, "Visiting and News: Gossip and Reputation-Management in the Desert," JECS, Vol. 6, No. 3 (1998): 503.

[54] *Prat. sp.* 19 (PG 87.2865-8).

[55] "Κῦρι ἀββα, κἀγὼ τὴν πολιτείαν ταύτην μετέρχομαι," *Prat. sp.* 19 (PG 87.2865-6).

[56] "Καὶ μετα τὸ ἀπελθειν αὐτὴν, ἤρξατο ὁ διάβολος πολεμειν με εἰς αὐτὴν, καὶ ἐμβάλλειν λογισμούς," *Prat. sp.* 19 (PG 87.2865-6); Wortley, "Grazers," 46.

[57] *Prat. sp.* 19 (PG 87.2865-6).

[58] "ἀπόλαυσαν ποιον οσον θέλεις τησ ἐπιθυμιας σου," *Prat. sp.* 19 (PG 87.2865).

[59] "Διηγήσατο ἡμῖν ὁ αββας Ἡλίας ὁ βοσκὸς," *Prat. sp.* 19 (PG 87.2865).

[60] Gleason, "Visiting and News," 503.

with Abba Macarios, bishop of Jerusalem, which might suggest a movement into this particular type of ascetic practice because of sour relations. Alternatively, perhaps the abba willingly engaged in this practice because he opposed the bishop in some way and this ascetic practice provided him with the means to subvert or oppose the bishop's authority. Regardless, both elements support the necessity of communal engagement in order for one's ascetic levels to be "proven," at the same time that they highlight possibilities of choice and freedom of movement and the freedom of Abba Elijah to redefine his relationship with the bishop. Further, in relating this tale not only about his practice of extreme withdrawal but also about his desire and ability to withstand the temptation set before him, the abba proves his level of ascetic dedication to a witness whose account becomes the means by which the author might also participate in the abba's ascetic behavior. Under the guide of our author, even after the abba has ceased to participate in the practice itself, the tale remains as evidence.

The abba's renunciation of sexual activity and subsequent temptation are fairly typical themes in the literature of the ascetic life, for an element of the ascetic program is to move the individual beyond the expectations of the average individual, which includes not only sexual activity but sexual temptation or desire.[61] But such temptations are not always so blatant, especially in beneficial tales, which have precious little time to tempt. More subtle is the account of the female grazer in *The Meadow*, a chaste version of the "repentant harlot" figure known in other accounts as "Mary of Egypt." Tales about this figure began circulating among eastern monastics in the sixth century,[62] very quickly becoming popular in the west as well. Several shorter accounts with varying distinctions in the details[63]—including that of Moschos'—will become combined, in time, into the longer, much more sensational account of *The Life of Mary of Egypt, the Former Harlot, Who in Blessed Manner Became and Ascetic in the Desert of the [River] Jordan*[64] attributed to Moschos' own companion, Sophronios.[65] The beginning of Moschos' account of a "Woman Religious" suggests less of an edifying tale and more of an opportunity for gossip, beginning thus: Moschos and Sophronios visit John the anchorite, who informs them that he heard Abba John

---

[61] Peter Brown, *The Body and Society: Men, Women, and Sexual Renunciation in Early Christianity* (Columbia University Press, 1988): 210–338.

[62] Benedicta Ward, *Harlots of the Desert: A Study of Repentance in Early Monastic Sources* (Kalamazoo, MI: Cistercian Publications, 1987): 26.

[63] E. Schwartz, *Kyrillos von Skythopolis* (Leipzig, 1939): 233–4; in *Lives of the Palestinian Monks*, trans. R.M. Price (Kalamazoo, MI: Cistercian Publications, 1987): 256–8.

[64] Alice-Mary Talbot (ed.), *Holy Women of Byzantium: Ten Saints' Lives in English Translation*, trans. Maria Kouli (Washington, DC: Dumbarton Oaks, 1996): 70–93. See also Cyril of Skythopolis, in Schwartz, 233–4.

[65] This is not without challenge; see Kouli, in Talbot, *Holy Women of Byzantium*, 66; she also references H. Delehaye, *L'Ancienne hagiographie byzantine: les sources, les premiers modèles, la formation des genres* [= SubsHag, 73] (Brussels, 1991): 53; F. Delmas, "Remarques sur la Vie de Sainte Marie l'Egyptienne," EO 4 (1900–1901): 37.

the Moabite say that there was once a nun who resided in the city and was very devout.⁶⁶ However, as this virgin⁶⁷ was resented by the devil, he placed desire in the heart of a young man. Foreseeing the young man's destruction,⁶⁸ she left the city and went into the wild, with only some water and "[beans,]"⁶⁹ off of which she lived for 17 years.⁷⁰ Although she saw many people in that time, they did not see her, which presents a problem that must be solved: if the ascetic project of one who is close to the ground is going to be proven—as we know it must—then how is that done? Abba Elijah solves the problem himself by giving his own account of his ascetic labors. In our nun's case, Abba John the Moabite reveals this to Abba John the anchorite, who claims that "in order that her virtuous conduct should not remain unknown"⁷¹ she encounters another anchorite who—unlike all the others— sees her and presses her for an explanation as to why she is "in this wild."⁷² Her instinct is to conceal the truth but then—when her visitor states that God had already revealed her identity—she confesses her tale, in response to which our anchorite "glorified God."⁷³

My purpose is neither to trace the historical development of this theme, to question why a pious woman must become a repentant harlot,⁷⁴ nor to offer a critical comparison of these texts.⁷⁵ Nevertheless it is worth highlighting a key difference between the simple tale of a pious grazing nun and Sophronios' later, much more extensive account of the repentance of a woman with an insatiable sexual appetite whose ascetic program is closely identified with divine punishment for what is clearly behavior judged by the author as deviant.⁷⁶ Unlike Mary of

---

⁶⁶ *Prat. sp.* 179 (PG 87.3049): 148–9.
⁶⁷ "παρθένῳ," *Prat. sp.* 179 (PG 87.3049).
⁶⁸ "καὶ τῆς τοῦ νέου ἀπωλείας," ibid.
⁶⁹ "λαβοῦσα εἰς ἓν μάλακιον ὀλίγα βρεκτά," ibid.
⁷⁰ "Ἔχω χάριτι Χριστοῦ ἔτη ιζ´." Ibid. Wortley claims that there is possibly only one text of a female "βοσκός": BHG 1322eb, *de vetula in spelunca* W886, in Wortley, "Grazers," 42. One might contest that our nun's beans disqualify her as a "βοσκός"; I offer that grazing off the same pile of beans for 17 years is as good as grazing from the same patch of grass. Évelyne Patlagean, "L'histoire de la femme déguisée en moine et l'évolution de la sainteté féminine à Byzance," *Studi Medievali*, 3.17 (1976): 597–623.
⁷¹ "ἵνα μὴ ἄγνωστος ἡ ἐνάρετος αὐτῆς μείνῃ πολιτεία," *Prat. sp.* 179 (PG 87.3049).
⁷² "εἰς τὴν ἔρημον ταύτην;" ibid.
⁷³ Ibid.
⁷⁴ Ward, *Harlots of the Desert*, 7–8; Efthalia Makris Walsh, "The Ascetic Mother Mary of Egypt," GOTR, Vol. 34, No. 1 (1989): 60; Patricia Cox Miller, "Is There a Harlot in This Text? Hagiography and the Grotesque," JMEMS, Vol. 33, No. 3 (2003): 429; R.M. Kerras, "Holy Harlots: Prostitute Saints in Medieval Legend," JHS, Vol. 1, No. 1 (1990): 3–32; Carolyn L. Connor, *Women of Byzantium* (Yale University Press, 2007): 78–93.
⁷⁵ See the Introduction, *Life of Mary of Egypt*, trans. Kouli, *Holy Women of Byzantium*, 63–8.
⁷⁶ Sophronios, *The Life of Mary of Egypt* 18 (PG 87.3709); Sophronios, *The Life of Mary of Egypt*, trans. Kouli, *Holy Women of Byzantium*, 80. It is worth noting that Moschos' nun resides in the desert for 17 years, equivalent to Mary's life of licentiousness.

Egypt's explanation for her life of repentance—"For more than seventeen years ... I was a public temptation to licentiousness, not for payment, I swear, since I did not accept anything although men often wished to pay me. I simply contrived this so that I could seduce many more men, thus turning my lust into a free gift"[77]— Moschos' account does not implicate the nun. In fact, it is quite the opposite. As with Abba Elijah above, the work of the devil causes desire, not any spiritual malaise of the ascetic. Unlike Sophronios' later tale, the nun of Moschos' account is not in the wilderness because of sin for which she needs to account or repent. In Moschos' tale we have a woman who seeks *not* to be an occasion of sin, not—as in Sophronios' *vita*—a woman who is attempting to make up for the many occasions in which sin has taken place and blissfully so. Sophronios' Mary as an icon of deep repentance is not found in the pious grazing nun we meet in this *Meadow* tale, for the pious grazer has done nothing for which she must repent.

To return to our female grazer's story, there are elements of this account that highlight its value as an independent tale within the greater context of *The Meadow*, and its unique contribution to the genre. First, it is worth noting that our grazer initially resides "in the Holy city"[78] and is clearly interacting with this young man,[79] although, in the style of a beneficial tale, precisely *how* they might know or interact with each other is absent from the text. Happily, we can count on Moschos and his method to tell us what we need to know. It is likely that if they were interacting in an impious manner then the devil would not be needed as a literary (and of course theological) device to move the tale along. Second, the relationship that does exist, no matter its degree, highlights and supports the variety of ascetic life available, the autonomy that this nun appears to have within whatever system she exists, and the level of spiritual proficiency that she has achieved. She is discerning enough that she not only concluded[80] what forces were at work, but the damage that would be done if she remained. There is nothing in the text that suggests that anyone else might make the decision on her behalf to go into the wild. She is not sent. She goes "into the wilderness,"[81] where she resides like "Truth in person standing all alone,"[82] a model of holiness and icon of wisdom rather than repentance. Further, she does not exhibit the traditional masculine qualities often required of women who choose such a life for themselves.[83] Unlike Thekla, Matrona, Marianos, or any other of the "transvestite

---

[77] Sophronios, *The Life of Mary of Egypt* 18 (PG 87.3709–12); Sophronios, *The Life of Mary of Egypt*, trans. Kouli, in Talbot, *Holy Women of Byzantium*, 80.

[78] "ἐν τῇ ἁγίᾳ πόλει," *Prat. sp.* 179 (PG 87.3049).

[79] "νέῳ τινὶ," ibid.

[80] "Θεωρήσασα," ibid.

[81] "εἰς τὴν ἔρημον," ibid.

[82] Fable 126. Ben Edwin Perry (ed.), *Babrius and Phaedrus*, LCL (Harvard University Press, 1975): 162–3.

[83] Miller, "Hagiography and the Grotesque," 420; Gillian Cloke, *This Female Man of God: Women and Spiritual Power in the Patristic Age, AD 350–450* (London: Routledge, 1995): 214–21; Gillian Clark, *Women in Late Antiquity: Pagan and Christian Lifestyles* (Oxford University Press, 1993): 126–30.

saints,"[84] our nun does not don male clothing; she is not told that she must become "male,"[85] nor is she mistaken for a man or some other kind of being, as happens in the Sophronios version[86] and in additional beneficial tales and hagiography with female holy women or anchorites.[87] When encountered, she is addressed simply as "Ἀμμᾶ."[88] Finally, we might be right to question why she is unable to engage in chaste relations with a man in the city but yet she is able to enter into conversation with Abba John. Perhaps this tale stands as testimony to the value of the desert as formational space for right relations.[89] She may dwell in the "Holy City,"[90] but it is a city nevertheless, and the devil resides there as comfortably as in the desert. But in a manner that we will find consistent over the course of this study of select beneficial tales, Moschos muddies the water: even as this tale upholds dichotomies of good/ evil and city/desert that one finds in earlier monastic tales, still there is no clear, sharp divide. Although she leaves the city because of the potential for sin, she leaves purity behind in the city; equally, she does not leave the city so that she might go to the desert and repent, but her purity accompanies her into the desert.

How does this nun prove her ascetic worth? Her ascetic program is proven primarily through the witness of the additional anchorite in the tale, an action that supports his ascetic worthiness at the same time. In order for her to be seen, she must be seen by one worthy to see her. Such an ascetic must be able to see her without temptation, without being prey to the devil, as was the young man.[91] This is possible only if the one whom she encounters has attained—like the nun—a certain level of spiritual wisdom. In the desert, then, the perfect opportunity exists for these two worthy individuals to find one another, to prove the ascetic program of each in the process; in doing so, as Valantasis above notes, their relationship creates a new culture. In the city—one might argue according to this text—this relationship is not possible, or at the very least not very remarkable.[92] Or, put another way, renunciation (of city, home, relations) is vital to see the Truth; and yet *how* one resides in the new city, the new home and among others proves precisely

---

[84] Patlagean, "L'histoire de la femme déguisée en moine," XI.

[85] *The Gospel According to Thomas*, trans. Bart Ehrman and Zlatko Plese, *The Apocryphal Gospels: Texts and Translations* (Oxford University Press, 2011): 335.

[86] Sophronios, *Life of Mary*, 10 (PG 87.3705–6); Sophronios, *The Life of Mary of Egypt*, trans. Kouli, in Talbot, *Holy Women of Byzantium*, 76.

[87] *Prat. sp.* 170 (PG 87.3035–8); see also *Vita Sanctae Pelagiae, Meretricis* (PL 73.663–72), in Ward, *Harlots of the Desert*, trans. Benedicta Ward, 60–75.

[88] *Prat. sp.* 179 (PG 87.3049).

[89] *Life of Mary*, 13–14, 37–40, trans. Kouli, *Holy Women of Byzantium*, 77–8, 90–92.

[90] "ἐν τῇ ἁγίᾳ πόλει," *Prat. sp.* 179 (PG 87.3049).

[91] "νέῳ τινὶ," ibid.

[92] Susanna K. Elm, "'Virgins of God': Variations of Female Ascetic Life," in Elm, *Virgins of God*, 25–59; James E. Goehring, "The Encroaching Desert: Literary Production and Ascetic Space in Early Christian Egypt," JECS, Vol. 1, No. 3 (1993): 293; E.A. Judge, "The Earliest Use of Monachos for 'Monk,' and the Origins of Monasticism," JAC, Vol. 20 (1977): 80.

what an ascetic is able to accomplish. Like our Abba Elijah, through channels of gossip the ascetic program of both nun and the one who "sees" her is proven to the author and to his companion as well.

Aside from elements of sexuality and gender, one finds a link between our abba, our pious nun and other "βοσκοί" in *The Meadow* in struggles with diet, geography and clothing, all specific factors that allow them the opportunity to prove levels of ascetic expertise and reveal different types of relations among anchorites. To cite a few examples, we find "[t]here was in the mountains an anchorite, exceedingly great before God, for many years grazing [a grazer]."[93] That the monastery fathers indicate knowledge of the anchorite's dietary practice—of which, along with relative proximity to their site, they are appropriately proud—betrays a necessary familiarity and intimacy.[94] Additional *Meadow* tales laud the dietary practices of anchorites, some of whom persist in their ascetic program for lengthy periods. Abba John, higoumen of Raïthou, relates to his brethren that "I have come by elders who lived seventy years and ate only grasses [herbs] and date-palms,"[95] while Abba Menas, higoumen of the Severian Monastery,[96] reported that Abba Sophronios lived as a naked grazer for 70 years alongside the Dead Sea, "eating only herbs/weeds, and partaking of nothing else."[97] In the cases of these particular individuals, there does not appear to be a standard diet beyond a combination of nourishments found within the environment where they live. Creativity in diet is present in tales about grazers exterior to *The Meadow*,[98] but regardless of the source, diet—as well as physical locations like the mountains, the desert or the shore of the Dead Sea—speaks to personal limits or license. Regardless, that the actions of the anchorites are known by the higoumen indicates that they know the anchorites or the anchorites have made themselves known physically or through some other means, even if only as a literary or theological ideal among those who wished them into existence. Finally, nudity—the popular garb of many grazers—assisted in removing the final barrier between the ascetic and the natural world. Again, we do not know if all such anchorites were naked or not; there is no reason to assume that they were. Nudity is often used to great effect in beneficial tales, and as this type of literature demands brevity, it is my suspicion that use of nudity

---

[93] "ὅτι Ἀναχωρητὴς εἰς τὰ ὄρη ταῦτα ἦν, πάνυ μέγας κατὰ Θεὸν, καὶ πολλὰ ἔτη ποιήσας Βοσκόμενος." *Prat. sp.* 84 (PG 87.2941–2).

[94] Approbation of an anchorite will be addressed in Chapter 4.

[95] "Εἶπεν πάλιν· Ἔρθασα γέροντας, ἀπὸ ἑβδομήκαντα ἐτῶν ποιήσαντας, βοτάνας καὶ φοίνικας ἐσθίοντας μόνον." *Prat. sp.* 115 (PG 87.2979–80).

[96] Joseph Patrich, *Sabas, Leader of Palestinian Monasticism: A Comparative Study in Eastern Monasticism, Fourth to Seventh Centuries*, DOS, 32 (Washington DC: Dumbarton Oaks, 1995): 162.

[97] "τὰς βοτάνας ἐσθίων μόνον, καὶ μηδενὸς ἑτέρου μεταλαμβάνων," *Prat. sp.* 159 (PG 87.3027–8).

[98] Cyril of Scythopolis, *Eythymii*, 38 (Schwartz, 57.7–8) and V. Sab, 11, 13; (Schwartz, 94.29 and 96.14–15, respectively) in Price, trans., *The Lives of the Monks of Palestine*, 53–4, 103 and 105, respectively.

is as intentional as each word selected. The naked anchorite challenges him or herself not to withstand the elements but to move beyond knowledge of them, as is demonstrated in the account of Abba Poemon, who has proven such a level of ascetic development that not only is he impervious to the weather, but impervious to the dangers presented to him by virtue of the fact that he sleeps with wild beasts who later kill him, as he foretells that they will.[99] In his case, his level of asceticism is proven not only by these acts, but in the transmission of them through Abba Agathonicus to Moschos.

If the activity of grazers—anonymous or named, male or female—brings us as close to the ground of ascetic practice as we can get, then the activity of a stylite moves us equally far in the other direction. It is worth ending this first section by bringing these two categories of highly specialized ascetic behavior into conversation with one another, as they do in *The Meadow* as well. One finds, for example, the account[100] of two grazers [who had] "much love for one another."[101] For many years they visit the stylite, but always together, never alone. When one grazer takes it upon himself to visit the stylite in secret, the stylite will not see him; he returns home, and on the way meets the other grazer, who was himself on his way to the stylite! When both grazers return to the column the stylite will see only the second of the two, informing him of his companion that "God rejects him, child."[102] The grazers return home and, days later, the first grazer dies.[103] As Derek Krueger has addressed so well the implications of a member of a clearly committed union breaking his vow of companionship and the implications of infidelity,[104] I wish only to draw attention to what this beneficial tale underscores by bringing a grazer to the base of the column. This tale illustrates the compendium of ascetic practices in Moschos' meadow and highlights how these diverse methods of ascetic activity are able to flourish in the same meadow: stylites are dependent entirely on the philanthropy of others,[105] grazers are dependent entirely on the earth; stylites are figures of stability, grazers are figures of instability. Yet both are living images of the philosophy and practice of asceticism; both are the "lilies" and "roses"[106] in the very distinct culture that *The Meadow* illustrates.

To conclude, I return to the goal of addressing how relations among ascetic figures contributed towards "proving" their ascetic life. In the first tale of Abba Elijah, personal interaction and the gathering of the tale stands as initial evidence of his ascetic program: that an individual would have something to teach is

---

[99] *Prat. sp.* 167 (PG 87.3033–4).

[100] *Prat. sp.* 129 (PG 87.2993–4).

[101] "ἀγάπην ἔχοντες πολλῶν πρὸς ἀλλήλους," ibid. Wortley translates this as "very attached to each other" (Wortley, *Spiritual Meadow*, 107), and Krueger as "had a great love for each other." Krueger, "Between Monks," 35.

[102] "Ὁ Θεὸς ἀποστρέφει αὐτὸν, τέκνον," *Prat. sp.* 129 (PG 87.2993–4).

[103] Ibid.

[104] Krueger, "Between Monks," 36.

[105] Caner, *Wandering, Begging Monks*, 247.

[106] "ῥόδων" and "κρίνοις," *Prat. sp.* PG 87.2851–2.

established by virtue of someone standing before them wanting a "word," a teaching, a tale. Lacking gossip or a social network, in order to prove one's ascetic program one might be forced to tell one's own story, as we saw with Abba Elijah; beyond that, one who receives the tale provides continued evidence by repeating or writing the account that they receive. This is taken further from the source in the case of the pious nun, whose encounter with one worthy to see her is repeated to another, and so forth, until it reaches the ears of one who will write it down. Additional grazers function in tales as "proof" of the ascetic worthiness of those who knew them: Abba Agathonicus, Abba Menas and Abba John each related accounts of the dietary and clothing practices, and the lengthy tenure of grazers known to them, which no doubt contributes to their authority, as they "know" one whose program is particularly extreme. Neither diet, dwelling, clothing nor other elements of the practices involved in grazing are consistent; what is consistent in the lives of the grazer is the control they seem to have over the ascetic program that they design, and the fact that the control includes the degree to which they will choose to interact with others. While each grazer's life might have a rule, there is no single rule for a grazer's life. Unlike the *Master*, grazers are not disrupting a world that is moving towards perfection; they are attempting to become one with a perfect world; they seek not the transformation of the environment, but to become enfolded within it.

In addition, we find also in the activity of Abba Elijah, our pious nun and the grazers mentioned above, further examples of what has been supported by scholarship on the topic of monastic life and movement: even among those close to the ground of asceticism there is some degree of social agency. By this I do not mean freedom *apart from* God; I mean merely the capacity that a person would have to make decisions for themselves. Neither patristic nor monastic anthropology would conceive of the autonomous actions of a person as existing independent of life in Christ, and I make no such argument on behalf of these texts. Any agency they might claim does not prevent them from relationships; through oral tradition and eye witness we learn that these figures remain very much in communion with other ascetics. As well, some leaders are identified as having themselves been grazers at one point or another, which suggests that the practice might be understood as one that builds character and authority.[107] Further, as they are not permanently grazers, it affirms creativity and autonomy because it is a practice into which people move in and out as their circumstances or will dictate.[108] As noted above, Wortley suggests that grazing is particularly defined and practiced within the Palestinian context of Moschos' era. But beyond defined, I would go further and suggest that it is no

---

[107] Arthur Vööbus, *History of Asceticism in the Syrian Orient: A Contribution to the History of Culture in the Near East*, Vol. I (Louvain: Secrétariat du Corpus CSCO, 1958): 150–57; Vol. II (1960): 22–35, 262–4.

[108] See *Prat. sp.* 21 (PG 87.2867–8). The death is seen by a trio of grazers, one of whom is the teller of the tale. He is identified initially as "ὁ ἡγούμενος," *Prat. sp.* 21 (PG 87.2868).

accident that Moschos includes so many tales of grazers. For Moschos this is a particularly admirable form of ascetic behavior as it models in its most developed form the type of ascetic practice in which Moschos and Sophronios engage; they are, to an extent, literary "βοσκοί." In the previous century and a half the geography of the Christian world had been transformed; was Moschos trying—through his own ascetic practice of literary grazing—to retain some shape of that geography by mapping the experiences and lives of those who populate the landscape in the wake of changing historical circumstances? The evidence is fairly convincing: they travel from site to site, though rooted to none; they glean what literary delicacies they can from many sites where they rest, nourished spiritually by tales they record; they are vulnerable to the elements, constantly exposed to economic, political and geographic challenges; and in the end, both parties remain largely known only by what they harvest to sustain themselves and their ascetic program.

"God's servants, working together"[109]: Improving the Ascetic Program

The work of Peter Brown, Philip Rousseau and John Wortley demonstrates that the history of engagement between ascetics and laity is known and documented in multiple sources from antiquity on.[110] But, Rousseau cautions, for a richer, fuller understanding of monastic history one needs to consider more than the unquestioning devotion to the orthodoxy and austerity of monastic luminaries. "One must examine the texts," he writes, "with an eye to the brief references within them to other, often different monastic movements, to interaction with secular and ecclesiastical authorities, and to practices that would necessarily lead to such interaction even if it is not expressly stated."[111] With this in mind, what does *The*

---

[109] I Corinthians 3.9. Material for this second section is drawn from Brenda Llewellyn Ihssen, "God's Servants, Working Together: Liminality and Laity in John Moschos' *Pratum spirituale*" (paper presented at the annual national meeting of the Byzantine Studies Association of North America, Brookline, MA, 2 November 2012).

[110] Peter Brown, "The Rise and Function of the Holy Man in Late Antiquity," in Peter Brown, *Society and the Holy in Late Antiquity* (University of California Press, 1989): 103–52; Peter Brown, "Town, Village and Holy Man: A Case of Syria," in Brown, *Society and the Holy*, 153–65; Philip Rousseau, "The World Engaged: The Social and Economic World," in James E. Goehring (ed.), *Ascetics, Society, and The Desert*, Studies in Antiquity and Christianity (Harrisburg, PA: Trinity Press International, 1999): 49–51; Philip Rousseau; "The Desert Fathers and Their Broader Audience," in Alberto Camplani and Giovanni Filoramo (eds), *Foundations of Power and Conflicts of Authority in Late-Antique Monasticism: Proceedings of the International Seminar Turin, December 2–4, 2004* (Leuven: Peeters, 2006): 90–91; Philip Rousseau, "The Identity of the Ascetic Master in the *Historia Religiosa* of Theodoret of Cyrrhus: A New Paideia?" MA, Vol. 11 (1998): 229–44.

[111] While Rousseau's statement is "A history of Egyptian monasticism," his account is not limited to Egyptian monasticism. Philip Rousseau, "The World Engaged," 43.

Meadow reveal to us about what is "not expressly stated" with regard to these relationships? Beyond this, what are the results of their interactions? I believe that in some of the tales a uniqueness exists that speaks to the creative relationships that are forged in Moschos' particular milieu.[112] Closer in kind to *apophthegmatic* material than lengthier hagiography, Moschos' beneficial tales demonstrate the presence of significant associations between laity and the professional religious that affords the modern reader a rare opportunity to explore boundaries that both categories drew around, erased or ignored altogether in their relations with one another.

Monastic figures in Moschos' *Meadow* were not exceptional in their civic engagements but were part of a tradition of public activity that includes working land owned by others for wages,[113] material production and trade in the cities,[114] interacting with magistrates[115] and even becoming involved in legal disputes over issues such as taxation, the placement or abandonment of children and wills.[116] Not to press the point too firmly, that an ascetic would engage with secular society in some form emerges as a customary, consistent, often troubling but certainly quite expected element of an ascetic life. As in contemporary collections of spiritually beneficial tales, hagiographies and *apophthegmata*, multiple ways in which monastic figures aided the lives of lay Christians are well documented in *The Meadow*, such as the bishop who anonymously hired himself out as a day laborer,[117] or the stern virgin who edified the soul of a noblewoman by repeatedly referring to her as a "rich fool,"[118] to the noblewoman's delight and surely to the benefit of her soul. Present also, but more atypical, is disclosure of the occasional dependence of monastic figures on laity for needs that move beyond fulfillment of basic corporeal requirements such as medical care or manual labor. When considering the collection as a whole[119] one recognizes in Moschos' accounts of early Byzantine monasticism that monks and lay people cannot avoid each other and they do not necessarily choose to do so. But interactions present challenges. Therefore this section seeks to analyze some of these interactions and their

---

[112] Regarding the dating of the text, see the Introduction.

[113] *APalph*, Macarius the Great 7 (PG 65.265–6); *APalph*, John the Dwarf 6, 35 (PG 65.205–6 and 65.215–16); in *The Sayings of the Desert Fathers: The Alphabetical Collection*, trans. Benedicta Ward (Kalamazoo, MI: Cistercian Publications, 1975): 86, 92 and 128–9, respectively. Caner notes that labor was not solely for subsistence, but served a sociological function, leveling pride and fostering solidarity. Caner, *Wandering, Begging Monks*, 45–6.

[114] *APalph* accounts: John the Dwarf 5, 30–31 (PG 65.205–6, 213–14); Isidore the Priest 7 (PG 65.221–2); Lucius 1 (PG 65.253–4); Macarius the Great 14 (PG 65.269–70); Megethios 1 (PG 65.299–300); Abba Poeman 9, 10, 11 (PG 65.323–6).

[115] *APalph*, Abba Poeman 9 (PG 65.323–4).

[116] Rousseau, "The World Engaged," 49–50.

[117] *Prat. sp.* 37 (PG 87.2885–8).

[118] "Μωροπλουσία," *Prat. sp.* 206 (PG 87.3097–8).

[119] For questions regarding the core of the *Meadow* text, see the Introduction.

challenges, and suggests that spiritual counsel, healing and training that monks receive from lay people through manual labor, medical care, education or shame speaks to the liminal boundaries that existed in the early Byzantine era between the secular and the religious. Ultimately, less structured forms of monasticism that operate along these liminal boundaries point towards creative interplay between laity and monastic, for the physical and spiritual benefit of a monastic figure who is temporarily a disciple of a secular "type" of interim abba.

Central to understanding these interdependent relationships that I propose exist between laity and monastics is the important relationship between the figures of the abba and disciple. I am not suggesting that secular figures *are* abbas as recognized by the institution of monasticism, but in an environment in which boundaries were fluid and creative expressions of monasticism were an option,[120] secular individuals independent of monastic communities appear to have been able to step forward intentionally or unintentionally as authoritative guides from whom a disciple might learn. To support these ideas I will identify and analyze passages from *The Meadow* that demonstrate this relationship of monk and lay person, passages in which I will explore the way these relationships model a bond between abba and monk with respect to the development of the virtue of obedience and the quality of discernment; finally I conclude by considering what these liminal monastic–lay boundaries teach us about the social history of the eastern empire.

The first tale I wish to address is of Theodore, a non-monastic monk.[121] Moschos and his companion Sophronios hear of Theodore from one Abba Jordanes the grazer, who reports that three anchorites went to visit Abba Nicholas at the Wadi Betasimos monastery. The anchorites note that near the abba sits one who is "foreign."[122] The notation of the proximity of the stranger to the abba indicates that though this person is unknown, nevertheless they are part of the gathering, although admittedly in a liminal way. While speaking about "salvation of the soul,"[123] Abba Nicholas turns to the stranger and attempts to move him closer, coaxing him to contribute to the discourse: "*You* say something to us,"[124] the abba entreats. The stranger demurs and questions how he, one "of the world,"[125] could contribute. When pressed again, the stranger says:

> For twenty years, Saturdays and Sundays excepted, the sun never saw me eating. I am the hired servant on the estate of a rich man who is unjust and greedy. I was with him for fifteen years, toiling night and day, and he would not pay me my wages, but treated me with considerable harshness. I said to myself: "Theodore,

---

[120] Claudia Rapp, "Ritual Brotherhood in Byzantium," *Traditio*, Vol. 52 (1997): 285–326; Krueger, "Between Monks," 28–61.
[121] *Prat. sp.* 154 (PG 87.3021–2).
[122] "Ξένων," ibid.
[123] "περὶ σωτηρίας ψυχῆς," ibid.
[124] "Εἰπὸν ἡμῖν τιποτοῦν καὶ σύ," ibid.
[125] "κοσμικόν," ibid.

if you endure this man, he is going to obtain the kingdom of heaven for you instead of the wages he owes you." So I kept my body free of contact with women until this day. "When we heard this," the grazer concludes, "we were greatly edified."[126]

This account has a few things to teach us about monastic identity, obedience and liminal space. First, clearly a more formal or organized practice of monastic life or even an ascetic program is neither limited to the monastery, nor limited to monks. The theme of the righteous lay person whose ascetic program is held up to curb arrogance is present in various other monastic texts. Perhaps the best known is found in the *Vita* of St Antony, to whom it is revealed that a medical doctor and a tanner are his spiritual equals.[127] While Theodore's identification and function as a righteous lay person is in no way an anomaly in the genre, what I find curious are the barriers that Theodore surmounts, compared to those of the medical doctor and tanner of Antony's experience. Theodore has taken clearly unfavorable circumstances and used them to shape a program for himself, lacking power, autonomy, opportunity or maybe even the discipline needed to do otherwise. For reasons unknown he is unable to commit himself to a monastic community; consequently he adapts a situation that suggests slavery at worst or oppression under a harsh patron at best as an opportunity to benefit his soul. Theodore adapts the harsh treatment in the following ways: he eats only on Saturdays and Sundays, which indicates a fasting schedule; his physical labor and endurance of the bodily harshness of his master is redolent of monastic austerities under the care of recognized elders; his virtual enslavement due to the failure of the greedy man to pay wages for his work is comparable with the renunciation of wealth or voluntary state of poverty; finally, after claiming that endurance of this unjust master will obtain for him the kingdom of heaven, Theodore keeps himself from women, which we can interpret as participating in the requisite chastity of the disciplined ascetic.

Theodore's practice of what I like to call "threshold monasticism" appears to be recognized and honored by the anchorites in three ways: the tale of Theodore is remembered and told by Abba Jordanes to his guests Moschos and Sophronios; this indicates to me that although Theodore was a stranger to the gathering initially, his dedication to his own thoughtful "rule" has resulted in his inclusion into monastic "kinship." Further, it is noted that what he says "greatly edified [benefited]"[128] the brothers; his tale gave them pause and taught them something, although of course we cannot know precisely what, nor are we probably supposed to. Finally, Theodore's ascetic program is neither questioned as inappropriate nor

---

[126] *Prat. sp.* 154 (PG 87.3021–2); Wortley, *The Spiritual Meadow*, 128.

[127] *APalph*, Anthony the Great 24 (PG 65.83–4). When Paphnutius learns of virtuous laity he concludes: "[i]n every walk of life, there are men pleasing to God, prompting God's love by deeds that are hidden to others." HME, xvi, 439B, in Russell, *Lives of the Desert Fathers*, 95–8.

[128] "ὠφελήθημεν μεγάλως," *Prat. sp.* 154 (PG 87.3021–2).

declared to be in any way deficient; no one lists essential characteristics that he has not cultivated or tasks he has not accomplished in his ascetic program. Of course the relative brevity of a beneficial tale allows for little opportunity to question, but we can be assured that if Theodore's dependence on a lay person for spiritual guidance were considered either counterfeit or heretical, the author would not hesitate to make this the point of the tale rather than the clear admiration of the grazers for his practice.

At the heart of the formative process of a disciple are conversation and the modeling of righteous behavior,[129] without which an elder has no standing. The cultivation and continuation of monastic life—no matter how sparsely or densely populated—is dependent on the transformation of a disciple into a mature ascetic within an environment that is both morally rigorous and intellectually challenging. Generally, an elder is recognized as discerning and upright, with the ability to identify the spiritual needs of the novice and respond accordingly with words and tasks of an edifying nature. It is easy to argue that the harsh master has no virtue as he appears to do nothing instructive, but if his vices aid in the cultivation of Theodore's virtue (which is how Theodore elects to understand the relationship), can we consider the harsh master's vices as virtues? I worry about the ramifications of such a claim even if only theoretically; I am not interested in making the dangerous argument that victims of abuse or unjust treatment are in a very good position to profit spiritually at the hands of their abusers; however, theologically, within the context of a beneficial tale it is easy to make that leap. That God's providence can be discerned in the evil actions of others or in moments of suffering has roots in scripture in the actions of Pharaoh,[130] Judas[131] and the suffering of Job, and is a topic of great interest in patristic theology.[132] While God's providence might be difficult to discern, nevertheless God's perfect justice is seen in the submission of Theodore's will to direction given, master to novice, without judgment on Theodore's part. Submission and obedience indicate trust that has been placed not so much in a harsh master or in a system that perpetuates abuse, but in a God who provides what is needed. In this way, Theodore cultivates a virtue of obedience, "the treasure of the monk."[133]

The second account I wish to consider is a spicy tale,[134] one that confirms that unchaste thoughts exist even among those who practice the angelic life. This

---

[129] Rousseau, "The Identity of the Ascetic Master," 237–8; Graham Gould, *The Desert Fathers on Monastic Community* (Oxford: Clarendon Press, 1993): 26–7.

[130] Exodus 4.21; 7.3, 13; 9.12; 10.1, 20, 27; 11.10; 14.4, 8. See Chapter 4.

[131] Matthew 10.4; Mark 14.10–11; Luke 22.3–5; John 6.71–2, 12.4–6.

[132] In short, for patristic theologians, God shapes providential plans around human choices; the choices are made by the creatures God *will* create. See Chapter 4.

[133] Hyperechius 8, Sentences 59, 139, in Gould, *Desert Fathers on Monastic Community*, 53.

[134] *Prat. sp.* 204 (PG 87.3093–6).

anonymous tale[135] relates that one who suffered a snake bite went to the city for medical care. A woman described as "devout"[136] and "fearing the Lord"[137] took him in and "she healed him."[138] Finding relief, the monk became infected by thoughts placed in his heart by the devil,[139] thoughts that compelled him to "touch her hand."[140] But this woman had the ability to discern the monk's desire, and though he did not even move to touch her she cautioned him nevertheless: "Not so father; you have Christ; be mindful of the regret and remorse and repentance, sitting in your cell."[141] Humiliated, he wanted to flee and "was not able to look into her face."[142] She responded by counseling him again, this time with encouragement: "'These did not come from your pure soul, but from a suggestion of an envious devil.' And in this way she healed him, without scandal, and sent him away, with provisions."[143]

It is worth noting that the image of this woman is completely positive. In addition to lauding her piety, the recipient of this tale learns that she is a healer with great skill, able to treat both the exterior and the interior of her patient. Beyond treatment, her ability to know what her patient needs demonstrates a level of discernment ("διάκρισις"), a quality without which asceticism would be of no benefit.[144] The cultivation of this virtue places her in good company with elders concerned with health and healing, such as St Pachomios, who through "discernment of spirits ... also tested the nature of the different states of health."[145] As we will explore more fully in another chapter, monastic texts related to health care often support a preventative approach that employed discernment rather than prognosis, which focuses on a predicted outcome of a disease rather than its

---

[135] "Ἔλεγὲν τις," *Prat. sp.* 204 (PG 87.3093–4).

[136] "ἡ γυνὴ εὐλαβὴ," ibid.

[137] "καὶ φοβουμένη τὸν Κύριαν," ibid.

[138] "καὶ ἐθεράκεθσεν αὐτὸν." Ibid.

[139] "ὁ διάβολος," ibid.

[140] "της χειρὸς αὐτῆς." Ibid.

[141] "Μή οὕτως, Πάτερ, Χριστὸν ἔχης· μνήσθητι τῆς λύπης καὶ μετανοίς, καὶ τῆς μετανοίας, ἧς μέλλεις μετανοεῖν καθήμενος ἐν τῷ κελλίῳ σου." *Prat. sp.* 204 (PG 87.3093–6).

[142] "μὴ δυνάμενος ἀτενίσαι εἰς αὐτήν," *Prat. sp.* 204 (PG 87.3093–4). Shame is an emotion or state with clear physical expression. Thomas J. Scheff, "Shame and community: Social components in depression," *Psychiatry*, Vol. 64, No. 3 (2001): 216.

[143] "οὐκ ἦν τῆς καθαρᾶς σου ψυχῆς διαλογίσασθαι ἐκεῖνα, ἀλλὰ τοῦ φθονεροῦ διαβόλου ἦν ἡ ὑποβολή. Καὶ οὕτως ἀσκανδαλίστως θεραπεύσασα αὐτὸν ἀπέλυσεν μετὰ εφοδίων." *Prat. sp.* 204 (PG 87.3095–6).

[144] Burton-Christie, *Word in the Desert*, 202–3.

[145] *V.Pach.*, G1.52 (F. Halkin, *Sancti Pachomii Vitae Graecae, Subsidia Hagiographica 19* (Brussels, 1932): 34; *The First Greek Life of Saint Pachomius*, in *Pachomian Koinonia*, Vol. 1, trans. Armand Veilleux (Kalamazoo, MI: Cistercian Publications, 1980): 332–3.

identification.[146] Aside from health care, discernment—referred to as "greater than all the virtues"[147]—was a virtue cultivated by an elder, one who presumably had the wisdom and experience to determine what and who was before their eyes. This woman's ability to discern properly is evident in the outcome of the tale, for she sees before her not merely prognosis ("If left untreated, he will touch me and this will cause sorrow and remorse and this could impact his salvation"), but diagnosis of all elements of illness that plague this monk: trauma of a snake attack; pain from a bite (which might include effects of mild poison or a contaminated puncture in an environment bereft of soap and the concept of bacterial infection); spiritual pain caused by carnal thoughts and subsequent shame that his thoughts are known by her. Discerning which healing he needs, the woman attributes unchaste thoughts to an unhealthy physical state that has left him vulnerable to manipulations. The tale concludes happily: "And in this way she healed him, without scandal, and sent him away, with provisions."[148]

This devout woman's abilities are not restricted to discernment and healing, for she possesses an even rarer quality: with the affection of Christ[149] she keeps the monk from wallowing in the aforementioned shame, a profoundly complex emotional condition that has the potential to leave scars far more damaging than any poison or bite a snake might inflict. Beyond the physical discomfort that it causes, shame, scholars note, is an emotion that has potential to undermine community.[150] We observe that the experience of shame caused him to wish to run and then to avert his eyes; in two ways the author indicates that shame prompts the monk to flee the community. Although that action is not taken, community is still weakened by his avoidance of her eyes. That a relationship is undermined suggests that there was a relationship to begin with. What I take from the aborted breech is that the devout woman is considered part of this monk's extended community, momentarily existing as an elder qualified to guide the brother in physical and spiritual healing.

Not all monks troubled with these thoughts receive such kind treatment, and I find this tale to be an interesting contrast to other beneficial tales in Moschos' *Meadow*, tales that offer divergent responses from lay persons to inappropriately amorous advances of monastics. In an account[151] that speaks to the temptations of the "οἰκουμένη," a brother was sent to a village to conduct business of the

---

[146] Andrew Crislip, *From Monastery to Hospital: Christian Monasticism & The Transformation of Health Care in Late Antiquity* (University of Michigan Press, 2005): 19.

[147] Note 106; see Gould, *The Desert Fathers on Monastic Community*, 46.

[148] "Καὶ οὕτως ἀσκανδαλίστως θεραπεύσασα αὐτὸν ἀπέλυσεν μετὰ ἐφοδίων." *Prat. sp.* 204 (PG 87.3095–6).

[149] "ἐν σπλάγχνοις Χριστοῦ," ibid.

[150] Scheff, "Shame and community," 217.

[151] *Prat. sp.* 205 (PG 87.3095–8).

community[152] and was lodged in the home of a devout secular person[153] who provided hospitality as an act of confidence on his part. The widowed daughter lodged with her devout father, and the brother became disturbed[154] by thoughts about her, which the audience is left to assume are thoughts of a sexual nature. The daughter, being "prudent,"[155] was mindful of this brother's thoughts and when she could no longer avoid him she sternly encouraged him to get to praying: "But I know that you monks do nothing without prayer. Get up then; pray to God, and what [God] puts into your heart, let us do that."[156] When this fails to calm his ardor, she turns his desire away with a description of the stench he will face if he persists in making advances on a menstruating woman.[157] Here we learn something of how women are understood as biological beings; that she is not a wretched woman is clear. That the author of the tale is put off by what she offers is also clear, for beyond the stench of menstruation she relates "similar things" not described. This leaves the audience free to imagine the horrors the brother must have faced, and leaves us also free to assume the author knew nothing of female biology beyond the "horror" of menstruation, and covers up his ignorance by shrouding the details in mystery.

Faced with what is clearly meant to reflect the ugly reality of his ignorant desire, he regretted his actions.[158] But the episode encouraged him not to be so ready to cast away his virtues and lose "the good things of eternity"[159] for the sake of "small pleasures" (a phrase that leads us to suspect that she does not entirely hate her status as widow).[160] The brother gave thanks for this woman's wisdom and for the way in which God employed her to prevent him from "a complete fall."[161] In what is likely another version of "monk-pressing-self-on-chaste-woman," a maiden keeps a monk at bay by initially attempting to reason with him, then by threatening him with having to provide for her financially and finally by informing him that if he does disgrace her she will kill herself and how would he like that on his conscience?[162] With that, she orders him back to the monastery, "for you will have much praying to do for me."[163] Finally, an anchoress, so tormented by unwelcome attentions of a youth overcome with lust,

---

[152] "ἐπέμπετο εἰς ἀποκρίσεις τοῦ κοινοβίου." *Prat. sp.* 205 (PG 87.3095–6).

[153] "τις κοσμικὸς εὐλαβὴς," ibid.

[154] "Εἰσερχόμενος οὖν καὶ ἐξερχόμενος ὁ ἀδελφὸς πρὸς αὐτοὺς, ἐπολεμήθη πρὸς αὐτήν." Ibid.

[155] "ἐκείνη δὲ συνετὴ οὖσα ἐνόησεν," ibid.

[156] "οἶδα δὲ ὅτι ὑμεῖς οἱ μοναχοὶ μηδὲν πράττετε ἐκτός προσεθχῆς. Ἐγείρου οὖν, εὖξαι τω Θεω, καὶ εἰ τί ἐμβαλεῖ εἰς τὴν καρδίαν σου, τοῦτο ποιήσωμεν." Ibid.

[157] "Ἐν τοῖς μηνιαίοις εἰμί," ibid.

[158] *Prat. sp.* 205 (PG 87.3095–6).

[159] "καὶ στερηθῆναι αἰωνίων ἀγαθῶν," *Prat. sp.* 205 (PG 87.3097–8).

[160] "μικρὰν ἡδονή," *Prat. sp.* 205 (PG 87.3095–6).

[161] "μὴ ἐάσαντι αὐτὸν τελείως ἐκπεσεῖν," *Prat. sp.* 205 (PG 87.3097–8).

[162] *Prat. sp.* 39 (PG 87.2889–92).

[163] "καὶ πολλά μοι ἔχεις εὔξασθαι." Ibid.

blinds herself when he reveals that he has been seduced by her eyes. Filled with remorse, he retreats to a monastic enclosure.[164]

Although the bright young woman, the wise widow and the anchoress put off their unwelcome suitors using quite different methods from that of the devout woman above, still they discern either the harsh words that the monks need to hear or the violent terms that these men must face; in doing so, the women force them to consider the consequences of impious thoughts that direct them towards impious actions, and they teach them not only that the response to temptation and lust begins with prayer, but also that such abuse will be matched with equal violence. Further, we learn something of the light in which sexual dalliances were cast. It may be that many did not think that one sexual encounter would damn anyone, an unpardonable sin through which salvation could be lost. But as Wortley reminds us that "salvation" *gained* in beneficial tales suggests more than future reward,[165] so too salvation *lost* might indicate a temporary state in this lifetime, more temporary than "salvation" suggests in a contemporary understanding of the term.

It is worth keeping in mind what we have considered in this chapter as we turn to the next chapter, which addresses the role of money in *The Meadow*; there too, we find no clear guidelines concerning how money should be handled, just as there were no clear guidelines regarding the types of societies that monastics and laity inhabit, or the types of relationships that might develop. But recognition of both parties was essential as each stood for something unique, something that supported the existence of the other. The monk, Peter Charanis writes, embodied spiritual ambitions of society,[166] which is why it was necessary to have the monk close by; that said, the pious lay person embodied the ambitions of the monk, which is why it was also necessary for a monastic figure never to draw themselves too far from the center of the polis, so far into the wild that they could not somehow be drawn back, even if only through memory.

In the end, there cannot help but be relationship with realms not so distinct, for such liminal spaces provide opportunity to "prove" levels of ascesis, or "improve" misdirection, for the desert was—as Maud Gleason notes in her charming article on monastic gossip—"a busy place, teeming with uninvited guests;"[167] this included not only laity but mobile monastics as well, seeking advice, cures, edification or any reason to chatter with—and about—one another.[168] This applied also to the village: a busy place, teeming with monks seeking advice, cures, edification or other reasons to be engaged in relationships with laity. Conflicting desires and

---

[164] *Prat. sp.* 60 (PG 87.2911–14).

[165] John Wortley, "What the Desert Fathers meant by 'being saved,'" *Zeitschrift für Antikes Christentum*, Vol. 12, No. 2 (2008): 322–43.

[166] Charanis, "The Monk as an Element of Byzantine Society," 63.

[167] Gleason, "Visiting and News," 501.

[168] Ibid.; see also Sally Engle Merry, "Rethinking Gossip and Scandal," in Donald Black (ed.), *Towards a General Theory of Social Control, Volume I: Fundamentals* (Orlando, FL: Academic Press, Inc., 1984): 271–302.

advice to withdraw from the world and at the same time to serve it, to rely on generosity and yet be generous, reveals the tension in which monks lived. As we will explore more thoroughly in the next chapter, ascetic mortifications created problems in equal proportion to the problems that they tried to solve, and monks often found themselves simply trading challenges. This tension is made all the more difficult when critical voices from within the tradition itself identified each choice as flawed or sinful.[169] We might be tempted, if we are willing to think creatively, to reconsider Antony's "desert made a city"[170] as Moschos' "city made a desert."

---

[169] John Chrysostom, *In Joannem hom.* 44.1 (PG 59.248–9). Conversely, Pseudo-Macarius' *Book of Steps* uses John 21.15–17 as defense for patronal support of sustenance and material needs of the monk, in Caner, *Wandering, Begging Monks*, 158–205; Philippe Escolan, *Monachisme et église: le monachisme syrien du IVe au VIIe siècle: un ministère charismatique* (Paris: Beauchesne, 1999): 182–225; Patlagean, *Pauvreté économique et pauvreté sociale*, 156–235; Jens-Uwe Krause, *Spätantike Patronatsformen im Westen des Römischen Reiches* (München: C.H. Beck, 1987): 8–67; Rousseau, *Ascetics, Authority, and the Church*, 206, n. 36.

[170] A word play on Chitty's famous *The Desert a City* and its origin in "the desert was made a city" from Antony's *Life*, *VV.A.* c.14 (PG 26.865–6); Gregg, *The Life of Antony*, 14, 42–3.

Chapter 2
Money in *The Meadow*:
Coin, Cost and Conversion[1]

Introduction

The late 2008 economic crisis in the United States that resulted in the collapse of financial institutions, the bailout of banks and businesses by the US government, and the subsequent decline in stock markets around the world culminated in various economic proposals for short- and long-term solutions, the appearance of the word "morality" in public discussions of finance[2] and a subsequent rise in religious activity.[3] This would not have come as a surprise to the bishops of late antiquity and the early middle ages, for as Basil, Ambrose, John Chrysostom and others in their position knew then, and as churches in North America have learned, a financial crisis can have moral signifcance and poverty can lead people to God. John Moschos knew this as well. In addition to the theology, history, esoteric sayings and witticisms thus encountered, one finds in *The Meadow* topics of wealth, poverty, lending, borrowing and other concerns of the market economy intimately tied up with matters of social and theological justice. Divine Economy sometimes includes precisely that.

With respect to Moschos and money, even if a sustained treatment of the passages related to finance has not yet emerged, the text has not been ignored; it is worth briefly noting some contributions—by no means exhaustive—to the conversation. Highlighting passages that address almsgiving, wages, loans, burial,

---

[1] I wish to thank my editor Sarah Lloyd and Ashgate for granting permission to publish a portion of this chapter in *Studia Patristica* (Leuven: Peeters Publishers, 2013). Material for this chapter is drawn from Brenda Llewellyn Ihssen, "Money in the Meadow: Conversion and Coin in John Moschos' *Pratam spirituale*" (paper presented at the XVI International Conference on Patristic Studies, Oxford, England, 9 August 2011).

[2] "Human Greed Lies At Root Of Economic Crisis," http://www.npr.org/templates/story/story.php?storyId=94930841&ps=rs (23 September 2008); Dick Meyer, "Wall St. Moral Rot: Spreading To Politics, Main St.?" http://www.npr.org/templates/story/story.php?storyId=95013900 (25 September 2008): Renee Montagne and Stephen Green, HSBC Holdings chairman and ordained Anglican priest: "Bankers Need A Moral Compass," http://www.npr.org/templates/story/story.php?storyId=123897141.

[3] Matt Bradshaw and Christopher G. Ellison, "Financial hardship and psychological distress: Exploring the buffering effects of religion," *Social Science & Medicine*, Vol. 71, No. 1 (2010): 202.

status, farming and the employment of ascetics,[4] Évelyne Patlagean consistently references Moschos' text—or texts written in Moschos' name[5]—in her important work on the development of poverty as an economic rather than a social concept, an important component of the relationship between church and society in the early medieval Byzantine world. Harry J. Magoulias' "The Lives of the Saints as Sources for Byzantine Agrarian Life in the Sixth and Seventh Centuries" employs material from edifying tales including Moschos' to support his claim that Byzantine hagiography provides a source for understanding how small farmers turned to saints in times of agricultural trial to assist peasants with a myriad of troubles, for everything from drought and debt to stubborn farm animals.[6] A plethora of examples demonstrates effectively the relationship between ascetic and farmer, a relationship based in part on economics and in part on affection. Angeliki E. Laiou, in her study of the role of the church in rural economy and economy of exchange,[7] notes select tales from *The Meadow* to highlight the way economic activities are recast in theological terms,[8] present also in George R. Monks' earlier study on Alexandrine economy.[9] Vincent Déroche's study of the hagiography of Bishop Leontius naturally draws apt comparisons between Leontius, Moschos and Sophronios, contemporaries in their interest in portraying God as active in startling moments and shadowy places.[10] Susan R. Holman makes use of a poignant tale from *The Meadow* to introduce and conclude a chapter highlighting the relationship between the hungry, impoverished lay person—in this case a Saracen Christian woman willing to prostitute herself for food[11]—and those who represent institutionalized religion, present in this particular account in the figure of a solitary monastic.[12] She notes elsewhere in a *Meadow* tale of almsgiving trickery that highlights the

---

[4] Patlagean, *Pauvreté économique et pauvreté sociale*, 54, 68, 177, 190, 202, 254, 261, 266–7, 271, 320, 354, 356, 359–60, 366, 400.

[5] Though she largely identifies the texts as being of Jean Moschos, she occaisionally notes: "Un récit mis sous le nom de Jean Moschos, par example ... " Ibid., 68, 261.

[6] *Prat. sp.* 24 (PG 87.2869); 154 (87.3021–3); 184 (PG 87.3056–7), respectively, in Harry J. Magoulias, "The Lives of the Saints as Sources for Byzantine Agrarian Life in the Sixth and Seventh Centuries," GOTR, Vol. 35, No. 1 (1990): 60–63.

[7] Angeliki E. Laiou, "The Church, Economic Thought and Economic Practice," in Robert F. Taft, S.J. (ed.), *The Christian East, Its Institutions and Its Thoughts* (Rome: Pontificio Istituto Orientale, 1993): see 444–6.

[8] *Prat. sp.* 185 (PG 87.3057–62); 186 (PG 87.3061–4); 189 (PG 87.3067–70); 193 (PG 87.3071–6); 203 (PG 87.3093–4); in Laiou, "The Church, Economic Thought and Economic Practice," 443–6.

[9] *Prat. sp.* 193 (PG 3071–6), in George R. Monks, "The Church of Alexandria and the City's Economic Life in the Sixth Century Author(s)," *Speculum*, Vol. 28, No. 2 (1953): 351.

[10] Vincent Déroche, *Études Sur Léontios De Néapolis* (Uppsala University Press: 1995).

[11] *Prat. sp.* 136 (PG 87.2999–3000).

[12] Susan R. Holman, *The Hungry are Dying: Beggars and Bishops in Roman Cappadocia* (Oxford University Press, 2001): 31; 63; Susan R. Holman (ed.), *Wealth and Poverty in Early Church and Society*, Holy Cross Studies in Patristic Theology and History, Vol. 1 (Grand Rapids, MI: Baker Academic, 2008): 105–7.

paradigm of the generosity of the poor for the shame of the wealthy,[13] which will be addressed below. Finally, Daniel Caner identifies select *Meadow* passages that note use of *eulogia/eulogiai* in his study on the idealization of religious wealth and the Christian development of a "gift."[14] The aim of this chapter is to bring Moschos' treatment of money in *The Meadow* into the larger conversation, to seek and identify connections between wealth, poverty and soteriology, which, to my knowledge, has not been done with these tales in a sustained way. Further, this chapter will consider how these tales suggest that honor, shame and the virtue of humility factor into the social intercourse of giving and receiving in the early Byzantine era, thus contributing to a more nuanced understanding of salvation.

Even a casual, surface read of the tales reveals that poverty is overwhelmingly present, to the degree that the state of poverty is itself part of the historical context of *The Meadow* as much as geography, war, politics and theology. All of these tales—whether they are about monks, farmers or naughty children—are collected against a background of constant awareness of and concern for poverty and its ill effects, with a large percentage of the tales dealing directly or indirectly with issues of poverty, wealth, hospitality, theft, generosity, alms, social services, investing, borrowing, debt, the exchange of goods or services, greed or *philanthropia*. For the purpose of organization, this chapter will identify select tales that fall under one of three themes that were grounded in contemporary patristic theology: (1) Christ present in the suffering poor; (2) poverty for the sake of salvation; and (3) the developmental stages of almsgiving in early centuries of Christianity.

Christ in the Suffering Poor

For Byzantine Christianity, the Incarnation of the *Logos* dominated theological discussion, and sources would have us believe that this transcended all levels of society. We may recall the oft-quoted adage from Gregory of Nyssa:

> If in this city, if you ask anyone for change, he will argue with you about whether the Son is begotten or unbegotten. If you ask about the quality of bread, you will receive the answer that "The Father is greater, the Son is less." If you suggest that you require a bath, you will be told that "there was nothing before the Son was created."[15]

---

[13] *Prat. sp.* 127 (PG 87.2987–92). Susan R. Holman, *God Knows There's Need: Christian Responses to Poverty* (Oxford University Press, 2009): 57.

[14] *Prat. sp.* 42 (PG 87.2896B–C); 125 (PG 87[3]:2988B); 41 (PG 87[3]:2896B); Daniel Caner, "Towards a Miraculous Economy: Christian Gifts and Material 'Blessings' in Late Antiquity," JECS, Vol. 14, No. 3 (2006): 334, 348, 350, respectively.

[15] Gregory of Nyssa, De deitate Filii et Spiritus sancti (PG 46.557).

With this type of spirited concern about the person of Jesus, it comes as no surprise that incarnational theology would extend to the marketplace, influencing the distribution of wealth and coloring the way in which the poor in society would be interpreted. After all, according to the gospel accounts, Jesus had a few things to say about money and how one was to treat the poor, and engaged in public acts of free charity and philanthropy. Jesus' and Paul's consistent attention to immediate, real human need by way of tax and debt relief is a powerful statement in a culture in which social services either do not exist, exist only on a small scale, or are unreachable for the majority of the population in need.[16] A central biblical passage for the first theme of "Christ present in the suffering poor" is a passage from the Gospel According to Matthew in which Jesus—surely fashioning this on Proverbs[17]—speaks of who will inherit, and why they will inherit, the kingdom of heaven: "Truly I tell you, just as you did it [provided food, drink, clothing and comfort] to one of the least of these who are members of my family, you did it to me."[18] This passage sets up more than an ethical injunction, for it contains within it the theological limits of the relationship between Jesus and humanity. For eastern Christianity, the Incarnation of the Logos—the theology of which is perfected early on in the theology of Athanasius[19]—implies that the previously broken relationship between the individual and God is restored in the person of Jesus and thus humanity—which is likewise restored to proper relationship with God—reflects the "image and likeness" in which it had originally been created. This restored relationship comes with a renewed purpose *in* the world and *for* the world, for if, as Chalcedonian theology claims, Christ is "of one substance with us in His humanity, 'like unto us in all things save sin,'"[20] then Jesus modeled perfect human activity in the world and for the world. The Matthew passage will be used reliably in patristic texts to highlight or emphasize ethical behavior, condemnation or mercy, depending on the circumstances and needs of the community to whom they are addressed. Gregory of Nyssa claims that blessings flow for the one who chooses to honor these words of Jesus, who has faith in his decree and sees in the poor and ill the face of God.[21] As John and Sophronios did, so too did Gregory live with famine, drought, disasters and disease; concerned with the lack of care available for those

---

[16] Bruce W. Longenecker, *Remember the Poor: Paul, Poverty, and the Greco-Roman World* (Grand Rapids, MI: Wm. B. Eerdmans Publishing Company, 2010): 60–107.

[17] Proverbs 19.17: "Whoever is kind to the poor lends to the Lord, and will be repaid in full." Even more explicit is Proverbs 28.27: "Whoever gives to the poor will lack nothing, but one who turns a blind eye will get many a curse."

[18] Matthew 25.31–46. For a history of interpretation of this passage, see Eric R. Severson, *The Least of These: Selected Readings in Christian History* (Eugene, OR: Cascade Books, 2007).

[19] Athanasis, *De incarnatione verbi* (PG 25.3–96); *On the Incarnation*, trans. A Religious of C.S.M.V. (Crestwood, NY: St Vladimir's Seminary Press, 1996).

[20] Chalcedonian Creed, *Acta Concilii* in Mansi; trans. in Robert Van Voorst, *Readings in Christianity* (Wadsworth, CA: 2001): 91–2.

[21] Gregory of Nyssa, In illud: Quatenus uni ex his fecistis mihi fecistis; On the Love of the Poor (GNO 9.1:111–27), trans. Holman, The Hungry are Dying, 200–201.

suffering, Gregory alleges that this "commandment is vital especially now, with so many in need of basic essentials for survival, and many constrained by need, and many whose bodies are utterly spent from suffering sickness. In caring for them, you will see for yourself the realization of good news."[22] Unlike his brother, Basil of Caesarea appeals neither to compassion nor to pity, but to the very question of inheritance and very human fear of punishment and hope for reward:

> Even in the last judgment, to which the Lord will call the just, those who give freely will hold the first rank; the one who nourishes will stand first in honor, the supplier of bread will be called before everyone else; the kind and bountiful will be escorted to life before all the other righteous. The one who distances himself from community and is asocial and stingy will be handed over to the fire before all [other] sinners.[23]

Like Gregory and Basil, John Chrysostom—of whom Brändle claims that this passage is the "integrative force" of his theology[24]—never hesitates to hold up the carrot of mercy, while noting identification of God with the poor: "The dignity of the one receiving, for it was God, was [received] by the poor."[25]

It is not likely that all of the monks or the lay people whom Moschos and Sophronios encountered were conversant in either Chalcedonian Christology or the sermons of those who supported it; in fact it is clear in *The Meadow* that many are greatly confused by theological questions of the day, and others do not even want to discuss them;[26] however, within several tales collected by our monks, the theology is reflected in the economic activity of individuals, and moments of charity become moments of evangelism for orthodox Christianity. In an environment rich with miracles and thick with desert theologians, Christ's injunctions to love God and love thy neighbor[27] become the operating principles. The most obvious manner by which one might demonstrate an orthodox theology—and the easiest in a time of empire-wide economic hardship—would be to engage in charitable activity rooted in the life of Jesus.[28] For example, John and Sophronios are told

---

[22] Gregory of Nyssa, *In illud*; in Holman, *The Hungry are Dying*, 200.

[23] Basil of Caesarea, *Homilia dicta tempore famis et siccitatis* (PG 31.303–28); in Holman, *The Hungry are Dying*, 191. Basil references the Matthew passage as well in the preface to his *Regulae brevius tractatae*. Basil of Caesarea, *Regulae fusius tractatae* (PG 31. 889–1052); *Long Rules*, in *Saint Basil: Ascetical Works*, trans. Sister M. Monica Wagner (Washington, DC: Catholic University of America Press, 1962): 22.

[24] Rudolph Brändle, "This Sweetest Passage: Matthew 25:31–46 and Assistance to the Poor in the Homilies of John Chrysostom," in Holman, *Wealth and Poverty in Early Church and Society*, 127–39. Rudolph Brändle, *Matth. 25,31-46 im Werk des Johannes Chrysostomos* (Tübingen: Mohr Siebeck, 1979).

[25] John Chrysostom, *Hom. in Mt. 79.1* (PG 57.61–2).

[26] *Prat. sp.* 26 (PG 2872) and 106 (PG 2965).

[27] Matthew 22.36–40.

[28] Chadwick, "Moschus and His friend Sophronios," 72.

a story of an unnamed charitable Christian woman in Nisbis who, when her pagan husband suggested that they loan their money and then live off the interest, convinced him to loan 50 *miliarisia*[29] to the "God of the Christians."[30] For, she claims, the Christian God will not only return the money with interest, but will double the capital.[31] She has him distribute the money to the poor outside of the church, informing him that "the God of the Christians receives these things, for these are all his,"[32] a clear reflection of a common patristic position that lending to the poor is lending to God because Christ is present in the poor. Within three months the couple have no money to pay their bills. When the husband returns to the church to claim his money he finds a single gold *miliarision* on the ground, which—after complaining about to his wife—he uses to buy fish, bread and wine. While preparing the fish for dinner the wife discovers a gemstone inside, which the husband trades for 300 *miliarisia*. The wife notes that the God of the Christians has not only returned their money, but has returned it six times over, which means that the interest that they received by investing in the poor in Christ rather than the secular market was 500 percent![33] Moschos writes: "And now persuaded by this miracle and learning the truth by experience, he became at once a Christian."[34]

It is tempting to label this as a poor person's fantasy or folklore, or to dismiss it altogether.[35] Unlike Bultmann, who disregards it outright as no more than a "legend,"[36] there is, according to Bauckham, a centuries-old history of tales about fish containing precious objects that bear some connection to the one who

---

[29] A *miliarisia* is a Byzantine coin. Philip Grierson, *Byzantine Coinage* (Washington, DC: Dumbarton Oaks, 1999): 2.

[30] "Τῷ Θεῷ τῶν Χριστιανῶν," *Prat. sp.* 185 (PG 87.3057–62).

[31] See: Matt 19.29; Mark 10.29; II Cor. 9.6–13. Chrysostom urges the lender to give money to the needy rather than lend it, for then God would return that investment with a better deal: "While this scarcely gives back a hundred; this a hundred times as much, and eternal life." *Hom. in Mt.* 56 PG 58.556. See also Chrysostom's *Homily 3* on Genesis, PG 53.33, referred to in Patlagean as an "investissement céleste." "Le thème de l'aumône comme investissement céleste est développé dans les homilés sur le bon usage de la richesse ou sur le prêt à intérêt, tandis qu'un récit naif de Jean Moschos l'illustre même au pied de la lettre, en montrant le don charitable rendu avec usure au donateur." Patlagean, *Pauvreté économique et pauvreté sociale*, 190.

[32] "ὁ Θεὸς τῶν Χριστιανῶν ταῦτα λαμβάνει. Οὗτοι γὰρ πάντες αὐτοῦ εἰσιν." *Prat. sp.* 185 (PG 87.3060).

[33] *Codex Just.* IV, 32.26 (1), *Corpus juris civilis*, S.P. Scott, trans., *The Civil Law* (New York, 1973): 82–3.

[34] "καὶ πεισθεὶς διὰ τοῦδε ταῦ θαύματος πείρᾳ μαθὼν καὶ οὕτως τὴν ἀλήθειαν, γέγονεν εσθεως Χριστιανὸς," *Prat. sp.* 185 (PG 87.3061).

[35] "Lorsqu'un personnage de Jean Moschos porte la pierre précieuse trouvée dans le ventre d'un poisson à un joaillier qui en propose 5 miliarisia pour commencer, et 300 pour finir, il s'agit, évidemment d'une fable." Patlagean, *Pauvreté économique et pauvreté sociale*, 171.

[36] Rudolf Bultmann, *The History of the Synoptic Tradition*, trans. John March (Oxford: Basil Blackwell, 1968): 34.

finds them; therefore we cannot discount the knowledge that the author would have had of this tradition.[37] But there are some interesting components to this beneficial tale. First, it is worth noting the allusion to the biblical tale in which necessary funds appears in the mouth of a fish; this reinforces the argument that God does not desire to impoverish God's people, but rather to provide for God's people.[38] Second, we are reminded that there are those who engage in simple loan transactions for profit, making their money by lending to others and living off the interest, a business against which the patristics speak quite harshly,[39] and a business from which the wife would like to retire.[40] Third, the husband learns "the truth" of the Christian God not because someone has taught him, not because he read it in the gospels or heard the preaching of an eloquent bishop; but he learns "the truth"[41] through experience, through actively engaging in giving money to the poor, which—worth noting—was an idea that he credits to his wife,[42] and by a clear profit from that transaction. It cannot escape notice that the couple profit *heavily* by this transaction,[43] a theme consistent in seventh-century hagiography, the "l'économie miraculeuse"[44] as coined by Déroche. While not *the* moral, certainly *a* moral of this tale is that God provides in this world with an act of miraculous wealth for those who engage in righteous behavior; they are rewarded (blessed?) with that which they would *not* have acquired had they engaged merely in regular market activity, for, according to Chrysostom, the activity of the market is based

---

[37] Richard Bauckham, "The Coin in the Fish's Mouth," in David Wenham and Craig Blomberg (eds), *The Miracles of Jesus*, Vol. 6 (Sheffield: JSOT Press, 1986): 237–44. W.F. Albright and C.S. Mann, *Matthew: A New Translation*, The Anchor Yale Bible, Vol. 26 (Yale University Press, 2011): 213. Although he acknowledges the connection between gold and the carp in Latin poetry, and the Vedic hymns in which fish bring riches, Gubernatis rejects the notion that "the legend of the fish with gold in its mouth, so common in Aryan legends" would be known in Judea. Angelo De Gubernatis, *Zoological Mythology: Or, Legends of the Animals*, Vol. II (London: Trübner & Company, 1968): 351–3.

[38] Matthew 17.24–7.

[39] Ambrose, *De Tobia* (PL 14, 0759B–0794B); trans. Lois Miles Zucker, *S. Ambrosii, De Tobia: A Commentary, with an Introduction and Translation* (Catholic University of America, 1933); Basil, *Homilia in psalmum 14* (PG 29.263–80); trans. Agnes Clare Way. *Saint Basil: Exegetic Homilies*. FC, 46 (Catholic University Press, 1963): 181–91; Gregory of Nyssa, *Contra Usurarios* (GNO 9.1.195–207); trans. Casimir McCambley, "Against Those Who Practice Usury," GOTR, Vol. 36 (1991): 287–302.

[40] Women lent as well. Brenda Llewellyn Ihssen, They Who Give From Evil: The Response of the Eastern Church to Moneylending in the Early Christian Era (Pickwick Publications, 2012): 97, n. 17.

[41] "τὴν ἀλήθειαν," *Prat. sp.* 185 (PG 87.3061).

[42] *Prat. sp.* 185 (PG 87.3061). Clearly she was the economist of the household.

[43] Laiou, "The Church, Economic Thought and Economic Practice," 446.

[44] Déroche, *Etudes sur Leontios de Neapolis*, 238–49; A.E. Laiou, "Trade Profit and Salvation in the Late Patristic and the Byzantine Period," in Holman, *Wealth and Poverty in Early Church and Society*, 249.

on deception,[45] such as we see clearly in this text as the money-changer initially offers only five *miliarisia* for a stone that he eventually concedes is worth three hundred.[46] Had they earned the standard interest they would have been enriched, but barely, and standard operating procedures never convince anyone of anything other than that the standard is preferable to chaos. While over-abundance granted in this present life—the "l'économie miraculeuse"[47]—convinces the husband of the very rightness of the decision to invest financially and spiritually in the Christian God, it might be the miracle but it is hardly the point: to lend ("δανείζω") the money to the Christian God they needed to distribute it to the poor. Therefore, between both the words of the wife and the actions of the husband, their tale supports the obligations of both parties—divine and human—as well as biblical passages on which the theology so heavily depends.

Proof that Christ is present in the poor, that lending or giving to the poor is giving directly to God, can take more than a lifetime to work itself through. While in Alexandria, John and Sophronios are told a story of Evagrios, a philosopher[48] who is fed up with a certain Bishop Synesios' attempts to convert him. Evagrios confesses that he is displeased with the following teachings: resurrection of the flesh; lending to the poor is lending to God; and those who give money to the poor build treasure in heaven which they shall receive—with interest—along with eternal life. After the philosopher is baptized he gives the bishop three coins and requests two things: first, that they be given to the poor; and second, that he be given a certificate that *guarantees* that he will receive them back in the next world, a certificate that is buried with him when he dies. After he has been dead and buried three days, he appears in a dream to the bishop and informs him that he has received what he was owed and that he has no further claim on the bishop, who is instructed to come to the grave, dig up his body, and collect the paper that he has signed, *post mortem*. In the presence of the dead man's sons, the clergy and leading citizens, the bishop has the tomb opened and they find the certificate with writing on it confirming "I accept and I have in this no further written pledge from you, in respect to the gold I gave you; or rather, through you, to Christ our God and Saviour."[49]

---

[45] John Chrysostom, *Homily on Almsgiving* (PG 64.436). The commonplace nature of theft in the marketplace is evident in *Prat. sp.* 200 (PG 87.3087–90). A patrician commissions a jewelled cross to offer to the church, and the apprentice adds his wages worth in gold to the cross. The patrician accuses the apprentice of tampering with the metal, and he is informed that the youth sought to share in the offering with the patrician. Chagrined, the patrician made the youth his son and heir. The astonishment of the patrician is an indication of the rarity of his actions.

[46] *Prat. sp.* 185 (PG 87.3060).

[47] Caner, "Towards a Miraculous Economy," 330; more on miraculous wealth below.

[48] *Prat. sp.* 195 (PG. 87.3077–80).

[49] "Ἔλαβον τὸ ἐν τούτῳ τῷ πιττακίῳ σου γεγραμμένον, καὶ ἐπληρώθην καὶ οὐδένα λόγον ἔχω πρὸς σέ, ἕνεκα οὗ δέδωκά σοι χρυσίου, ἤγουν διὰ σοῦ, Χριστῷ τῷ Θεῷ καὶ Σωτῆρι ἡμῶν." *Prat. sp.* 195 (PG. 87.3080).

Analysis of this tale must begin with a caveat that John is clearly not interested in telling us everything. First, the text does not tell us why a man who is opposed to Christian teachings was baptized, which suggests either that he converts to silence the bishop's attempts to convert him or that John assumes that we will know that the philosopher has had a change of heart. But the baptism seems to come at the same time as he makes this financial "deal" with the bishop and requests the document, which implies that, regardless of his baptism, he is reserving final judgment until he is able to meet his maker and find out for himself if this Christian philanthropy business is nonsense or not. Second, there is no argument or even a discussion about this certificate, which naturally raises questions about the practice of issuing certificates that would establish what people would get when they got to heaven. It certainly reflects the level of anxiety that people who donated or gave to the poor experienced about what, exactly, they would get back, and when they would get it. In this case the bishop has his official draw up a document that would satisfy that the philosopher would get his "due" in the end. A curious action, this is not without precedent: in another tale we find a bishop having a false letter of credit against the church written by the legal officer—even going so far as to "age" the documents—to satisfy a difficult financial situation, in this case the restoration of public honor for a man who has lost his fortune through no fault of his own.[50] To return to our philosopher, finally, we learn from this tale that giving to God via the poor seemed distasteful to some members of society, and we can be fairly sure that he is not the only one who feels this way. It is almost refreshing to see evidence *not* of stinginess, but of the very real and reasonable struggle with generosity that many must have had in the face of the radical suggestion to give something to one who has proven themselves a poor manager of funds or a victim of fate. Regardless, he was willing to gamble that the God of the Christians would pay up; according to the text, God did, and God's reception of the money via the poor is revealed publicly to those who gathered to witness the exhumation of the body. If anyone present was doubtful of God making good on a promise, a notarized document from God would surely suffice. This particular type of tale is noted by Laiou as a tale of "shifting realities and values,"[51] evidence that the church did not necessarily follow its own legislation, and that it certainly engaged in business and banking.

---

[50] *Prat. sp.* 193 (PG 3071–6); this appears to be a popular tale in Alexandria, for Bishop Leontius includes in his *Life of John the Almsgiver* the identical story, which the translators note and omit from the tale. Leontius of Neapolis, *A Supplement to the Life of John The Almsgiver*, in Dawes and Baynes, *Three Byzantine Saints*, 244. Worth noting, Leontius also writes that Patriarch John discreetly directs the man in charge of the distribution of alms to give a foreign resident who had been robbed of 15 pounds of gold because "[t]he Saint was very sorry for him—for he was one of the prominent foreign residents." The patriarch might also have been acting out of a sense of embarrassment that this prominent foreign resident was a victim of theft in his apostolic city. Leontius of Neapolis, *A Supplement to the Life of John The Almsgiver*, in Dawes and Baynes, *Three Byzantine Saints*, 218.

[51] Laiou, "The Church, Economic Thought and Economic Practice," 444.

The final text to consider that most explicitly reflects this theme is a tale that John and Sophronios acquire while in Antioch, of a man identified only as a "φιλόχριστος."[52] As the head of a social service in the city, he would provide the impoverished with whatever they lacked. Of note, he would import linen undergarments from Egypt, which he distributed in accordance with Matthew 25.36, quoted in the text: "I was naked and you clothed me."[53] An individual identified only as a "ἀδελφὸς"[54] came to the distribution of clothing several times, and when he came the fourth time the righteous man chastised him, ordering him to refrain from taking any more as there were plenty of others in need. Shamed, the poor man left. That night, the righteous man had a vision in which he was standing before Jesus, who lifted his own tunic and showed him four undergarments, demonstrating that the supervisor had actually been giving the undergarments to Christ, present in the poor. The supervisor fell to the ground prostrate before Jesus and begged forgiveness for having accounted the circumstances as a man might (with the implication that God might account the circumstances in a different way,[55]), "and thereafter in simplicity and joy he furnished all things to those asking."[56]

We learn in this text about the philanthropic institutions of the city of Antioch; this man is not distributing from his own wealth, but from the resources of someone or something else. Social services or civic duties (*leitourgiai*) were established in cities in the empire, services often provided by the church for those in need of accommodation, food, health care, clothing or comfort, distributed to the poor who gathered in need.[57] Canon law enshrined the role of philanthropy in the city,[58] and bishops were the models of the expected philanthropic behavior.[59] While it seems evident that the righteous man is to be understood as a Christian, it is not evident that the poor people to whom he distributes the undergarments are. Prior to his outburst his hand is restricted. But his unrighteous spirit towards a man he

---

[52] A "friend of Christ." 12, Nissen, "Unbekannte Erzählungen," 367.
[53] "γυμνὸς ἤμην καὶ περιεβάλετέ με." Nissen, "Unbekannte Erzählungen," 367–8.
[54] Ibid., 368.
[55] "ὅτι ὡς ἄνθρωπος τοῦτο ἐλογισάμην." Ibid.
[56] "καὶ ἔκτοτε ἐν ἁπλότητι καὶ χαρᾷ πᾶσι τοῖς αἰτοῦσι παρεῖχεν." Ibid.
[57] Holman, The Hungry are Dying, 31–63.
[58] Canon 59 of the *Ecclesiastical Canons of the Same Holy Apostles* equates deprivation with murder. Roberts and Donaldson, ANF 7, 503; see also Canon 17 of *The Canons of the 318 Holy Fathers Assembled in The City of Nice, in Bithynia*, and Canons 8 Canon 11 of *The Fourth Ecumenical Council: The Council of Chalcedon*. Philip Schaff and Henry Wace (eds), *The Seven Ecumenical Councils*, NPNF 14 (Peabody, MA: Hendrickson Publishers, 1999): 36–8, 273–4 and 276–7, respectively.
[59] Demetrios Constantelos, Byzantine Philanthropy and Social Welfare (Rutger's University Press, 1968): 67–87; Holman, The Hungry are Dying, 31–63; Claudia Rapp, Holy Bishops in Late Antiquity: The Nature of Christian Leadership in an Age of Transition (Berkeley, CA: University of California Press, 2005); Andrea Sterk, Renouncing the World Yet Leading the Church: The Monk-Bishop in Late Antiquity (Cambridge, MA: Harvard University Press, 2004).

perceived as greedy is chastised by Jesus, who counts the undergarnments out loud,[60] but then assures him that what had been provided for the poor had become, in fact, Christ's own attire.[61] The result of his encounter with the actual recipient of the undergarments is that from this point on the righteous man's generosity is truly motivated by righteousness and extends to all in need—Christian or not—without questioning their motives.[62] The poor, in this case, became for the righteous man a public means by which he might invest in the body of Christ on an altar of poverty, or, as John Chrysostom writes, on the altar of the bodies of the poor: "This altar is composed of the very members of Christ, and the body of the Lord becomes your altar ... venerable because it is itself Christ's body ... This altar you can see lying everywhere, in the alleys and in the agoras and you can sacrifice on it anytime."[63]

Poverty for the Sake of Salvation

If Christ is present in the poor because of shared humanity, and if Christ is also God by nature, failure to aid the poor carries severe implications, for the failure to lay one's offering on the "altar" of the poor is to fail to bring one's offerings to God. In the early centuries of Christianity there were plenty of opportunities to put this into practice; Christianity developed in a society in which the poor formed both a large and visible part of society, and it responded quickly to the needs of the poor in the forms of organized social services and charity[64] as well as the more individualized and less regulated redemptive almsgiving,[65] an activity that bound lay Christians together in mutual service to one another.[66] In addition to the aforementioned canonical law and office of the episcopate as the model of philanthropy, monastic houses, hermitic figures and lay persons also adopted their own methods of philanthropic management to conform to the expectations to divest themselves of wealth for salvation at the same time that they managed their

---

[60] "ἰδοὺ ἕν, ἰδοὺ δύο, ἰδοὺ τρία, ἰδοὺ τέτταρα," Nissen, "Unbekannte Erzählungen," 368.

[61] Ibid.

[62] Ibid.

[63] Chrys., *Hom. 20.3 in Ep 2 ad Cor.*, trans. M.J. De Vinne, "The Advocacy of Empty Bellies" (UMI Dissertation Services, 1995): 82–3, n. 108.

[64] Geoffrey D. Dunn, David Luckensmeyer and Lawrence Cross (eds), *Prayer and Spirituality in the Early Church: Poverty and Riches* (Strathfield, Australia: St Paul's Publications, 2009); Steven J. Friesen, "Injustice or God's Will? Early Christian Explanations of Poverty," in Holman, *Wealth and Poverty*, 17–36; Peter Brown, *Poverty and Leadership in the Later Roman Empire* (Brandeis University Press: 2002).

[65] Roman Garrison, Redemptive Almsgiving in Early Christianity (JSNT supplement, Sheffield, 1994); Richard Finn, Almsgiving in the Later Roman Empire: Christian Promotion and Practice (313–450) (Oxford University Press, 2006).

[66] William Countryman, *The Rich Christian in the Church of the Early Empire* (New York: Edwin Mellon Press, 1980): 118.

own earthly prosperity. Passages of scripture most often referenced to support this activity are found in Luke, Matthew and Mark, primarily Luke 14.26–33 on the renunciation of possessions,[67] and Matthew 19.24–5, on the barrier created by wealth: "Jesus said ... 'Truly I tell you, it will be hard for a rich person to enter the kingdom of heaven. Again I tell you, it is easier for a camel to go through the eye of a needle than for someone who is rich to enter the kingdom of God.'"[68] A much-discussed passage, what is fairly unambiguous in this statement is that while a rich person might be saved, nevertheless wealth can be a hindrance; further, while wealth is a good thing, it is only good if it is being used.[69] The renunciation of wealth, then, in addition to the practical assistance that it provided to the poor, served to indemnify against the loss of salvation of the one who gave. This notion that the wealthy and poor might benefit each other's physical and spiritual well-being—one by giving and one by receiving—emerges in the mid-second-century *Shepherd of Hermas*, which addresses wealth and its benefits and detriments through several themes. Of primary importance is self-sufficiency; that which is in excess, that which might have gone to purchase food, clothing, land or items of luxury or leisure, is instead required to be put to another use:

> Therefore instead of lands, purchase afflicted souls, as each is able, "and look after widows and orphans," and do not despise them, and spend your wealth and all your establishments for such fields and houses as you have received from God. For, for this reason did the Master make you rich, that you should fulfill these ministries for him. It is far better to purchase such lands and houses, as you will find in your own city, when you go to it. This wealth is beautiful and joyful, and has neither grief nor fear, but has joy.[70]

Renunciation and the embracing of poverty for the sake of salvation is revealed in the hospitality practices of eastern monastic houses. Monasteries provided food, health care, bathing houses and money to lay persons, becoming sites of both physical and spiritual rest for those living in the world.[71] We read in Basil's

---

[67] Note Pachomius' method: "He introduced them to the life gradually. First, they had to renounce all the world, their parents, and themselves, and follow the Saviour who taught them doing so, for this is to carry the Cross." *The First Greek Life of Pachomius*, in *Pachomian Koinonia: The Life of St. Pachomius and His Disciples*, Vol. I, trans. Armand Villeux (Kalamazoo, MI: Cistercian Publications, 1980): 312.

[68] See also Mark 10.23–5.

[69] Chrysostom, Hom. In. Acts of the Apostles, Justo González, Faith and Wealth: A History of Early Christian Ideas on the Origin, Significance, and Use of Money (Eugene, OR: Wipf and Stock Publishers, 1990): 212, n. 6.

[70] *Shepherd of Hermas*, trans. Kirsopp Lake, in *The Apostolic Fathers*, Vol. 2 (Harvard University Press, 1997): 1.6; 1.8–9.

[71] Constantelos, *Byzantine Philanthropy*, 88–110.

Longer Rules— the standard upon which Byzantine *typika*[72] will be constructed— that monks must "choose to have treasure in heaven alone, so that we may keep our heart there."[73] Basil understands renunciation not merely as the renunciation of wealth or property, but as taking place on several levels: renunciation of passions, then "property, vainglory, life in society, useless desires."[74] Sometimes these injunctions were taken to such a degree that monks themselves ran dangerously close to extreme levels of poverty, as a passage from the Greek life of Pachomius suggests: "Since they [the monks] used to give away in alms whatever they had, it happened once that they ran short of bread. The divine Pachomius wanted to sell two blankets which one of the monks brought with him when he renounced the world, to buy wheat."[75]

Clearly, engaging in the practice of the distribution of wealth for the good of salvation puts the giver at risk in this lifetime; however, patristics consistently encourage monastics and laity to consider giving to the impoverished as a risk worth taking. Chrysostom suggests that this might be accomplished by restructuring how people understand their role in the present society and how that role affects the afterlife; renunciation of one's goods for the sake of salvation is stated explicitly in his *Homily 5* from Matthew: "lend to Him who returns interest greater than the principle ... Lend where your return will not be death, but life instead of death."[76]

Lending for life, however, can sometimes invite the possibility of death, as John and Sophronios learn while reading together with an elder some stories from a text known as the *Paradise*, which appears to be a series of edifying tales very much like the text Moschos himself will compose. They read of a monk who, when he discovers that thieves left a purse behind in his cell, runs after them and gives them what they overlooked.[77] Amazed by the depth of his charity, they recognize him as a "man of God,"[78] and "repented."[79] The requisite level of philanthropy has been extended and the monk has done what is required as he works out his salvation in fear and trembling, but the monk has also put himself at physical risk by running after the thieves and giving them the final bit of coin that they overlooked in their robbery.

---

[72] *Typika* are Byzantine monastic foundation documents. John Thomas, Angela Constantinides Hero and Giles Constable (eds), *Byzantine Monastic Foundation Documents:* A Complete Translation of the Surviving Founders' Typika and Testaments (Washington, DC: Dumbarton Oaks, 2000): 44.

[73] Basil of Caesarea, Regulae fusius tractatae; Long Rules, in Wagner, Ascetical Works, 256.

[74] Ibid., 253.

[75] *The First Greek Life of Pachomius*, in *Pachomian Koinonia, Volume One: The Life of Saint Pachomius and His Disciples*, trans. Armand Villeux (Kalamazoo, MI: Cistercian Publications, 1980): 39.324. Satoshi Toda, "Pachomian Monasticism and Poverty," in Dunn, Luckensmeyer and Cross, *Poverty and Riches*, 198.

[76] John Chrysostom, *Hom. in Mt. 5* (PG 57.61-62.j).

[77] *Prat. sp.* 212 (PG 87.3103–6).

[78] "Ἀληθῶς, οὗτός ἄνθρωπος τοῦ Θεοῦ ἐστιν," *Prat. sp.* 212 (PG 87.3105).

[79] "μετενόησαν," *Prat. sp.* 212 (PG 87.3105).

They might very well have killed him, or he might have starved, with nothing left to buy food—but he would only have gotten to heaven that much sooner. Convinced by his philanthropy, their response is immediate verbal recognition of that which is holy—the monk—and subsequent conversion. The second monk—the elder who is reading the story with John and Sophronios—relates that he asked God to allow him to follow in this holy man's example. Shortly after, he himself was robbed, and he cheerfully led the thieves around his cell, courteously showing them all they might have.[80] Such extreme levels of poverty for the sake of salvation appear in many tales in *The Meadow*, and while there are examples of magnanimous giving,[81] giving by the poor to the poor takes place far more often, and the numerous examples testify the dedication that lay people and monks had for this practice, as well as the fact that it takes very little to demonstrate this virtue: John writes of the elder who would sow at night the fields of men too poor to hire oxen,[82] of the elder who gave his last loaf of bread to a beggar,[83] of the anchorite who fasted all week and gave what he earned to the poor,[84] of the monk who allowed himself to be robbed of his cloak in the winter,[85] and of the compassion of Abba Sisinios for the "Saracen" women who, when he asked her why she "play[ed] the harlot," replied "Because of hunger."[86] At bare minimum, if one has nothing to offer, one at least offers hospitality; under these circumstances, rich is not an adjective that describes one's worth, but one's ability to extend mercy. To do otherwise is unmerciful, and—to return to our Chalcedonian Christology—violates the nature of Christianity, according to John Chrysostom: "Do not tell me that you cannot watch after others. If you are Christians, what is impossible is for you not to watch after them ... If you claim that a Christian is not able to be of service to another, you insult God and call God a liar."[87]

That Christians fail to be of service to one another, John and Sophronios learn, is revealed in the tale of an Alexandrine girl whose wealthy parents die when she is young; they leave her provided for financially, but she is not baptized.[88] One day she meets a man so heavily in debt that creditors have made his life unbearable, and he intends to hang himself. She offers him all her money and he pays his creditors. However, she is now impoverished and turns to prostitution, to

---

[80] This particular tale has a humorous ending: when John asked the elder if he ran after the thieves and gave them more, the elder replied, "No, God forbid." *Prat. sp.* 212 (PG 87.3105). The Greek in the PG is obscured, but the Latin reads: "Non; avertat hoc Deus."

[81] *Prat. sp.* 186 (PG 3061–4); more on this below.

[82] *Prat. sp.* 24 (PG 87.2869–70).

[83] *Prat. sp.* 9 (PG 87.2859–60). This action models perfectly an exhortation from Basil of Caesarea: "Even if you possess only one loaf of bread, and the beggar stands at the door, bring the one loaf out of the storeroom." Basil, *Homilia dicta tempore famis et siccitatis*, in Holman, *The Hungry Are Dying*, 190.

[84] *Prat. sp.* 13 (PG 87.2861–2).

[85] *Prat. sp.* 68 (PG 87.2917–18).

[86] "Ὅτι πεινῶ." *Prat. sp.* 136 (PG 87.2999–3000).

[87] Chrysostom, *Hom. in Act. Apost.* 20.4 (PG 60.163).

[88] *Prat. sp.* 207 (PG 87.3097–100).

the scandal of those who knew her parents. Eventually she falls ill, is filled with remorse and wishes to be baptized.[89] When her neighbors refuse to help her, angels appear, take her to the church, have the clergy baptize her and return her home dressed in white. The pope,[90] who has had this brought to his attention, realizes that this is divine work. Like the majority of the tales in *The Meadow*, this tale does not give us everything we need to know, and sometimes vices are present when we wish for virtues: for example, with all this talk of charity and mercy, why will the neighbors not assist her? Hagiographic analysis would suggest that this is the opportunity for the activity of God to be manifest in the work of the angels disguised as public officials and clergy. But it is not the activity of the angels that saves her. When questioned by the pope, he asks not what she *believes*, but "what good have you done?"[91] After informing the pope that she financially freed a man about to hang himself out of despair from his debt, Moschos writes, she "fell asleep in the Lord,"[92] released from sins voluntary and involuntary.[93] According to this text it is not baptism that offers cleansing; it is her deed of charity in a world in which a pious action redeems grave sin. What distinguishes this from the purchase of salvation is repentance: charity without repentance no more buys salvation than repentance without charity.[94]

A final example of poverty for the sake of salvation is a curious tale of a virtuous anchorite who beseeches God to make known God's judgments.[95] According to the tale, God permitted an idea to come to the anchorite[96] that he should visit another anchorite some distance away. While traveling, the elder meets an angel disguised as a monk, who, while they are traveling, performs many atrocious acts: he makes a silver dish disappear,[97] strangles a young boy[98] and rebuilds a crumbling wall like a laborer.[99] When the elder finally confronts the angel-monk about his actions, the angel-monk replies that the silver dish was the inheritance of a man who had *not* been just, therefore it was taken from the Christ-loving man because he was a just man, in order that he not lose grace on account of the dish.[100] The child, the angel-monk explains, was a child of a good man, and yet had the child lived he

---

[89] *Prat. sp.* 207 (PG 87.3097).

[90] "Pope" refers to the Alexandrine patriarch, whose title is the same as the Roman pontiff.

[91] "Εἰπέ μοι, θύγατερ, τί πέπρακταί σοι ἀγαθόν;" *Prat. sp.* 207 (PG 87.3100).

[92] "Καὶ ταῦτα εἰποῦσα ἀνεπαύσατο ἐν Κυρίῳ." Ibid.

[93] *Prat. sp.* 207 (PG 87.3100).

[94] James 2.20–24.

[95] VI, Mioni, "Il Pratum Spirituale," 87–8.

[96] "παρεχώρησεν ἐλθεῖν αὐτῷ λογισμόν," IV, Mioni, "Il Pratum Spirituale de Giovanni Mosco," 87.

[97] Ibid.

[98] Ibid.

[99] Ibid.

[100] "τὸ δὲ πατελίκιν ἐκεῖνο ἀπὸ ἀδίκου κληπονομίας αὐτῷ κατελείφθη· ἵνα οὖν μὴ χάριν τοῦ πατελικίου ἐκείνου ἀπολέσῃ τὸν μισθὸν τῶν ἄλλων ἀγαθῶν, ἰδοὺ ἠφάντωσα

would have been an instrument of Satan and so his early death was "to ensure the salvation of his father" and, it is implied, the son as well.[101] The wall he rebuilt because the owner's grandfather had left money in the wall, and if the wicked owner were to get his hands on that money he would be even more of a plague on his community than he was already.[102] And with that explanation concluded, the angel-monk orders the elder: "Now go to [your] cell."[103] In this interesting— and slightly disquieting— tale, money, material goods and even life are denied individuals who might otherwise come to spiritual harm through their possession. A damaging and disturbing conclusion that one could draw from this tale is that those who "have not" might very well have not because they would come to harm if they "had." There is tremendous potential for abuse in this case: one might well draw the conclusion that people are impoverished and remain in those circumstances because they *might* sin if given the opportunity (i.e. the material means to do so). However, one might argue that the lack of free will afforded to individuals who are denied is balanced by the thoughtful activity of the agent of God in the guise of a monk; in Moschos' world, Christians were counseled to consider themselves as foreigners; thus the emphasis on that which is eternal rather than ephemeral makes more sense. One must also be mindful that this is a text collected and composed by a monk, whose very occupation is renunciation. In this context, perhaps poverty might be a blessing, providing the means to salvation.

While poverty for the sake of salvation very often means an investment in the celestial life beyond the life of the flesh, some *Meadow* tales suggest that the concept of salvation is nuanced.[104] Select tales advocate that God rewards those who obey God's law with salvation in the form of freedom from destitution, shame or imprisonment. For example, in one tale, a merchant learns that a woman is prostituting herself for food for her husband because he was imprisoned for a shipwreck that financially ruined his family and others.[105] Moved by her hardship, the merchant gives the woman the gold owing to redeem her husband. After the merchant is later slandered, deprived of his property, put into prison, and threatened daily with death, in a series of dreams he sees the woman whose husband he earlier redeemed, and she assures him that she will intercede on his behalf. The merchant's property and position are restored, after which the woman appears a final time and informs him that "for the sake of God, you respected my body. Behold, I have delivered you from danger. So you see how kindly God deals with men. That is how you dealt with me, and I have extended my mercy

---

αὐτὸ καὶ ἔστι τὸ ἔργον αὐτοῦ καθαρόν." IV, Mioni, "Il Pratum Spirituale de Giovanni Mosco," 88.

[101] Ibid.

[102] Ibid.

[103] "Ἄπελθε οὖν εἰς τὸ κελλίον." Ibid.

[104] John Wortley, "What the Desert Fathers meant by 'being saved,'" ZAC, Vol. 12, No. 2 (2008): 322–43.

[105] *Prat. sp.* 186 (PG 3061–4).

towards you."[106] Clearly a tale that promotes charity and virtue, what is granted to the merchant, the woman and the man through their shared virtue is a mutual restoration—or salvation—of property, freedom and honor.

Shipwrecks, prisons and money-managers factor into many of these tales, demonstrating the far-reaching activity of God and creditor, as well as the degree to which the ruination of life and reputation by one party might require the salvific activity of the other. Further, the tales demonstrate the degree to which one's honor could be taken as easily as one's fortune, and that honor could—sometimes— be found among thieves. For example, when a sailor-merchant lost his cargo, creditors threw him into prison and confiscated his property. His wife would daily bring him bread and eat with him, and while she was thus engaged a person of reputation saw and desired her. He sent for her and she came, thinking he would help her. He promised to discharge their debts if she would sleep with him, to which this sharp-witted woman replied that as her body belonged to her husband, he should ask him. Not swayed by the promise of freedom in exchange for sexual enslavement of his wife, the husband rejected the offer. A condemned prisoner overheard this pious exchange and was so moved by their honor [ἐλευθερίαν] that he offered them hidden wealth, which the woman used to discharge their debts and procure her husband's release. The priest telling this story informed Moschos and Sophronios that "Behold, even as they were faithful to the mandate of God, thus did our Lord and God display great mercies on them."[107] That the money they received from a highwayman who died for his crimes was procured by thefts and murders was of no account: either it is assumed that the chastity and piety of the other couple appear to have cleansed the money of taint, or Moschos is not concerned with reflecting on this question, although many others will.[108]

That poverty is *not always* a blessing or the path to salvation is evident in some tales that propose that one's salvation might be at risk without money. For example, in a tale mentioned briefly above,[109] a wealthy young man is left a large inheritance, but loses it all as a result of problems related to the common risks of trade that are beyond his control. Apollinarios, the pope of Alexandria, knew the young man's parents and wished not to embarrass him with an offer of help out of his destitution. Disturbed by the reduction in this man's status, upset and embarrassed that the young man was sad in his countenance and in seedy

---

[106] *Prat. sp.* 186 (PG 3064); Wortley, *Spiritual Meadow*, 159. See also: *Prat. sp.* 200 (PG 87 3087–90) and *Prat. sp.* 201 (PG 87 3089–90).

[107] "Ἰδοὺ ὥσπερ ἐφύλαξαν οὗτοι τὴν ἐντολήν τοῦ Θεοῦ· οὕτως ἐμεγάλυνεν τὸ ἔλεος αὐτοῦ εἰς αὐτοὺς ὁ Κύριος καὶ Θεὸς ἡμῶν." *Prat. sp.* 189 (PG 87.3069).

[108] The relationship between the church and the world will naturally lead to questions and reflection on moral value and money. The ultimate conclusion will be that some money is, in fact, dirty, and it often is linked with how the money is gained (i.e. prostitution, theft, robbery, unjust taxing etc.). Laiou, "Wealth, Trade and Profit in Early Byzantium," 257–63.

[109] *Prat. sp.* 193 (PG 87.3071–6).

clothing,[110] the pope devises a plan to have the chancellor draw up and physically "age" a false letter of credit against the church that favored the father of the young man. The chancellor then pretended he had only recently found the document, although the young man's father had been dead for ten years. The young man took the paper to the pope, who pretended to be angry that the letter had not been presented earlier. After much back and forth, the young man was happy to forgo any interest on the false debt, and happily accepted 50 pounds of gold, which he used to recover his status and benefit his soul.[111] Did the pope fear that this man would lose his soul without money? Would he be so dishonored by his financial status that he would fall away from Christianity? In this incidence, the redemption of the man's honor is linked to the health of his soul. Therefore this tale begs the question: salvation from what? It is natural to assume that eternal damnation is the correct response, if passages in the *Apophthegmata Patrum* suggest that the salvation of one's soul might mean something other than eternal salvation. I would claim that this tale suggests that "benefited greatly his soul"[112] means salvation from the social stigma of poverty and reduced social status.

Almsgiving: Who Gets to Give?

Evagrius Scholasticus, author of the *Historia Ecclesiastica*, wrote that Pope Gregory of Antioch distributed funds so liberally that "whenever he went out in public, great numbers followed after him."[113] *The Meadow* includes beneficial tales of Pope Gregory, and confirms that he excelled in "almsgiving, forgiveness, tears."[114] Rather cheekily, the fathers who related this noted that they had many opportunities to test these virtues.[115]

In the Graeco-Roman world, liberality such as Pope Gregory displayed was a sign of the virtuous character of the giver. Giving had little to do with the one in need and everything to do with the one who gave. The one who distributed money must judge appropriately the circumstances and virtue of the one who received, and the challenge was to give precisely, Aristotle claimed, "to the right people, and the right amounts and at the right time."[116] According to Plato, proper distribution was an exchange that took place among those of a similar worthy character, and

---

[110] *Prat. sp.* 193 (PG 87.3071–6).

[111] "μετὰ καὶ τοῦ μεγάλως ὠφεληθῆναι τὴν ψυχὴν." *Prat. sp.* 193 (PG 87.3076).

[112] Ibid.

[113] In fairness, Evagrius worked for Pope Gregory. Evagrius Scholasticus, *Hist.eccl.* V.6.; trans. Michael Whitby, *The Ecclesiastical History of Evagrius Scholasticus* (Liverpool University Press, 2000): 262.

[114] "ἐλεημοσύνην, ἀμνησικακίαν, δάκρυα." *Prat. sp.* 140 (PG 87.3003–4).

[115] Ibid.

[116] Aristotle, *Nicomachean Ethics*, 4.1.25–7, trans. J.A.K. Thompson (Penguin: 1955): 83.

being hungry or impoverished disqualified one from being worthy: "The man who suffers from hunger or the like is not the man who deserves pity, but he who, while possessing temperance or virtue of some sort, or a share thereof, gains in addition evil fortune ..."[117] Endorsed by Cicero and Pliny the Younger, liberality bound a suitable person together to "his kindred, his relations, and his friends."[118] The destitute need not apply.[119] "Significantly," Garrison writes, "within the broadly classified popular morality of the Graeco-Roman tradition, we find no specific exhortations to the rich that they should give to the poor;"[120] rather, he argues, Christianity will inherit from the Graeco-Roman way of distributing alms a preoccupation with self-interest more than redemption of sin. A markedly different attitude towards the poor is found in the Hebrew scriptures, from which Christianity will also inherit several themes: first, one should seek to imitate the benevolence grounded in God's character; in this case, one might argue, almsgiving functions as an expression of love and/or compassion. Second, devotion to God involves sacrifice; and finally, reward and punishment are tied up with—and eventually replace—sacrificial offerings in that the one who offers will be rewarded, while the one who fails to do so will face the wrath of God. An important stage in the development of redemptive almsgiving, according to Garrison, is preference in the Early Church for the Septuagint, with its translation of "righteous" in Daniel 4.27 as ἐλεημοσύνη, suggesting clearly that compassion for the poor is demonstrated by financial contributions to them.[121]

It is neither my desire nor obligation to provide a history of almsgiving, and yet the developmental stages of this important social and economic activity in the history of early Christianity are particular to *The Meadow* because all of the stages—alms as maintenance of status, alms grounded in sacrifice, alms as representative of God's character (i.e. love and/or compassion for the poor) and alms connected to punishment and reward—are present in the beneficial tales, and one can find theological support for all stages. Consistent with *The Meadow* in

---

[117] Plato, *Laws*, 11.936B, trans. R.G. Bury, Vol. II (Cambridge: William Heinemann, 1926): 465. Plato envisioned a state without the unseemly sight of the indigent: "There shall be no beggar in our State; and if anyone attempts to beg, and to collect a livelihood by ceaseless prayers, the market-stewards shall expel him ... he shall be driven across the border by the country-stewards, to the end that the land may be wholly purged of such a creature." Plato, *Laws*, 11.936C, in Bury, 465.

[118] Pliny, *Letters*, 9.30, trans. William Melmoth, Vol. II (Harvard University Press, 1953): 247.

[119] A.R. Hands, *Charities and Social Aid in Greece and Rome* (Cornell University Press, 1968): 62–76; Countryman, *The Rich Christian in the Church*, 103–7.

[120] Garrison, Redemptive Almsgiving, 41. Hendrik Bolkestein, Wohltätigkeit und Armenpflege im vorchristlichen Altertum; ein Beitrag zum Problem "Moral und Gesellschaft" (Utrecht: A. Oosthoek Verlag, 1939): 114. Den Boer notes "relief was not explicitly recommended ... as a virtuous act." W. Den Boer, Private Morality in Greece and Rome: Some Historical Aspects (Leiden: E.J. Brill, 1979): 169.

[121] Garrison, Redemptive Almsgiving in Early Christianity, 45–52.

general, analysis of the almsgiving tales suggests that there is no paradigm for almsgiving overall, other than that they consistently reveal the vulnerability of those struggling to be charitable and self-sufficient. In this way, the spectrum of Christian practice and belief is demonstrated, and the social and cultural elements that Christianity inherited remain, even as participants in the process sometimes interpret the experience in different ways, and struggle with the way others do as well. For example, social tension around almsgiving and status is evident in a tale of an elderly woman who practiced almsgiving by giving two *lepta* to everyone in the church out of her want.[122] When an amma brings her kinswoman—a relative of Emperor Maurice—to the church, the amma informs her kinswoman that if the elderly woman presents her with alms, she "take them, [be] not proud."[123] Although the kinswoman is put off by this request, she does as she is told by the elderly woman: "Take these, eat."[124] The coins are used to purchase vegetables, which, when eaten, "were sweet as honey."[125] Although the reception of alms by one beneath her status was distressing to the kinswoman, the honeyed taste of the vegetables is acknowledged by the kinswoman as evidence that the alms were necessary for her wellbeing. Although the kinswoman's station was above that of the elderly woman, acceptance of the alms allowed her—forced her? moved her?—into a different type of relationship with this elderly woman who challenges the kinswoman with this offering. The kinswoman found herself humbled before the elderly woman's higher spiritual status,[126] and Baxter and Margavio note the important relationship that exists between honor and economy: "Honor is central to character development and self-definition and helps maintain social stability as the concern for reputation and status moderate aggressive and opportunistic economic behavior." [127] Consequently, the elderly woman's move was a social move that could have forced or tipped the kinswoman into anger as easily as humility.

Alms rooted in sacrifice is demonstrated consistently through *Meadow* tales, concerned as many of the tales are with the complete renunciation of ascetics who remain engaged in the needs of society at the same time they are apart from it (distinct, of course, from the less dangerous renunciation of *private* property when entering a monastery). When, in "The Wondrous Charity of an Holy Elder,"[128] a

---

[122] *Prat. sp.* 127 (PG 87.2987–92).

[123] "λάβε, αὐτὰ, μὴ ὑπερηφανίσῃς." *Prat. sp.* 127 (PG 87.2991–2).

[124] "Λάβε ταῦτα, καὶ φάγε." Ibid.

[125] "ὅτι γλυκέα ἦσαν ὡς τὸ μέλι." Ibid.

[126] The Phrygian Galatian woman is identified as "old woman," (μία γραῖα) an age of vulnerability and repulsion in the Roman world. Tim G. Parkin, *Old Age in the Roman World: A Cultural and Social History* (Baltimore, MD: Johns Hopkins University Press, 2003): 86. Mary Harlow, *Growing Up and Growing Old in Ancient Rome: A Life Course Approach* (London: Routledge, 2002): 127–30.

[127] Vern Baxter and A.V. Margavio, "Honor, Status and Aggression in Economic Exchange," *Sociological Theory*, Vol. 18, No. 3 (2000): 413.

[128] *Prat. sp.* 9 (PG 87.2859–60).

beggar refuses the elder's offer of bread, the elder shows him that he has nothing else to offer; stricken by the elder's complete and utter poverty, the beggar appears to suffer an existential crisis: he empties his sack on the floor of the cell and leaves.[129] That the elder has nothing and yet gives daily suggests either that he is engaged in daily renunciation and alms or commerce;[130] does this elder's focus on owning nothing but distributing everything actually betray avarice? Basil addressed this precise practice in the *Regulae brevius tractatae*: the monastic figure that consistently redistributes is not truly withdrawn from the cares of the secular world and risks exposure to—and thereby infection by—materialism,[131] and on occasion monastic figures will be disciplined for this activity.[132] This interpretation of alms as sacrifice took multiple forms in *The Meadow*, demonstrating effectively how renunciation often complicated rather than concluded a monk's relationship with money[133] and was often as much about humility as about renunciation.[134]

Creative as well as compassionate approaches towards almsgiving in *The Meadow* demonstrate the reflection of God's character and the benevolence of those who cared for the poor. Abba Leontios'[135] almsgiving practices, for example, speak to the intention he brings to this practice: if the beggar were blind he would put the coins into their hand, but if they had sight the abba would leave the money at the base of a column or on the steps, so that they would "find" it. When questioned, he replied that it was not he who did the giving but "the Mother of God who nourishes me and them."[136] He merely distributes them on her behalf, and arranges

---

[129] That the beggar has a *sack* filled with items suggests he is a thief and not a beggar; perhaps the elder's renunciation has stimulated a vocational crisis. *Prat. sp.* 9 (PG 87.2859–60).

[130] Finn, Almsgiving in the Later Roman Empire, 93.

[131] Basil, *Regulae brevius tractatae* 91, 100 and 101 (PG 31.1145B, 1152B–C and 1152C–1153A); *The Asketikon of St. Basil the Great*, trans. Anna M. Silvas (Oxford University Press, 2005): 322–9.

[132] When Simeon is caught distributing his food to the poor, this activity is reported to the abbot as a violation of their rule: "[T]his man wants to undo the monastery and certainly the rule you handed down to us ... [w]e were taught to fast till sun-down, but he eats only on Sundays, and the bread and pulse he receives he secretly gives to the poor." *The Life & Daily Mode of Living of the Blessed Simeon the Stylite by Antonios*, 6; *The Lives of Simeon Stylites*, trans. Robert Doran (Kalamazoo, MI: Cistercian Publications, 1992): 89.

[133] On poverty and vulnerability, see David Brakke, "Care for the Poor, Fear of Poverty, and Love of Money: Evagrius Ponticus on the Monk's Economic Vulnerability," in Holman (ed.), *Wealth and Poverty in Early Church and Society*, 82–7.

[134] An elder engaged in continuous renunciation and care by sowing fields for those with no oxen, assisting travelers with food, water, clothing or labor. *Prat. sp.* 24 (PG 87.2869–70); we read also of the bishop who worked as a laborer when the city was damaged by an earthquake. *Prat. sp.* 37 (PG 87.2885–8). Patlagean, *Pauvreté économique et pauvreté sociale*, 33.

[135] *Prat. sp.* 61 (PG 87.2913–14).

[136] "μου ἡ Θεοτόκος, ἡ καμε καὶ αὐτοὺς τρέφουσα." Ibid.

it so that all the alms are offered in such a way that ideally no one suffers shame for having received them, an interesting alternative to the elderly woman above.

Alms connected to punishment is revealed in beneficial tales that suggest that the temptation to hoard was strong in monastic houses, and suggest a link to the parables of growth with abundance of fish, bread and wine. While at the monastery of Abba Theodosios at Skopelos,[137] John and Sophronios learn that customarily orphans and the poor came to the monastery on Maundy Thursday to receive an offering of wine, bread, honey and coins.[138] As grain was becoming scarce, the monks convinced the abba to discontinue the customary alms. On Good Friday, however, they discovered what grain they had in their possession had germinated and all of it—more than they would have distributed—had to be thrown out. The abba admonished them severely for many reasons: for wasting food; for ignoring the commandment of the founder of the monastery; for failing to trust in God; and for failing to "bring comfort to the poor, our brothers."[139] Ultimately, failing to invest in God by virtue of distributing alms to those in need brought ruin beyond the initial investment, and they were found to have "robbed" God instead. By trusting in the granary rather than God, the monastery lost not just the 500 pecks of grain they would have given to the poor, but the entire 5,000 pecks that they had been storing. In a supplementary tale, a monastery that finds itself suddenly enriched with a gift of gold neglects its barley production, and it is not until they distribute the gold that their fields are fertile once again.[140] Their capitulation into a state of avarice stems the fertility provided by providential productivity, granted to those who pledge to care for the poor.

Retention versus distribution for individuals and monasteries was consistently a struggle, and had the power to disrupt not only the spiritual state of the individual, but the environment overall. Different practices emerged in the centuries before Moschos' time about proper procedures to caution against spiritual disruption. For example, at Shenoute's White Monastery all property became the permanent possession of the monastery, from which some portion would be distributed to charity, and although a monk might leave, his property would not.[141] Not all

---

[137] *Prat. sp.* 85 (PG 2911–14).

[138] Some monasteries engaged in alms distribution from their surplus. Finn, *Almsgiving in the Later Roman Empire*, 93.

[139] "καὶ τοὺς ἀδελφοὺς ἡμῶν τοὺς πτωχοὺς παρημυθήσασθαι." *Prat. sp.* 85 (PG. 2943–2944).

[140] I, Mioni, "Il Pratum Spirituale de Giovanni Mosco," 83.

[141] "[W]hoever comes in to be a monk with us shall from the first renounce everything which he has and make it over to the fellowship of God and the service of the poor; and that neither he nor any man related to him shall be able to go back and ask for anything ..." Besa, "31. On Those Who Have Renounced Their Constancy," in *Letters and Sermons of Besa*, trans. K.H. Kuhn, CSCO, Vol. 157 (Louvain: Imprimerie Orientaliste, 1956): 101. Brakke, "Care for the Poor, Fear of Poverty, and Love of Money," in Holman (ed.), *Wealth and Poverty in Early Church and Society*, 76. Finn, *Almsgiving in the Later Roman Empire*, 91–2; Elm, *Virgins of God*, 301.

monasteries followed this procedure. In a later tale attributed to *The Meadow*, when a wealthy man was tonsured he was encouraged to distribute his wealth not to the monastery—which had no need—but to the poor, for the novice needed to "follow the commandment of the Lord: go and distribute to our brothers, the poor, and according to [God's] true commandments, you shall have treasure in heaven."[142] The brother tried to press the money on the elder to do this for him, and the elder finally agreed but hid the money instead. Eventually the newly tonsured brother became resentful over the loss of gold to the degree that he was disruptive to the community. The elder returned the gold to the brother who, admonished at how this money had prevented his spiritual development, returned to the monastery, greatly edified.[143] No doubt this tale is representative of incidents in which the distribution of an estate to the monastic institution was not accompanied by an actual renunciation of the wealth on the part of the monastic. Perhaps for this reason Basil counsels in *Regulae brevius tractatae* that one either distributes funds personally or allows this to be done by a trusted agent.[144]

Stages of alms and reward are found in a beneficial tale that might more fittingly be called a beneficial romance:[145] a young man's father is so generous with his almsgiving that he leaves his son no inheritance beyond the son's verbal preference to have Christ as his guardian rather than a patrimony. Having chosen Christ, the young man is reduced to poverty. A woman of high rank, wishing to find a worthy husband for her daughter, informs this young man that his guardian [Christ] selected him to marry her daughter and thus receive a Christian bride and riches "that you rejoice in both in the fear of God,"[146] transforming his earthly ties from consanguineal to conjugal. Good works aside, the failure of a wealthy father to provide a patrimony for his son would be a loss for more than just the son, the justification of which would need to be balanced by a father's piety and the son's inheritance of that piety. The freedom of the individual sometimes countered the interest that the church might have in inheriting either property or funds, and family did not fail to get involved.[147] One might argue that it is the father who distributes the alms, but as it is his son's inheritance that he gives "without sparing," the son chooses this inheritance. In the end the son is doubly rewarded with both bride and his wife's family fortune, a move that reminds us that renunciation could operate in this world as a method of professional—as well as social—advancement.

---

[142] "ἀλλὰ κατὰ τὴν ἐντολὴν τοῦ κυρίου· πηγαίνετε καὶ διάδος αὐτὰ ἀδελφοῖς ἡμῶν τοῖς πτωχοῖς, καὶ κατὰ τὰς ἀψευδεῖς αὐτοῦ ἐντολὰς ἕξεις θησαυρὸν ἐν οὐρανῷ·" 13, Nissen, "Unbekannte Erzählungen," 369.

[143] Ibid., 370–71.

[144] Basil, *Regulae brevius tractatae* 9 (PG 31. 941–2).

[145] *Prat. sp.* 201 (PG 87.3089–90).

[146] "ἵνα χρήσῃ ἀμφοτέροις μετὰ φόβου τοῦ Θεοῦ." Ibid.

[147] Laiou, "The Church, Economic Though and Economic Practice," 438. Jack Goody, *The Development of the Family and Marriage in Europe* (Cambridge, 1983): 83–102; A. Laiou, *Mariage, Amour et Parenté à Byzance aux XIe–XIIIe Siècles* (Paris, 1992): 170.

The majority of beneficial tales that contain references to alms are concerned primarily with the redistribution of wealth, goods and services. In an environment in which the greater portion of the population is perched precariously on the edge of destitution, and in an environment of clearly fluctuating populations, there seems to be a general desire in several tales on the part of individuals to balance commodities along with the movement of migrants, vagrants, the impoverished, thieves and beggars. This process invites the kinswoman into relationship with the poor, the poor and the kinswoman into relationship with the destitute. Further, it invites the monk or elderly woman to participate in the activity of the clergy or the monastic community, even when they are not part of that system in any kind of official way. To this end, the individual almsgiver moves beyond the management of a church hierarchy that attempted to control movement of profits and thus the relationships between the clergy and the poor, and the wealthy and their non-religious social duties.[148]

While the motivations behind almsgiving in the *The Meadow* seem primarily to aid those with need and to honor the command to "Sell all that you own and distribute your money to the poor,"[149] nevertheless John and Sophronios learn that almsgiving is also a pious deed that might very well compensate for a lifetime of unrighteous behavior or a wicked deed.[150] Emperor Zeno, known for his liberality in other sources, harmed a woman by harming her daughter[151] and took refuge in counsel given by Daniel to King Nebuchadnezzar.[152] When the mother pressed the Mother of God for justice against Emperor Zeno, the Mother of God refused, informing the mother that while she had tried to do justice on the mother's behalf, she was prevented because "he [Zeno] was much [given to] almsgiving."[153] Redemptive almsgiving is, of course, a well-established practice and classic method for making amends for sinful activity; as early as the first half of the second century, Garrison writes, "the doctrine of redemptive almsgiving was gaining broad acceptance within the church,"[154] and patristic literature both eastern and western

---

[148] "For the wealthy must assume secular obligations, and the poor must be supported by the wealth of the churches." *Codex Theodosianus*, 16.2.6 (326), in *The Theodosian Code and Novels*, trans. Clyde Pharr (Princeton University Press, 1952): 441. Brown, *Poverty and Leadership*, 31.

[149] Luke 18.22.

[150] A theme also in Leontios. Déroche, *Études Sur Léontios De Néapolis*, 279.

[151] We are left to wonder how, precisely, Zeno harmed the girl; Moschos' silence on the matter suggests that it is not fitting for us to know. *Prat. sp.* 175 (PG 87.3034–44).

[152] "Therefore, O king, may my counsel be acceptable to you: atone for your sins with 'ἐλεημοσύνῃ,' and for your iniquities by mercy to the oppressed ..." Daniel 4.27.

[153] "Ἦν γὰρ ἐλεήμων πάνυ." *Prat. sp.* 175 (PG 87.3034–44). In a critical character sketch, Evagrius Scholasticus notes Zeno's charity. *Hist.eccl.*, III.8; Whitby, *Ecclesiastical History*, 142.

[154] Garrison, Redemptive Almsgiving, 135.

will make full use of the theme.[155] But while bishops' sermons are addressing the need for those fully engaged in secular society—most especially those whose occupations might very well force them into corrupting opportunities every single day—redemptive almsgiving is given almost no heed in *The Meadow*. It is not the distribution of the alms that is redemptive; rather, the attention to the ascetic life, a life that provides consistent opportunity for almsgiving, is redemptive.

It is worth ending with a modern question: do we find in Moschos' a critique of systems that kept people in poverty? It is unlikely Moschos would challenge a system that kept people impoverished, if only that it might allow for charity to be practiced by those who seek to invest not in the market but in heaven, who lay their offerings on the altar of the poor in whom Christ is present. For John, the greater likelihood is that his critique would be aimed at diversity of belief; despite the poverty and suffering present in his *Meadow*, what is truly wicked and shameful is the existence of multiple Christological claims. For John, the presence of heterodoxy in the empire—not poverty or greed—prevented Christians from truly being Christian to one another.

---

[155] Boniface Ramsay, "Almsgiving in the Latin Church: the Late Fourth and Early Fifth Centuries," TS, Vol. 43 (1982): 241–7.

Chapter 3
Medical Management in *The Meadow*: Curing, Enduring and Identity Formation[1]

Introduction

In the medical landscape of the early medieval Byzantine Empire, disease and illness as by-products of life in the flesh were understood by patristic theologians and monastics as participation in God's saving activity and interaction in the created world, otherwise known as the divine economy. In some cases, cures for diseases were neither sought nor granted if the illness that it caused was interpreted as being beneficial for the soul. For example, Abba Joseph of Thebes claims that although renunciation of worldly possessions and obedience are two honored deeds before the Lord, he elects for a third option: "But I have chosen sickness."[2] In the absence of the opportunity for martyrdom, Abba Joseph's choice to embrace ill health as a particular type of ascesis demonstrates a consistent and legitimate pattern of ascetic activity that develops within monastic life.

The development of ascetic illness does not mean, however, that monks are never on the receiving end of medical treatment, nor does it mean that health care was neither promoted nor supported within monastic environments, as we learn in John of Ephesus' alarming tale of Abba Aaron's bout of gangrene of the genitals.[3] Further, the vast numbers of individuals who turn to monastic figures for medical and non-medical healing indicates a willingness and necessity to address seriously medical needs for themselves, their monastic communities and their lay sisters and brothers. When considering incongruent attitudes towards the medical management of the body and the relationship that the ill or healthy body has with spiritual management, characteristically Moschos' *Meadow* does not present overall a consistent response to maladies; rather, both physical and psychological health challenges in Moschos' collection appear to be organized into two categories

---

[1] Material from for this chapter is drawn from Brenda Llewellyn Ihssen, "Curing and Enduring: Medical and Spiritual Management of Non-Ideal Bodies in John Moschos' *Spiritual Meadow*" (paper presented at the annual national meeting of the American Academy of Religion, Chicago, Illinois, 17 November 2012).

[2] Joseph of Thebes, *APalph* (PG 65.241). The Greek passage in my PG is difficult to read, but the Latin—*Ego vero infirmitatem elegi* ("Ἐγὼ δὲ τὴν ἀσθένειαν ᾑρησάμην")—can be translated "But I have chosen sickness/weakness."

[3] John of Ephesus, *Lives of the Eastern Saints*, 38 (PO 18.643–4); Stephen of Lybia, *HL* 24.

that require that ill health be either cured or endured. This chapter suggests that select beneficial tales from Moschos' *Meadow* demonstrate that alongside widespread acceptance of ill health as endurable were beliefs about ailments that were curable, to the end that the medical and spiritual management of suffering or healing contributed to the construction of religious and social identity in the early medieval Byzantine Empire. This claim will be supported with evidence from *The Meadow* that address various ailments, and will consider corroborating evidence from additional contemporary tales and patristic texts as appropriate.

Henry Magoulias' oft-quoted and noted article, "The Lives of Saints as Sources of Data for the History of Byzantine Medicine in the Sixth and Seventh Centuries,"[4] as well as work of distinguished scholars Évelyne Patlagean,[5] Owsei and Lilian Temkin and all of the fine scholars represented in the Dumbarton Oaks *Symposium on Byzantine Medicine*,[6] demonstrates effectively how hagiography is a valuable resource for learning about the study of medicine. In addition to revealing to us the types of diseases with which physicians were concerned, hagiography also highlights the suffering of the ill and the many elements that illness entails: fear, pain, humiliation, shame, disgust and isolation. To wit, hagiography can tell us how people suffered physically and emotionally due to ill health, as well the methods of medical and spiritual management of bodies during times of epidemic disease, social distress[7] and increasing pressure from imperial and ecclesiastical hierarchs determined to define and manage the "holy."[8] Because Moschos assembled his tales during an age when all levels of society struggled not only with poverty, disease and famine but also with questions of political and religious kinship,[9] this chapter will conclude by suggesting that Moschos' text presents a unique picture of the complicated relationship between personal agency and divine intercession, a relationship that allows both bodies with diseases to be cured and diseases to be

---

[4] H.J. Magoulias, "The Lives of Saints as Sources of Data for the History of Byzantine Medicine in the Sixth and Seventh Centuries," BZ, Vol. 57, No. 1 (1964): 127–50.

[5] Patlagean, *Pauvreté économique et pauvreté sociale*, 101–12.

[6] John Scarborough (ed.), *Symposium on Byzantine Medicine*, DOP, Vol. 38, (1984). Hereafter DOP, Vol. 38.

[7] Anthony Kaldellis, "The Literature of Plague and the Anxieties of Piety in Sixth-Century Byzantium," in Franco Mormando and Thomas Worcester (eds), *Piety and Plague: From Byzantium to the Baroque*, Sixteenth Century Essays and Studies (Truman State University Press, 2007): 1–22; Magoulias, "Lives of the Saints as Sources of Data," 127–50; Patlagean, *Pauvreté économique et pauvreté sociale*, 101–12; Susan Ashbrook Harvey, "Physicians and Ascetics in John of Ephesus: An Expedient Alliance," DOP, Vol. 38: 87–93.

[8] Phil Booth, "Saints and Soteriology in Sophronius Sophista's *Miracles of Cyrus and John*," SCH, Vol. 45 (2009): 53.

[9] Averil Cameron, "New Themes and Styles in Greek Literature: Seventh–Eighth Centuries," *The Byzantine East and Early Islamic Near East I*, 85, 88. See also Philip Wood, *"We have no king but Christ": Christian Political Thought in Greater Syria on the Eve of the Arab Conquest* (Oxford University Press, 2010): 12–16.

endured to contribute to the creation of religious and social identity.[10] Further, it is my hope that this chapter will provide an opportunity for scholars in the fields of Byzantine social history and historical theology to make connections with those who engage in academic conversations around what constitutes a healthy body, how health, disease and illness contribute to religious and social identity, or with scholars who work with religious interpretations of suffering, illness and disease. The first part of the chapter will consider an early Christian theology of health and healing, a theology that will inform monastic life in the early Byzantine period. The matrix within which Christian medical care practices emerge is considerable: the pagan philosophical notion of the physician as compassionate healer, the theological milieu of Jewish charity, the social milieu of dislocation, displacement, disease and imperial brutality,[11] and the monastic milieu, in which individuals who gathered together in a social network independent of their families were forced to construct attitudes towards health care that accounted for their renunciation of those who would have traditionally provided medical care for one who suffered.[12] Therefore it is worth considering the theological basis for health-care activity in the desert. The second and third parts of this chapter will consider Moschos' beneficial tales regarding health and healing; illness and disabilities addressed include those regarded as worthy of curing, such as breast cancer,[13] infertility[14] and snake bites.[15] Illnesses and disabilities addressed also include those worth enduring, including edema,[16] leprosy,[17] fever[18] and blood poisoning.[19]

A Theology of Health and Healing

Medical anthropologists claim that there are distinctions in the way a culture defines bodily health and, beyond this, approaches to the therapeutic treatments of ill health differ as well. According to Kleinman, western medicine traditionally

---

[10] J. Haldon, "The Works of Anastasias of Sinai: A Key Source for the History of Seventh-Century East Mediterranean Society and Belief," in Averil Cameron and Lawrence I. Conrad (eds), *The Byzantine East and Early Islamic Near East I: Problems in the Literary Source Material* (Princeton, NJ: Darwin Press, 1992): 143–5.

[11] Amanda Porterfield, *Healing in the History of Christianity* (Oxford University Press, 2005): 45.

[12] Andrew Crislip, *From Monastery to Hospital: Christian Monasticism & The Transformation of Health Care in Late Antiquity* (University of Michigan Press, 2005): 39–67.

[13] *Prat. sp.* 56 (PG 87.2909–12).

[14] Ibid. 114 (PG 87.2977–80).

[15] Ibid. 124 (PG 87.2985–8).

[16] Ibid. 8 (PG 87.2857–8).

[17] Ibid. 14 (PG 87.2861–2).

[18] V, Mioni, "Il Pratum Spirituale de Giovanni Mosco," 86–7.

[19] *Prat. sp.* 10 (PG 87 2859–60).

focuses on causes and cures;[20] in other words, what is the problem and how is the problem solved in order that bodily functions and activities might be restored as fully as possible? For cultures less oriented towards such methods, medical care concentrates more on the removal or management of symptoms. Further, they note the distinction between "curing disease" (disordered biology) and "healing illness" (management of problems shaped by disease).[21] According to John J. Pilch, a biblical scholar, this latter method of medical care is a reorientation of meaning for the one who suffers and for their community, which does not necessarily mean that the individual is cured of their medical condition.[22] By way of example, Pilch refers to John 9.1–41, in which Jesus' disciples ask him the following question about a man born blind: "Rabbi, who sinned, this man or his parents?" Unconcerned with the answer to that question, Jesus informs them that neither of them sinned, and that sin is not the point. According to the distinctions that the medical anthropologists and Pilch are making, the disciples, by trying to identify the root of the man's problem, are, one could argue, asking scientific questions (what is the problem and how is it solved?), while Jesus' response removes the symptoms and reorients meaning, which suggests that those questions do not help. It also affirms that scientific methods—in this case, the asking of critical questions—were actively practiced in an age often erroneously derided for its unscientific methods.[23] But regardless of method, the point remains: in Jesus' age, medical care was focused primarily—though not exclusively—on the alleviation of suffering to the degree that an individual might be returned to "purposeful living"[24] for themselves and their community. How "purposeful living" is understood in the monastic setting will aid in the distinction between a medical malady that must be "cured" (a problem to be solved) and a medical malady that must be "endured" (a problem to be borne). I highlight the healing ministry of Jesus[25] and its incorporation into the mission of Christianity not because I wish to trace the history of healing in the Christian religion—which has been done elsewhere—but because precisely how ill health is managed in *Meadow* tales is close in many ways to how ill health is

---

[20] H. Tristram Engelhardt Jr, "The Concepts of Health and Disease," in L. Arthur Caplan, H. Tristram Engelhardt Jr and James J. McCartney (eds), *Concepts of Health and Disease: Interdisciplinary Perspective* (Reading, MA: Addison-Wesley, 1981): 31–45; see also Arthur Kleinman, *Patients and Healers in the Context of Culture: an Exploration of the Borderland between Anthropology, Medicine, and Psychiatry* (Berkeley, CA: University of California Press, 1980): 82.

[21] Kleinman, *Patients and Healers in the Context of Culture*, 82.

[22] John J. Pilch, *Healing in the New Testament: Insights from Medical and Mediterranean Anthropology* (Minneapolis, MN: Fortress Press, 2000): 13–15; see also Kleinman, *Patients and Healers in the Context of Culture*, 356–61.

[23] But this is an argument for another paper. Marcel Sendrail, *Histoire Culturelle de la Maladie* (Toulouse: Privat, 1980): 167ff.

[24] Pilch, *Healing in the New Testament*, 14.

[25] Porterfield identifies 72 accounts of exorcisms and healings in the canonical gospels, 41 distinct events. Porterfield, *Healing in the History of Christianity*, 21.

managed in that John passage. Although some of the Moschos texts demonstrate a desire to "cure" (remove) a disease, and some demonstrate a desire to manage symptoms, regardless, they reflect less of an interest in understanding ill health as a manifestation of divine punishment or blessing based on personal or inherited moral choices, less of an interest with ill health as an offense against cultural or social norms; rather, in their brevity, the tales of health care move quickly to either management or acceptance of ill health.

In the gospel accounts, healings are equated with the restoration of relations, a theme that draws from the Israelite understanding of illness, suffering and disease linked to God's condemnation for sin, and healing linked to repentance and evidence of forgiveness. Generally, the Hebrew nation did not have a negative attitude towards physicians, and in the Hellenistic period there is evidence of professional Jewish physicians; however, Yahweh was the only true healer. Although the Jews eschewed magical medical practices, natural methods of healing were employed, including prayer, fasting and repentance.[26] Surely influenced by Jewish exhortations to extend charitable care to those in need and aid in the restoration of right relations with God and community, Jesus' healing ministry will emerge in an empire populated well into the fourth century with shrines dedicated to the healing gods Isis, Asklepios, Pan, Serapis and Hygieia,[27] evidence of the ancient and enduring connection between divine will and bodily suffering. Traditional healing shrines remained active after the legalization of Christianity, even after Theodosius made Christianity the religion of empire; consequently, Christianity benefited from vocabulary, territory, buildings, ritual and imagery of healing shrines all across the empire, from Egypt to Britain.[28] Although this general continuity with the classical past continues well into the apostolic and patristic periods of Christian history,[29] and although notable early

---

[26] See: Ps. 32.3–5; 38.1–11; Isa. 38.1–6; 2 Sam. 12.16–23; II Kings 20.7). Gary B. Ferngren, *Medicine & Health Care in Early Christianity* (Baltimore, MD: Johns Hopkins University Press, 2009): 23–4.

[27] Hector Avalos and Rodney Stark both conclude that simple, accessible, free or cheap healing won more followers to Christianity than competing, expensive healing cults of Isis and Asklepios. Hector Avalos, *Health Care and the Rise of Christianity* (Grand Rapids, MI: Baker Academic, 2010): 87; Rodney Stark, *The Rise of Christianity: How the Obscure, Marginal, Jesus Movement Became the Dominant Religious Force in the Western World in a Few Centuries* (San Francisco, CA: Harperone, 1997): 73–94; see also John Dominic Crossan, *The Birth of Christianity: Discovering What Happened in the Years Immediately after the Execution of Jesus* (San Francisco, CA: HarperSanFrancisco, 1998): 291–302.

[28] Vivian Nutton, "Galen to Alexander, Medical Practice in Late Antiquity," DOP, Vol. 38: 7; see also Porterfield, *Healing in the History of Christianity*, 48–9; see also Ferngren, *Medicine and Health Care*, 136–8.

[29] Demetrios J. Constantelos, "Physician-Priests in the Medieval Greek Church," GOTR, Vol. 12, No. 1 (1967): 149.

Christian leaders and intellectuals such as Bishop Ignatius of Antioch,[30] Cyril of Jerusalem[31] and Origen[32]—among others—will make free use of the theme of "*Christus medicus*,"[33] still many Christians accepted natural causation of diseases and maladies, and believed ailments were curable by natural means.[34] Interest in engaging in this ministry separates them from philanthropic practices of the empire, a philanthropy not based on concern for marginalized members of society, and one that neither included social services for those ill or in need[35] nor did much more than pity them.[36] In imitation of the behavior of a God who pitied the poor,[37] motivated by the parable of the Good Samaritan[38] and in *imago Dei* of the incarnate God,[39] aid and healing were distributed and granted by Christians to those whom they believed were also in the image of God, even if they had no means to pay for therapeutic benefits of pragmatic medical and non-medical care Christian physicians and lay caretakers offered. In addition to diagnosis, medication or surgery,[40] they offered a gentle touch, companionship, a meal, a bit

---

[30] Ignatius, bishop of Antioch, "To the Ephesians," 7.2 (PG 5. 649); Ignatius, "Ignatius to the Ephesians," in *The Apostolic Fathers*, Vol. I, trans. Kirsopp Lake (Harvard University Press, 1998): 181.

[31] Cyril of Jerusalem, *Catechesis* 10.13 (PG 33.677).

[32] Origen, *Adnotations in librum III regum* 15.23, in Ferngren, *Medicine and Health Care*, 27.

[33] *Christus medicus* was employed across the frontiers of empire, "un thème dominant dans la prédication du grand évêque d'Hippone." P. Monceaux, "Une invocation au Christus medicus sur une pierre de Timgad," *Comptes-rendus des séances de l'Académie des Inscriptions et Belles-Lettres*, Vol. 68, No. 1 (1924): 78. According to Arbesmann, some 40 texts in Augustine reference the healing or salvific work of the "Divine Physician." Rudolph Arbesmann, "The Concept of 'Christus Medicus' in St. Augustine," *Traditio*, Vol. 10 (1954): 2–3; H. Schipperges, "Zur Tradition des 'Christus Medicus' im frühen Christentum und in der älteren Heilkunde," *Arzt und Christ* 11 (1965): 15. The term is also in Jerome, who uses medical language in his writing. Arthur Stanley Pease, "Medical Allusions in the Works of Jerome," HSPh, Vol. 25 (1914): 73–86.

[34] Ferngren, *Medicine and Health Care*, 59.

[35] Brown, *Poverty and Leadership*, 1–44; Ferngren, *Medicine and Health Care*, 87; Hands, *Charities and Social Aid in Greece and Rome*, 77–88; Holman, *The Hungry are Dying*, 6–12 and Paul Veyne, *Bread and Circuses: Historical Sociology and Political Pluralism* (London: Allen Lane, the Penguin Press, 1990): 19–34; 101–14.

[36] Glanville Downy, "Who is my Neighbor? The Greek and Roman Answer," ATR, Vol. 47 (1965): 5.

[37] Ferngren, *Medicine and Health Care*, 87; see also N.W. Porteous, "The Care of the Poor in the Old Testament," in J.I. McCord and T.H.L. Parker (eds), *Service to Christ: Essays Presented to Karl Barth on his 80th Birthday* (Peterborough, UK: The Epworth Press, 1966): 25–36; see also Garrison, *Redemptive Almsgiving*, 46–7.

[38] Luke 10. 25–37.

[39] Holman, *The Hungry are Dying*, 27–30.

[40] To be clear, I do not mean to suggest that all Christians believed alike on this issue. Tatian, a second-century Mesopotamian convert and student of Justin Martyr, rejected medication ("φαρμακεία") as belonging to the demonic realm (but his problem was with demons, not with drugs). Tatian, *Oratio* 18.1; p. 19 ll. 25–6, in Owsei Temkin, *Hippocrates*

of clean water to drink or wash, the anointing of oil on the lips, ears and eyes, prayer, a blanket for warmth or a quiet place to sleep without fear, all of which served to bolster the emotional and physical health of the individuals, and the reputations and numbers of Christians.[41] But while non-medical healing in early and early medieval Christian communities seems to be greatly misunderstood as ignorant reliance on quaint but meaningless ritual rather than a legitimate form of non-evasive health care,[42] Porterfield notes the importance of such simple healing methods, that "[f]or people drawn to Christianity, hopes of dispelling isolation, suffering and fears of sickness and death coalesced around the person of Jesus and his victorious power of healing."[43] The distribution of goods and services to those whose physical needs had been previously ignored and the elevation of their status served as a powerful social challenge to leading pagan patrons of late antiquity, and a theological challenge to those who would argue against the value of the body and the humanity of Christ. In a society quite far from politically and economically healthy, the ill health of an individual was often the norm, and frequently Christian doctrines were of secondary importance to the need for basic health care.[44] Doctors failed and money was scarce, but there was always free-healing, nursing or even just compassion to be found at the hands of those who identified God as the "chief physician."

Whether in reference to God, to doctors, philosophers or theologians, medical language enters colorfully into patristic literature (sermons, letters and the like) for a variety or reasons: first, many eastern Christian theologians were educated in rhetoric, which included the study of Hellenistic philosophers, some of whom understood themselves as "physicians of the soul." This was a particularly favored theme of Stoics, Skeptics, Cynics and Epicureans, who all believed that the healing

---

in a World of Pagans and Christians (Baltimore, MD: Johns Hopkins University Press, 1995): 121–5.

[41] Nutton notes that Christian charity was distinguished from other groups in primarily three ways: first, it was directed to any in need; second, the number of those involved in care for others was considerable; and third, there was a specific mandate to care for the ill in texts contemporary with the early years, such as the *Apostolic Constitutions*. Vivian Nutton, *Ancient Medicine*, SAS (New York: Routledge, 2005): 289–303. Canonical texts also point to the injunction to offer therapeutic care, including James 5.13–15, I Timothy 5.23 and Mark 6.13. Samellas' take on Christian charity and subsequent popularity is slightly cynical: "Whether the new faith won converts by exploiting the emotional vulnerability of the afflicted will remain a plausible but unverifiable conjecture." Samellas, *Death in the Eastern Mediterranean*, 72.

[42] Bonnie J. Miller-McLemore, "Thinking Theologically About Modern Medicine," JRH, Vol. 30, No. 4 (1991): 288–9.

[43] Porterfield, *Healing in the History of Christianity*, 47. Crislip notes the distinction between medical and non-medical treatments in the early Christian era, which are his designations for treatment that draws on the skill of the physical (medical) or the link between healer and divinity (non-medical). Crislip, *From Monastery to Hospital*, 21.

[44] Stark, *The Rise of Christianity*, 73–94.

of the soul was essential for the healing of afflictions.[45] And while a Hellenistic concept of the "physician of the soul" becomes transformed into a theological concept that refers to priests, prophets[46] and the person of Christ,[47] the medical profession as a model of ministry not just for trained physicians but also from one Christian to another[48] will expand even as the theological value of the physical body rises. Second, many eastern Christian theologians were educated in medical arts or at very minimum mindful of them,[49] including Basil of Caesarea,[50] Gregory of Nazianzus[51] and Patriarch Photios.[52] Gregory Nazianzus' brother Caesarius was a prominent physician who studied in Alexandria, the site of the finest medical educations in antiquity, and Susan Holman notes that at Caesarius' death Gregory inherited his brother's estate, which would probably have included medical books.[53] Third, illness itself—either directly or indirectly—affected the personal

---

[45] "[U]nless the soul is cured ... there will be no end to our afflictions." Cicero, *Tusculan Disputations* (3.13), in Martha C. Nussbaum, *The Therapy of Desire: Theory and Practice in Hellenistic Ethics* (Princeton University Press, 1994): 317; Judith Perkins, *The Suffering Self: Pain and Narrative Representation in the Early Christian Era* (London: Routledge, 1995): 153–6; Darrel W. Amundsen, *Medicine, Society, and Faith in the Ancient and Medieval Worlds* (Baltimore, MD: Johns Hopkins University Press: 2000): 133; Samellas, *Death in the Eastern Mediterranean,* 70–115; Ludwig Edelstein, "The Relation of Ancient Philosophy to Medicine," in Owsei Temkin and C. Lilian Temkin (eds), *Ancient Medicine: Selected Papers of Ludwig Edelstein* (Baltimore, MD: Johns Hopkins Press, 1967): 360–66.

[46] Temkin, *Hippocrates in a World of Pagans and Christians,* 143.

[47] Irenaeus, *Adversus Haereses* 3.5.2 (PG 7.359): Origen, *Esplanatio super psalmum tricesimum septimum, Homily I* (PG 12.1369C–D); Gregory Nazianzus, *Oration* 7 (PG 35.755–8); *Oration* 18.29 (PG 35.1019–22); *Oration* 38.14 (PG 36.327–8); Susan Blackburn Griffith, "Iatros and Medicus: The Physician in Gregory Nazianzen and Augustine," in F. Young, M. Edwards and P. Parvis (eds), *Orientalia. Clement, Origen, Athanasius. The Cappadocians. Chrysostom,* Vol. 41 (Leuven: Peeters, 2006): 319–20.

[48] Gregory Nazianzus, *Oration* 33.6 (PG 36.221–2) and *Oration* 34.2 (PG 36.214); Griffith, "Iatros and Medicus," 320.

[49] Sister Mary Emily Keenan, "St. Gregory of Nazianzus and Early Byzantine Medicine," BHM, Vol. 9 (Johns Hopkins Press, 1941): 9–14; Constantelos, "Physician-Priests," 151.

[50] Gregory the Presbyter, *Vita S. Patris Nostri Gregorii,* 10.256 (PG 35); Holman, *The Hungry are Dying,* 29; Constantelos, "Physician-Priests," 151.

[51] Keenan, "St. Gregory of Nazianzus and Early Byzantine Medicine," 13–14; John McGuckin, *Saint Greogry of Nazianzus: An Intellectual Biography* (Crestwood, NY: St Vladimir's Seminary Press, 2001): 46–7; Constantelos, "Physician-Priests," 151.

[52] Photios includes medical volumes in the texts that he has read in his *Bibliotecha veterum partum,* or "Μυριοβίβλιον" (PG 103.9–356); Constantelos, "Physician-Priests," 151.

[53] McGuckin, *Saint Greogry of Nazianzus,* 44; Holman, *The Hungry are Dying,* 30; José Janini Cuesta, *La Antropología y la medicina pastoral de San Gregorio de Nisa* (Madrid: Consejo Superior de Investigaciones Científicas, 1946): 31–2.

and professional lives of many patristic writers, who wove medical terminology together with biblical typologies, and in doing so constructed theological claims around frail bodies that starved to death or burned with fever and died. Gregory of Nyssa documented extensively his and Basil's sister Macrina's painful demise, comparing her in her illness to Job;[54] Basil, who traces the stages of starvation in its torturous delay, exhorts Christians to feed the poor "as Joseph fed Jacob;"[55] finally, Gregory Nazianzus and John Chrysostom boldly equate the degraded bodies of the leper with Lazarus the beggar, and in doing so recast the outcast no longer as the refuse of society but as "a gold coin beside the road, but even more valuable."[56] Such theological constructions encourage humane attitudes towards the ill in imitation of God's attitudes towards humanity. The most effective cure for alleviating pain, Gregory Nazianzus writes, is compassion:[57] moderate and painless treatments were to be encouraged over those that brought greater pain[58] and those who suffered were not to be despised.[59] But any treatment would be of little value if the bodies of those who were the recipients of medical care were not transformed within this theology. Operating as a complement to the good work of the physician was inherent belief in the goodness of the created world, proven in the incarnation event: if the created world is good, if the body is a part of a good created world, then the body is by extension at best good and at worst morally neutral. Further, disease exists in a world that is fallen, but God—Basil will claim—has not abandoned the world, and will grant clemency that provides medicine beneficial to the body: "And when we were commanded to return to the earth whence we had been taken and were united with the pain-ridden flesh doomed to destruction because of sin

---

[54] Gregory of Nyssa (PG 46:960–1000); Gregory of Nyssa, *A Letter from Gregory, Bishop of Nyssa, On the Life of Macrina*, trans. Joan M. Peterson, in *Handmaids of the Lord: Holy Women in Late Antiquity & The Early Middle Ages* (Kalamazoo, MI: Cistercian Publications): 65.

[55] Basil of Caesarea, *Tempore famis et siccitatis*, 8 (PG 31.326); Basil of Caesarea, *In Time of Famine and Drought*, trans. in Holman, *The Hungry are Dying*, 192.

[56] John Chrysostom, "Sixth Sermon on Lazarus and the Rich Man/On the Earthquake," ed. and trans. Catherine P. Roth, *Saint John Chrysostom: On Wealth and Poverty* (Crestwood, NY: St Vladimir's Seminary Press, 1984): 108. For a moving treatment of Cappadocian transformative theology around disease and, particularly, leprosy, see "Diseased and Holy: The Peri Philōptochias Sermons and the Transforming Body," in Holman, *The Hungry are Dying*, 135–67. See also Gregory Nazianzus, *Oration 14: On the Love of the Poor and Those Afflicted with Leprosy* (PG 35.857–909); *St. Gregory of Nazianzus: Select Orations*, trans. Martha Vinson; The Fathers of the Church series, 107 (Washington, DC: The Catholic University of America Press, 1963.): 39–71.

[57] Gregory Nazianzus, *Oration* 17 (PG 963–82).

[58] Gregory Nazianzus, *Oration* 40.9 (PG 36.369–70).

[59] Gregory Nazianzus, *Oration* 14.10–15 (PG 35.869–76); see also Basil, *Homilia in illud: Destruam horrea mea* (PG 31.261–78), and *Tempore famis et siccitatis* (PG 31.303–28).

and, for the same reason, also subject to disease, the medical art was given to us to relieve the sick, in some degree at least."[60]

And yet the texts demonstrate that despite clear support for attention to ill health on the part of theologians and monastic overseers, the development of "illness asceticism" accompanies the development of monastic practice. Like lay Christians, monastic figures also suffered from medical problems, sometimes unintentionally as a result of their enthusiastic ascetic rigors and other times for quite unrelated reasons. Regardless of the cause, sources indicate that their own infirmities required medical management as much as anyone else's did, and sometimes creative methods were employed to address the ill health of individuals whose bodily practices might lean to the extreme. In a most tender account, Bishop Theodoret of Cyrrhus, ever mindful of the monks entrusted to his care, encouraged the anchorite James of Cyrrhestica to abandon the heavy shackles that seemed to function as an oven for his fever: "On perceiving this tremendously heavy load, I begged him to assist his sick body, which could not bear at the same time both the voluntary load and the involuntary infirmity. 'At the moment, father,' I said, 'the fever is doing the work of the iron; when it abates, let us at that stage impose on the body again the labor from the iron.'"[61] Further, the sensitive bishop sent crowds packing when they congregated to gaze at James during a time of great intestinal distress, one which produced contradictory impulses that coupled a natural desire to evacuate his bowels with the horror of doing so in front of a crowd.[62] While Theodoret would probably agree with Gregory of Nazianzus and John Chrysostom when they claim that illness strengthens character and patience, tests virtue, provides a model for others, curbs pride and demonstrates commitment to the theology of bodily resurrection,[63] Theodoret clearly drew the line when James' ascesis became a side-show attraction for those seeking to humiliate the anchorite.

This level of ascetic activity alongside the challenges of ill health and the good bishop's caution puts one in mind of the subjects of marriage, virginity and fasting, for as with these topics ecclesiastical leaders will have to work diligently to assure

---

[60] Basil, *Regulae fusius tractatae*, Q.55, "Whether recourse to the medical art is in keeping with the practice of piety" (PG 31.1046); in Wagner, *Ascetical Works*, 211. Basil is not the only one who will make this claim; see also Origen, *Contra Celsum* 3.13 (PG 11.935–6); Origen, *Contra Celsum*, trans. Henry Chadwick (Cambridge University Press, 1953): 135.

[61] Bishop Theodoret of Cyrrhus, *Historia Religiosa*, 21.8 (*Sources Chrétiennes* 257; Paris, Éditions du Cerf, 1977–79, 81–3); "James [of Cyrrhestica], in *A History of the Monks of Syria*, trans. R.M. Price (Kalamazoo, MI: Cistercian Publications, 1985): 136.

[62] Bishop Theodoret of Cyrrhus, *Historia Religiosa*, 21.5 (*Sources Chrétiennes* 257, 77–9); in Price, *A History of the Monks of Syria*, 135.

[63] Gregory Nazianzus, *Letters* 31 (PG 37.67–8); Gregory Nazianzus, *To Philagrius* (Letter 31), in *Gregory of Nazianzus*, trans. Brian E. Daley, *The Early Church Fathers* (London: Routledge, 2006): 176. John Chrysostom elaborates on 12 reasons why it is acceptable for a Christian to "take a little wine for the sake of your stomach" (I Tim. 5.23); *Concerning the Statues*, *Homily 1* (PG 49.15–34); John Chrysostom, *Concerning the Statues, Homily 1*, NPNF Series 1, Vol. 9 (Peabody, MA: Hendrickson, 1999): 331–44.

their charges that there is to be no boasting in illness, even as illness itself can aid in ascetic discipline. Andrew Crislip, in his study of health and illness among monastics,[64] notes that responses to the question of degree of responsibility that an ascetic might have to care for their body and maintain bodily health vary greatly, and criticism of illness as an ascetic practice often begins within the ascetic community itself. As he is so often the model, here too, Antony the Great's *vita* as composed by Athanasius presents the model of health based on ascetic rigor. Not despite his ascetic endeavors but because of them, by the end of his life Antony "possessed eyes undimmed and sound, and saw clearly. He lost none of his teeth— they simply had been worn to the gums because of the man's great age. He also retained health in his feet and hands, and generally he seemed brighter and of more energetic strength than those who make use of baths and a variety of foods and clothing."[65] Antony's harsh ascesis functions for Athanasius as a strengthening of the soul and evidence of his right belief, and thus Antony becomes the ideal monastic figure in all things: in this way, the clear bodily health of the ascetic was a reflection of the right theology that he maintained,[66] problematic for those without Antony's constitution.[67] Crislip notes that Basil the Great, Evagrius of Pontus and Amma Syncletica are among those who would agree that "those without Antony's constitution" would include just about every other ascetic, and that illness can, in fact, work in the opposite direction by promoting an intense obsession with the body rather than transcendence of the same.[68] To counter this, monastic organizers and bishops such as Basil the Great—who experienced ill health for a great deal of his life and founded the famous Caesarean *Basileias*[69]—will encourage moderation

---

[64] Andrew Crislip, "'I Have Chosen Sickness': The Controversial Function of Sickness in Early Christian Ascetic Practice," in Oliver Freiberger (ed.), *Asceticism and Its Critics: Historical Accounts and Comparative Perspectives*, American Academy of Religion Cultural Criticism Series (Oxford University Press, 2006): 179–209.

[65] Athanasius, *Vita S. Antonii*, 93 (PG 26.973–4); in *The Life and Affairs of Our Holy Father Antony*, trans. Gregg, in *Athanasius: The Life of Antony and The Letter to Marcellinus*, 98.

[66] Crislip, "'I Have Chosen Sickness,'" 183.

[67] Evidence suggests many were without Antony's constitution as defined by Athanasius, such as Palladius, *Historia Lausiaca* 35.11–12, in *Palladio, La Storia Lausiaca*, Testo critico e commento a cura di G.J.M. Bartelink (Milano: Fondazione Lorenzo Valla, A. Mondadori, 1990): 174.

[68] Crislip, "'I Have Chosen Sickness,'" 186–97.

[69] Gregory of Nazianzus, *Oratio* 43 (SC, No. 384, trans. Jean Bernardi (Paris: Les Éditions du Cerf, 1992): 116–307); Sozomen, *The Ecclesiastical History*, 6.34 (PG 67.1397). Rousseau writes that the system was probably already in place, but Basil made more permanent arrangements for the poor. Philip Rousseau, *Basil of Caesarea* (Berkeley, CA: University of California Press, 1994): 139–40, 375; Stanislas Giet, *Les idées et l'action sociales de saint Basile* (Paris: Librairie Lecoffre, 1941): 417–23; Holman, *The Hungry are Dying*, 74–5; Demetrios J. Constantelos, *Byzantine Philanthropy and Social Welfare*, 154–5; Nutton, "Galen to Alexander," 9–10; Ferngren, *Medicine and Health Care*, 126.

and uniformity.⁷⁰ Basil also, as mentioned above, assures monks that the medical arts are a gift from God to be placed at the service of one in need:

> In as much as our body is susceptible to various hurts, some attacking from without and some from within by reason of the food we eat, and since the body suffers affliction from both excess and deficiency, the medical art has been vouchsafed us by God, who directs our whole life, as a model for the curse of the soul, to guide us in the removal of what is superfluous and in the addition of what is lacking. Just as we would have not need of the farmer's labor and toil if we were living amid the delights of paradise, so also we would not require the medical art for relief if we were immune to disease.⁷¹

It is worth noting that Basil does not mention—although he seems to suggest it—that an individual's physical infirmities might very well be caused by their own extreme mortification, and thus he cautions elsewhere that "[t]he best rule and standard for a well-disciplined life is this: to be indifferent to the pleasure or pain of the flesh, but to avoid immoderation in either direction, so that the body may neither be disordered by obesity nor yet rendered sickly and so unable to execute commands."⁷²

Ever mindful of essential unity of body and soul and therefore the importance of the health of both, fifth-century Bishop Diadocus of Photike states unequivocally that "[t]here is nothing to prevent us from calling a doctor when we are ill."⁷³ That said, he affirms that one is not to place hope for healing in the hands of doctors, but in "our true Saviour and Doctor, Jesus Christ."⁷⁴ To those unable to access physicians in times of illness, they can draw consolation from the desert and from the illness itself; those who refrain from seeking medical attention for illnesses or those who enjoy good health are to refrain from the temptation to boast that they have no need of medical attention, a concern Evagrius and Amma Syncletica share. Beyond potential for pride in refraining from engaging with doctors when ill, or even pride in good health, Evagrius and Syncletica see asceticism that leads to

---

⁷⁰ Basil, "An Ascetical Discourse" (PG 31.875–6), in Wagner, *Ascetical Works*, 211–12. Vincent Desprez, *Le Monachisme Primitif: Des origines jusqu'au concile d'Éphèse*, Spiritualité Orientale n° 72 (Abbaye de Bellefontaine, 1998): 361–2.

⁷¹ Basil, *Regulae fusius tractate*, Q.55, "Whether recourse to the medical art is in keeping with the practice of piety," (PG 31.1043–4): in Wagner, *Ascetical Works*, 330–31.

⁷² Basil the Great, *Ascetica* (PG 31.875–6), "An Ascetical Discourse," in Wagner, *Ascetical Works*, 211.

⁷³ "Διαδόχου ἐπισκόπου Φωτικῆς τῆς Ἠπείρου κεφάλαια γνωστικὰ ρ'," 53 (SC 5); Diadoque de Photice, *Œuvres Spirituelles*, Édouard des Places, ed., SC 5 (1955): 114–15; *The Philokalia: The Complete Text Complied by St. Nikodemos of the Holy Mountain and St. Makarios of Corinth*, Vol. 1, trans. G.E.H. Palmer, Philip Sherrard and Kallistos Ware (London: Faber and Faber, 1983): 268.

⁷⁴ "Διαδόχου ἐπισκόπου Φωτικῆς τῆς Ἠπείρου κεφάλαια γνωστικὰ ρ'," 53 (SC 5); des Places, 114-15; in Palmer, Sherrard and Ware, 268.

illness—or an understanding of asceticism that leads the ill to become sicker—as demonic and tyrannical.[75] Ultimately this undermines the goal of ascetic behavior, which is the control of the passions,[76] rather than pride in the ascetic activity itself.

Despite consistent counsel for moderation, illness as a contributing factor to an ascetic program remains embedded in the tradition, and even as ascetics are many times battling illness, the presence of the ill seeking healing from the hands of the ascetic becomes a cornerstone of the genre of hagiography. Beneficial tales, however, do not as often address the topics of illness and healing as do their more elaborate hagiographic cousins; Wortley suggests that this is because monks were more accepting of illness as a method of ascetic activity as well as a sign of God's favor.[77] While I agree, I think that it is also worth noting that it might point to the relatively good health many ascetics may have enjoyed. It is common knowledge that a moderate and healthy diet, supportive community, care for the spiritual self, a regimen of physical activity and mental stimulation are all factors that encourage general good health management, and the texts suggest that many monastic figures lived lengthy lives.[78] Further, authorial intention may play some role in the fewer beneficial tales on illness primarily because the construction of a fuller hagiographic treatment of a holy person often is connected with the desire to promote a cult following, a component of which includes the necessity of healing miracles. Consequently, people of all stations of life—from outcasts to emperors—find themselves benefiting from the healing mercies of holy people. Beneficial tales, on the other hand, are closer to the sayings of desert ascetics in this case in that although lay Christians are present, and—as seen in the previous chapter—are incorporated into the daily lives of monastic figures, nevertheless the author is preserving beneficial tales for a purpose other than for the promotion of a cult following.[79]

---

[75] *Praktikos* 40 (SC 592–3); *The Praktikos*, in *Evagrius Ponticus: The Praktikos. Chapters on Prayer*, trans. John Eudes Bamberger (Kalamazoo, MI: Cistercian Publications, 2006): 27; *V. Syncleticae* 98; Pseudo-Athanasius, *The Life and Activity of the Holy and Blessed Teacher Syclectica*, trans. Elizabeth A. Castelli, in Vincent L. Wimbush (ed.), *Ascetic Behavior in Greco-Roman Antiquity: A Sourcebook* (Minneapolis, MN: Fortress Press, 1998): 305.

[76] Crislip, "'I Have Chosen Sickness,'" 196.

[77] John Wortley, "Getting Sick and Getting Cured in Late Antiquity," *Washington Academy of Sciences* Vol. 90–93 (2004): 91.

[78] Hirschfeld, "The Secret Diet of Monks," 26.

[79] See, for example, the *Miracles of St. Artemios* (Crisafulli and Nesbitt, 76–225), or the *Miracles of Cyrus and John* (PG, 87.3373–696) by Sophronios, who wrote to promote the cult. John Duffy, "Byzantine Medicine in the Sixth and Seventh Centuries," DOP, Vol. 38: 23; John Duffy, "Observations on Sophoronius' Miracles of Cyrus and John," JTS, Vol. 35, No. 1 (1984): 71–90. Philip Booth, "Saints and Soteriology in Sophronius Sophista's *Miracles of Cyrus and John*," *Studies in Church History*, Vol. 45 (2009).

Medical Management in Early Medieval Byzantium: Curing

Medicine in the age of Moschos was not, as has been insultingly suggested, "a mumbling of incantations."[80] In the early Byzantine era, hospitals were located in highly populated areas where trade, travel and political activity took place, although they had developed in the eastern empire initially within monastic houses.[81] Aside from the pragmatics of placing a hospital in a site where people might benefit, it must also be acknowledged that the development of pilgrimage contributed to the growth of sites of rest and healing; even as many traveled miles to seek a cure at a holy site, still, institutions needed to be created to accommodate the requirements of those who were traveling and fell ill or remained ill if—for example—Holy Unmercenaries were not listening.[82] Evidence suggests that Byzantine hospitals followed the monastic model and served all levels of society, from the poverty-stricken to imperial figures,[83] and were not restricted—as in the Roman hospitals—to select groups or the army.[84] Until the tenth century, many hospital administrators and physicians were also members of the clergy, though this would change in time.[85] Byzantine physicians proved themselves quite adept at diagnosing illnesses[86] and had a variety of *materia medica* at their disposal by way of recipes, lexica and substances of plant, mineral and animal origin,[87] even if they were not able to solve medical problems or employ methods to the degree that would satisfy a physician or patient of our age. "The practice of ancient

---

[80] F.H. Garrison, *An Introduction to the History of Medicine* (Philadelphia, 1921): 111. Athanasios Diamandopoulos identifies this attitude towards the intellectual energy of the day in "The effect of medicine, in particular the ideas about renal diseases, on the 'well-being' of Byzantine citizens," in Michael Grünbart et al., *Material culture and well-being in Byzantium (400–1453): proceedings of the international conference (Cambridge, 8–10 September 2001)* (Wien: Verlag der Österreichischen Akademie der Wissenschaften, 2007): 93.

[81] Timothy S. Miller, "Byzantine Hospitals," DOP, Vol. 38: 57–8; Crislip, *From Monastery to Hospital*, 100–142; Peregrine Horden, "The Earliest Hospitals in Byzantium, Western Europe and Islam," JIH, Vol. 35, No. 3 (2005): 364–5.

[82] Miller, "Byzantine Hospitals," DOP, Vol. 38: 56–8; Gary Vikan, "Art, Medicine and Magic in Early Byzantium," DOP, Vol. 38: 66.

[83] Miller, "Byzantine Hospitals," 58.

[84] Nutton, "Galen to Alexander," 9; Horden, "The Earliest Hospitals," 372–3.

[85] Wortley observes that the hospital in Jericho in *Prat. sp.* 6 (PG 87.2857–8) was run by monks from Saint Sabas; Wortley, *The Spiritual Meadow*, 235. See also Miller, "Byzantine Hospitals," 58–62; Constantelos, "Physician-Priests," 141–8; Demetrios J. Constantelos, "Clerics and Secular Professions in the Byzantine Church," BΘ, Vol. 13 (1985): 382–7.

[86] Scarborough, "Introduction," DOP, Vol. 38: x; John Wortley, "Getting Sick and Getting Cured," 103. Note also the diagnosis and medical skill involved in the treatment of the presbyter Aaron, the aforementioned sufferer of gangrene of the genitals. John of Ephesus, *Lives of the Eastern Saints*, 38 (PO 18.641–5); Harvey, "Physicians and Ascetics in John of Ephesus," 87–93.

[87] Jerry Stannard, "Aspects of Byzantine Materia Medica," DOP, Vol. 38: 205–11.

medicine," Ferngren writes, "cannot be easily reconciled with modern ideas of medical professionalism, a factor that pertains to the distinction that is often made between caring (delivering palliative care) and curing (providing medical therapies). In a society that lacked both medical licensure, with its restrictions on who could practice medicine, and any defined nursing profession, the boundary was fluid."[88] It is edifying to note that in recent scholarship on illness, disease, medicine and sciences in the general history of the Byzantine Empire the above-mentioned "Gibbon-esque" attitudes towards medical practices[89] of a once great civilization have given way to appreciation for creative and intellectual talents of Byzantine physicians, skilled professionals who incorporated a dynamic blend of medical theory, magic and tradition into their practices,[90] and evidence that Byzantine physicians were involved—like monastics—in the "real life of their time."[91] That said, the "real life" of the age of Byzantine physicians was one in which it was readily believed that the only true healer was Christ and any other type of healing was simply an alternative.[92] This belief sometimes manifested itself in language that works so hard to press the point that the modern reader might very well be misled.[93] The absence of doctors in *The Meadow* in no way indicates hostility to the medical profession, unlike what one finds on occasion in the *Life of St. Theodore of Sykeon*, who at times encourages people to ignore their

---

[88] Ferngren, *Medicine and Health Care*, 127.

[89] Scarborough notes a variety of insults, including Majno's problematic claim that Nestorian physicians are among the crowds of the "unknown," in G. Majno, *The Healing Hand: Man and Wound in the Ancient World* (Harvard University Press, 1975): 422; Garrison's likening of Byzantine medicine to a "mumbling of incantations and spells," Garrison, *An Introduction to the History of Medicine*, 111; Singer and Underwood's claims that Byzantine medical writers were "mere compiles," C. Singer and E.A. Underwood, *A Short History of Medicine* (New York, 1962): 67; and, finally, that "Medicine of any pretence to a scientific quality thus passed … into slumber." T.C. Allbutt, *Greek Medicine in Rome* (New York, 1970): 394. John Scarborough, "Introduction," DOP, Vol. 38: ix.

[90] Ibid.; see the physician Alexander of Tralles' willingness to address talismans that his patients preferred to medicines or enemas; John Duffy, "Byzantine Medicine in the Sixth and Seventh Centuries," DOP, Vol. 38: 25–7; Chryssi Bourbou, *Health and Disease in Byzantine Crete (7th–12th Centuries AD)*, MMM (Farnham, UK: Ashgate, 2010): 25–8.

[91] A. Kazhdan, in collaboration with S. Franklin, *Studies on Byzantine Literature of the Eleventh and Twelfth Centuries* (Paris: Editions de la Maison des sciences de l'homme, 1984): vii.

[92] Vivian Nutton, "Galen to Alexander, Aspects of Medicine and Medical Practice in Late Antiquity," DOP, Vol. 38: 5. Peregrine Horden, "Saints and Doctors in the Early Byzantine Empire: The Case of Theodore of Sykeon," in W.J. Sheils (ed.), *The Church and Healing: Papers Read at the Twentieth Summer Meeting and the Twenty-First Winter Meeting of the Ecclesiastical History Society* (Oxford: Basil Blackwell, 1982): 10; Barry Baldwin, "Beyond the House Call: Doctors in Early Byzantine History and Politics," DOP, Vol. 38: 19; see also Constantelos, "Physician-Priests," 150; Magoulias, "Lives of Saints as Sources of Data," 135–6.

[93] Duffy, "Byzantine Medicine in the Sixth and Seventh Centuries," 24.

advice.[94] It is worth remembering that ascetic healers were often the last option of the ill, rather than first choice; perhaps Theodore resented this order.

The "real life" of both Byzantine physicians and monks of Moschos' day also included medical and psychological challenges of the great pandemic of bubonic plague, which troubled the waters of the eastern Empire for nearly 200 years. The introduction to this study noted briefly the effects of the "Plague of Justinian," the first of three pandemics known to history. The roots of this version of the plague are found in the Nile delta, whence it quickly spread along land and sea trade routes throughout the Roman Empire, and appeared roughly each decade. From 541 until the mid-eighth century it appeared often without warning, disappearing as mysteriously as it arrived.[95] Although Christianity developed in the wake of—and partly as an antidote to—much of the suffering that diseases such as various plagues brought to society,[96] religious and medicinal skills have historically proven to be rarely any match for such grand-scale epidemic disease.[97] Physically, descriptions of the disease include fever and swelling of the glands ("buboes"), with death following swiftly upon the appearance of such symptoms. Psychologically and theologically reviews are mixed: Byzantine authors characteristically refrained from making categorical statements about the role of God in historical events such as widespread illness, but that did not prevent them from commenting on the increase in pious actions—even if contrived—such as appeals to saints both living and dead, or fleeing to churches at the outbreak of disease.[98]

---

[94] See "Théodore Comme Thaumaturege, Médecin et Directeur D'Ames," 145–7, in Géorgios, *Vie de Théodore de Sykéôn*, trans. André-Jean Festugière, *SubsHag* 48 (Bruxelles, Société des Bollandistes, 1970): Vol. I, 113–17, and Vol. II, 118–22.

[95] Lester K. Little, "Life and Afterlife of the First Plague Pandemic," in Lester K. Little (ed.), *Plague and the End of Antiquity: The Pandemic of 541–750* (Cambridge University Press, 2007): 3; Cameron, "New Themes and Styles in Greek Literature," 82–3; Lois N. Manger, *A History of Infectious Diseases and The Microbial World* (Westport, CT: Praeger, 2009): 9; see also Biraben, *Les Hommes et la peste*, for a table that traces the movement of the Justinian plague across the territory of the empire. Jean-Noël Biraben, *Les Hommes et la peste en France et dans les pays européens et méditerranéens: Tome I: La peste dans l'histoire*, CS, Vol. 35 (Paris: Mouton, 1976): 1: 27–32.

[96] Porterfield, *Healing in the History of Christianity*, 45; Stark, *Rise of Christianity*, 73–94.

[97] Little, "Life and Afterlife of the First Plague Pandemic," 25.

[98] During the first stage of the pandemic, Justinian declared that sodomy and blasphemy caused plagues and natural disasters, and took legal measures to eradicate these sins from his regime. Justinian, *Novel ii*, in *Novellae*, ed. Krueger, Mommsen, Schöll, Kroll, Justinian, *Corpus Iuris Civilis: Novellae* (New Jersey: The Lawbook Exchange, Ltd, 2010): 381–3; see also, Scott, *Civil Law*, 16.288–9. John of Ephesus, *Lives of the Eastern Saints*, PO, 1923. John claims that plague is a reforming tool, although Kaldellis notes that his logic is contradictory. Anthony Kaldellis, "The Literature of Plague and Anxieties of Piety in Sixth-Century Byzantium," in Franco Mormando and Thomas Worcester (eds), *Piety and Plague: From Byzantium to the Baroque*, Sixteenth Century Essays and Studies (Truman State University Press, 2007): 10. Procopius, *Wars* 2.22–3, and *The Secret History*,

Indisputably the plague had an effect on early Byzantine society at multiple levels, but despite the near constant presence of this disease in the Byzantine east for two centuries, Moschos says relatively little about either the plague or its effects. Unlike John of Ephesus, Procopius,[99] Evagrius[100] or hagiography,[101] Moschos' tales do not present any plague narrative,[102] nor does he appear to be interested in either theological speculation about divine activity and disease or clarifying God's role in the historical reality of illness beyond reporting the interpretation of ill health as it is presented by the one telling the account to Moschos. In any case, interpretations vary: in general, Byzantine Christians were not consistent in their language of God and historical agency. But two things are worth noting: first, Moschos was born and raised during the age of "Justinian's plague" and thus we can conclude that plague and the effects of plague shaped his life in significant respects, even if we cannot measure those ways in the same way that we can measure demographic decline, breakdown in urban and rural agricultural production and economic transactions, lack of military personnel that contributed, in part, to enemy incursions into the empire, resultant deportation and migration, and additional health problems that accompany the disease, such as malnutrition, starvation and infant mortality.[103] Second, tales that Moschos collected and composed—in addition to those later added—were, as with poverty, written against a backdrop of illness, disease and the effects of general ill health, and therefore "plague" (if it was indeed always understood that way) may very well have formed such a consistent presence that one would not find it even worth mentioning.

"It shall be healed"

The first element to consider in texts from the *Meadow* that address medical cures is that curing is the norm. Despite the important role that suffering plays in an ascetic life, a general sweep of the passages treating ill health in the *Meadow* suggests that ill health was not necessarily equated with a state of holiness, monastic figure or not. When a distraught young man (whose crime will be revealed in

---

4.1, 18.44. Procopius was skeptical of "fear-induced pietism." Kaldellis, "Literature of Plague," 15–17.

[99] Procopius, *Wars*, ii.23.1; *Secret History* xviii.44.

[100] *Hist.eccl.*, IV.29.

[101] For example, *The Life of St. Theodore of Sykeon* 8, 40, 45 (Festugière, Vol. I: 7, 36, 40–41, respectively); in Dawes and Baynes, *Three Byzantine Saints*, 91, 117, 120–21, respectively.

[102] Few beneficial tales mention the plague. Two accounts—*Prat. sp.* 131 (PG 87.2995–6) and *Prat. sp.* 132 (PG 87.2995–6)—are set against the background of the plague, but they are about unique knowledge and power of the holy man, rather than disease or illness.

[103] Dionysios Stathakopolous, "Crime and Punishment: The Plague in the Byzantine Empire, 541–750," in Lester K. Little (ed.), *Plague and the End of Antiquity*, 114–18; see also Allen, "The Justianic Plague," 16–20.

the next chapter) appears at the Giants' Monastery, Abba John assures him that healing requires understanding the disease in order that the doctor can apply what is needed: "But if you wish to be healed, tell me the truth concerning your deeds, so I can apply penances appropriate to these ... and to each the medication due."[104] Obviously the young man's misery is an indication that he is spiritually unwell, and we find this argument elsewhere in the texts. Here, however, the abba acknowledges that health is something that the young man must want, and that health is something that is possible for him to achieve, with the abba's assistance, of course. As stated earlier, brevity of beneficial tales prevents the opportunity for turning a simple series of events into an extensive theological treatise; but the material at hand allows us to conclude with some degree of security that "healed" is a state that Abba John believes is achievable for a miserable young man whose history and sins the abba does not yet know.

Abba John is not the only one who believes that the restoration of health is either achievable or desirable, as Moschos and Sophronios learn when they are told of a great elder who had a disciple named John who excelled in discernment.[105] After the death of the elder the disciple received a vision in which he was told that "if you place your hand on any suffering, it shall be healed."[106] The next morning a man arrived and begged John to cure his wife "who had cancer in her breast."[107] Breast cancers are not uncommon in antiquity and they are noted with some degree of frequency in Greek and Roman texts along with abscesses and inflammatory mastitis, which carry a considerably better prognosis than carcinoma.[108] After appropriate claims of unworthiness, John, under duress, put his hand on her breast,

---

[104] "ἐπιτίμια" (Gk), "*epitimia*" (Ltn), or "suitable penances" should here be understood not in the sense of absolution; the context rather suggests a healing of the one suffering from the disease caused by their sin, and points towards the development of the church as the hospital of the soul. "Ἀλλ' εἰ θέλεις ἰατρείας τυχεῖν, εἰπέ μοι εἰς ἀλήθειαν τὰς πράξεις σου, ὅπως κἀγὼ ταύταις ἁρμόζοντα προσάγω τὰ ἐπιτίμια ... καὶ ἕτερον τὸ τοῦ πλεονέκτου βοήθημα." *Prat. sp.* 78 (PG. 87.2933). The Latin of Fra Ambroggio adds: "Et ne tibi plurima vitia enumerem, quemadmodum in corporalibus infirmitatibus variis varia quoque remedia adhiberi conspicimus, ita et animæ vitiis, quæ plurima sunt, medicina quoque varie succurrit." "*And, not to mention the many vices,* [just] *as in the various bodily weaknesses various remedies* [are] *to be applied accordingly, so too* [for] *the vices of the soul* [there are] *a great many medicines that, in various ways, comes to their rescue.*"

[105] *Prat. sp.* 56 (PG 87.2909–12).

[106] "Ἐν οἱοδήποτε ἂν τὴν χεῖρά σου ἐπιθῇς πάθει, θεραπευθήσεται." *Prat. sp.* 56 (PG 87. 2909–10).

[107] "εἰς τὸν μαστὸν αὐτῆς καρκίνον." The PG has "καρκίνον" (Gk) and "*cancri*" (Ltn). *Prat. sp.* 56 (PG 87.2909–10).

[108] Don Brothwell, "The Evidence for Neoplasms," and A.T. Sandison and Calvin Wells, "Diseases of the Reproductive System," in Don Brothwell and A.T. Sandison (eds), *Diseases in Antiquity: A Survey of the Diseases, Injuries and Surgery of Early Populations* (Springfield, IL: Charles C. Thomas, 1967): 343 and 512–13, respectively; Pauline Thompson, "The Disease That We Call Cancer," in Sheila Campbell, Bert Hall and David

"and sealed the disease, and she was healed."[109] There are several elements worth considering in this beneficial tale, and I will focus on diagnosis and procedure.

Unlike Aetios of Amida's sixth-century explanations of the treatment of breast cancers, abscesses and ulcers,[110] John's procedure appears to be pain-free. According to *The Meadow* this cancer—a tumor traditionally cut off or out— is healed/cured by God through John's mere touch, a method that perhaps has links with the gospel account of Jesus and the hemorrhaging woman,[111] and a tale from Cyril of Scythopolis.[112] But what interests me is not so much where John touches her, but the way in which he touches her. The text does not indicate that this touch causes her any degree of pain at all, though it is worth noting that her pain might not be mentioned because it might not be thought worthy of mention, her "experience" not being considered valid.[113] But according to the account, John does not make her suffer any more pain than she presumably has already experienced. Peregrine Horden notes that with the exception of mysterious healing saints such as St Artemios, who performed surgery during incubation,[114] most traditional holy persons who offer healing do so in ways that refrain from drawing blood,[115] abandoning the paradox and troubling dilemma that one who heals must harm one who is already suffering.[116] But while the by-product of bodily pain that comes with disease might be welcome to anyone who seeks to use that for the benefit of their soul, as far as we can tell the wife with breast cancer is not an ascetic. This is, however, because she does not speak for herself or ask for healing, which leads us to a question: does she even want to be healed? That John heals

---

Klausner (eds), *Health, Disease and Healing in Medieval Culture* (New York: St Martin's Press, 1992): 1.

[109] "καὶ σφραγίσαντος τὸ πάθος, παραχρῆμα ἐθεραπεύθη," *Prat. sp.* 56 (PG 87.2912).

[110] Aetios of Amida, Ch. 37–50, in *Aetios of Amida: The Gynaecology and Obstetrics of the VIth Century, A.D.*, trans. James V. Ricci (Philadelphia, PA: The Blakiston Company, 1950): 46–54.

[111] Mark 5.25–34.

[112] "62. The Woman with a Haemorrhage," 164.2–9 (*Kyrillos von Skythopolis*, ed. Eduard Schwartz (Leipzig: J.C. Hinrichs, 1939): 163–4); Cyril of Scythopolis, *The Lives of the Monks of Palestine*, trans. R.M. Price (Kalamazoo, MI: Cistercian Publications, 1991): 173.

[113] Elizabeth A. Clark, "The Lady Vanishes: Dilemmas of a Feminist Historian after the 'Linguistic Turn,'" CH, Vol. 67, No. 1 (1998): 6.

[114] *The Miracles of St. Artemios: A Collection of Miracle Stories by an Anonymous Author of Seventh-Century Byzantium*, trans. with commentary by Virgil S. Crisafulli and John W. Nesbitt (Leiden: E.J. Brill, 1997): 22, 25, 44; 131–7, 145–7, 219–23, respectively.

[115] Peregrine Horden, "The Case of Theodore of Sykeon," 9.

[116] Edelstein, "The Relation of Ancient Philosophy to Medicine," 363. Edelstein also quotes Epictetus, who asks "But are there not paradoxes in the other arts? And what is more paradoxical than to lance a man in the eye in order that he might see?" Epictetus, *Dissertationes* I, 25, 32–3 [Loeb]; in Edelstein, "The Relation of Ancient Philosophy to Medicine," 363.

her does not mean that she wishes for healing to take place. Her silence does not prove that she is engaged in a type of ascetic behavior that seeks to avoid physical healing for the sake of the soul (as we shall see below), but even as she receives the benefit of John's sacrifice to asceticism, it is John's suffering that alleviates her suffering, not her own.

Concerning diagnosis, how does John know what to do with this woman brought before him? How does he know to touch her rather than send her away? Earlier in this beneficial tale we learn that the disciple has been granted this gift of healing due to his discernment ("διάκρισις"), a trait openly recognized by John's elder before the elder dies, and a trait that will place John in the company of the previously studied woman in *Meadow* tale 204, whose methods of discernment allowed her to heal both the spiritual and physical maladies of her patient.[117] According to Andrew Crislip, diagnosis of disease was *not* the traditional task of physicians; they did not engage in diagnosis, but in prognosis.[118] Put bluntly, a physician did not ask themselves "What is wrong with this patient?" but "In light of what is wrong with this person, how long will it take them to die?" which does not suggest a preventative approach. Monastic literature related to health care, on the other hand, reveals that monks engaged in health care employed the method of discernment rather than prognosis; discernment, or the diagnosis of disease, was how monastic health-care providers distinguished between angelic and demonic forces that caused ill health, between various types of natural causes of disease, or even if someone needed any treatment at all.[119] This was a quality that was not left to anyone other than an elder, one who presumably had the wisdom and experience to determine what and who was before their eyes. In addition to the fact that this ability for discernment is recognized and fostered in John by his elder, we see also in this beneficial tale the outcome of that ability, for John sees before him not merely the prognosis ("If left untreated, she will die in pain, the family will suffer"), but we can conclude that he discerns all of the elements of illness that her disease is causing: an anxious husband whose desperation might betray what we have seen already, that healing at the hands of a holy person was often the last-ditch effort when all had failed with physicians;[120] perhaps John sees a couple whose resources have been depleted along with their hopes; further, perhaps he sees a woman whose disease probably causes her to suffer physically a pain that she has not willingly adopted for the sake of an ascetic program. Or, if she is intentionally suffering, perhaps John wishes to cure the undue strain her ascetic program is placing on the family. For whatever reason, John does not merely cure

---

[117] *Prat. sp.* 204 (PG 87.3093–6); see Chapter 1.
[118] Crislip, *From Monastery to Hospital*, 18–19.
[119] Ibid., 19.
[120] PG 87.3.3948, in Dominic Monteserrat, "'Carrying On the Work of The Earlier Firm': Doctors, Medicine and Christianity in the *Thaumata* of Sophronios of Jerusalem," in King, *Health in Antiquity*, 233.

her, but cures the entire situation, restoring not only her breast but most probably the health of her family as well.

"Who is your father?"

We should not assume that John's initial reluctance to heal the woman of cancer is an indication that he has no desire to help her. That an ascetic figure would need to be coaxed into activity is merely a demonstration of—and therefore confirmation of—their humility. We see such modesty present in a *Meadow* tale of Abba Daniel,[121] who, according to John and Sophronios, was approached by a young man in the market. The young man begged the good elder to come to his home and pray over his wife, "for she is sterile."[122] Eventually the elder agreed; he entered the home, prayed and the wife became pregnant. Either Moschos or the teller of the tale (Abba John of Petra) is careful to note that it was by the will of God that she becomes pregnant, not by her desire, the husband's desire or the abba's. As the short tale develops we learn that some men use the occasion of their wife's pregnancy to accuse the elder of unchaste behavior with the wife, for it is actually the man who "is barren,"[123] they claim, demonstrating the human need to find someone at fault of barrenness.[124] Determined to address this, after the baby is born the abba requests that the young father prepare food and invite friends and neighbors;[125] at the conclusion of the meal the abba took the infant in his arms and asked: "Who is your father?"[126] The infant indicates verbally and through gesture that his father is the man who had begged the abba for prayer, and God, the "guardian of truth," was praised by everyone there. And thus we learn that the point of this beneficial tale is not really about healing this woman's infertility; rather, it is about healing the problems that accompany infertility, problems that are larger than one woman's inability to conceive a child.

The inability of a woman to conceive a child is never simply about conception; it is also about social pressure. We know today that infertility is often accompanied by feelings of grief, depression and a sense of isolation[127] that lingers even when a committed partner is present, and there is no reason to think that women in antiquity did not also experience these emotions. But, in addition, pregnancy in antiquity carried different types of familial and civic import, especially during

---

[121] *Prat. sp.* 114 (PG 87.2977–80).
[122] "ὅτι στεῖρα ἐστίν." *Prat. sp.* 114 (PG 87.2977).
[123] "ὅτι Ἀληθῶς ὁ νεώτερος ἄγονός ἐστίν." Ibid.
[124] This also suggests one belief about fertility in the Greek world, that it was the man who implanted the child in the woman, whose uterus merely carried the child to term. Jane F. Gardner, "Aristophanes and Male Anxiety: The Defense of the *Oikos*," in *Women in Antiquity*, GRS, Vol. 3 (Oxford University Press, 1996): 147, 151–2.
[125] *Prat. sp.* 114 (PG 87.2980).
[126] "Τίς ἐστίν ὁ πατήρ σου;" *Prat. sp.* 114 (PG 87.2980).
[127] Anonymous, "What Price A Baby?" JPN, Vol. 37, No. 5 (1999): 7.

times of population decline due to war or widespread disease. To supplement the need to provide citizens for the empire, there was added anxiety to produce not just heirs,[128] but *authentic* heirs. Sociologist Rodney Stark notes that despite continual pronatalist legislation, philosophical endorsements and financial subsidies[129] designed to encourage population growth among declining numbers of pagan Roman citizens, all of these factors combined appear to have done little to solve problems caused by lack of interest in marriage itself or the prevalence of unsafe abortion practices, ineffective or poisonous contraceptives and the abandonment of children less than perfect, or female.[130] "A final factor," Stark writes, "in favor of high Christian fertility was an abundance of women who were far less likely to be infertile."[131] But Stark's claim that Christian women were "less likely to be infertile"[132] by virtue of their religious affiliation does not mean that they were necessarily more fertile. In fact, texts that indicate the continued presence of anxious women at the sites of holy persons, begging saints to pray for a pregnancy, suggests that even "fertile" Christian women struggled to either become or remain pregnant. The shrine of St Euphrosyne, for example, specialized in the healing of fertility,[133] and Michael Goodich notes that many saints pressured to marry and produce children find much of their ministry devoted to attending to the needs of those in the world who want children or who suffer from childbirth pains.[134] In response to Stark's chapter on Christianity among women in the Roman world, Elizabeth Castelli, in "Gender, Theory, and The Rise of Christianity," notes that a

---

[128] The amount spent annually on fertility treatments makes it abundantly clear that having *one's own* child continues to exert pressure. Mark P. Connolly, William Ledger and Maarten J. Postma, "Economics of Assisted Reproduction: Access to Fertility Treatments and Valuing Live Births in Economic Terms," HF, Vol. 13, No. 1 (2010): 13–18; Karen C. Lee, "Fertility Treatments and the Cost of a Healthy Baby," NWH, Vol. 15, No. 1 (2011): 15–18.

[129] Richard I. Frank, "Augustus' Legislation on Marriage and Children," *California Studies in Classical Antiquity*, Vol. 8 (1975): 41–52; Beryl Rawson, "The Roman Family," in Beryl Rawson (ed.), *The Family in Ancient Rome: New Perspectives* (Ithaca, NY: Cornell University Press, 1986): 5, 9, 25.

[130] Stark, *The Rise of Christianity*, 115–22. Stark cites a discovery in Ashkelon sewers of close to 100 infant skeletons as evidence that Romans and Greeks were prone to favoring infanticide. Archaeologists conclude that the infants had been dropped into sewers either at birth or shortly after. Lawrence Stager, "Eroticism and Infanticide at Ashkelon," *Biblical Archaeological Review*, Vol. 17, No. 4 (1991): 47. However, I would note that the contents of the sewer date to the sixth century CE, in an area heavily Christian.

[131] Stark, *The Rise of Christianity*, 126.

[132] Ibid.

[133] Alice-Mary Talbot, "Pilgrimage to Healing Shrines: The Evidence of Miracle Accounts," DOP, Vol. 56: 153–73.

[134] Michael Goodich, "Sexuality, Family, and the Supernatural in the Fourteenth Century," JHS, Vol. 4, No. 4 (1994): 501–2; Susan Ashbrook Harvey, "Women in Early Byzantine Hagiography: Reversing the Story," in Lynda L. Coon, Katherine J. Haldane and Elisabeth W. Sommer (eds), *That Gentle Strength: Historical Perspectives on Women in Christianity* (University Press of Virginia, 1990): 43.

variety of factors could have accounted for fertility and infertility rates, including sexual abstinence,[135] spiritual marriages[136] or even medical procedures aimed at increasing fertility (which I marvel that women even survived).[137] High praise of virginity, chastity, sterile marriages and monastic life also greatly influenced and validated the desire for some women to avoid—or attempt to avoid—the marital state and the marital bed,[138] a condition that served only to preserve from sin those who could not endure the ascetic life.

By Moschos' era expectations about marriage and childbearing had changed somewhat, but women were still under great social pressure to fulfill the roles of wife and mother as society dictated, as the eighth-century *Ecloga* of Leo will attest.[139] The desire to have a child—a male child[140]—meant that women would resort to all types of behaviors to force their family to conform to standards set by those exterior to their own homes,[141] and sometimes their actions took a tragic turn. For example, Moschos includes among his *Meadow* a tale of a Byzantine widow named Mary who had two children;[142] her desperation for financial protection in

---

[135] Elizabeth Anne Castelli, "Gender, Theory, and The Rise of Christianity: A Response to Rodney Stark," JECS, Vol. 6, No. 2 (1998): 256; Elizabeth A. Clark, "Antifamilial Tendencies in Ancient Christianity," JHS, Vol. 5, No. 3 (1995): 356–80; Évelyne Patlagean, "Sur la limitation de la fécondité dans la haute époque Byzantine," *Annales* (1969): 1355.

[136] Dyan Elliott, *Spiritual Marriage: Sexual Abstinence in Mediaeval Wedlock* (Princeton University Press, 1993): 55–93.

[137] Aetios of Amida, Chapters 26–31, in Ricci, *Aetios of Amida*, 36–40. Basil of Caesarea notes that abortion often led to the death of fetus and patient. Basil, "To Amphilochius, On the Canons," in *Saint Basil: The Letters*, Vol. 3, trans. Roy J. Deferrari (Harvard University Press, 1926): 188.2, and "Sonorus' list of causes for [abortion] make one wonder how anyone ever managed to have a baby." Gillian Clark, "Roman Women," in Ian McAuslan and Peter Walcot (eds), *Women in Antiquity*, GRS, Vol. 3 (Oxford University Press, 1996): 38–40.

[138] "La procréation n'est donc pas la justification unique ou suffisante du mariage. L'état le plus élevé, le plus souhaitable, est la virginité, libre des peines de la vie charnelle, et promise à une félicité spirituelle dont l'éloge hante la littérature du temps." Patlagean, "Sur la limitation de la fécondité dans la haute époque Byzantine," in Évelyne Patlegean, *Structure sociale, famille, chrétienté à Byzance, IVe–XIe siècle* (London: Variorum Reprints, 1981): 1357; Évelyne Patlagean, "Birth Control in the Early Byzantine Empire," in Robert Forster and Orest Ranum (eds), *Biology of Man in History* (Baltimore, MD: Johns Hopkins University Press, 1975): 5–6.

[139] Angeliki E. Laiou, "The Role of Women in Byzantine Society," in Angeliki E. Laiou, *Gender, Society and Economic Life in Byzantium* (Aldershot, UK: Ashgate, 1992): 233–4.

[140] Patlagean, "Sur la limitation de la fécondité dans la haute époque Byzantine," 1366.

[141] Judith Herrin, "In Search of Byzantine Women: Three Avenues of Approach," in Averil Cameron and Amélie Kuhrt (eds), *Images of Women in Antiquity* (Wayne State University Press, 1983): 172; Patlagean, "Birth Control in the Early Byzantine Empire," 12–13.

[142] *Prat. sp.* 70 (PG 87.2927–9).

the form of a second husband leads her to kill her two children in the hope that he will then accept her as a wife. As it would have fallen to her new husband to provide for those children as his own, she tries unsuccessfully to remove the obstacle that is preventing his interest in marrying her. Horrified by her actions, he refuses her altogether. The conclusion of the tale finds Mary as dead as her children, but while this beneficial tale has a clear moral purpose in its faulting of Mary, it speaks also to the frightening lengths to which women would go for financial security for themselves and freedom for their children.[143]

"Brother John, arise"

Like most medical maladies in the *Meadow*, infertility and cancer remain with us in the twenty-first century. Infertility—male or female—is diagnosed as a disease that currently affects one out of every eight couples, and the science of infertility is a multi-billion-dollar industry.[144] Breast cancer, as well, kills nearly 50,000 women each year in the United States.[145] The final example to be addressed in this section of diseases worth curing is selected from among a list of many conditions of ill health that—like the first two—are known to contemporary society, even if they are not always understood in the same way. Malnutrition and dehydration,[146] fevers,[147] paralysis,[148] a mystery "incurable disease" which—though no doctor can cure it and it is "incurable"—is cured,[149] sinful thoughts,[150] depression[151] and

---

[143] Herrin, "In Search of Byzantine Women," 173; Mary's situation seems to support Patlagean's observation regarding how women and their health were viewed, which is that "La santé des femmes, mentale autant que physique, est vue comme fragile, incertaine, spécifique." Evelyne Patlagean, "Introduction," in Évelyne Patlagean (ed.), *Maladie et Société à Byzance* (Spoleto: Centro italiano di studi sull'alto medioevo, cop. 1993): XIII.

[144] National Infertility Association, http://www.resolve.org/about/funding-vital-research.html.

[145] Centers for Disease Control and Prevention, http://www.cdc.gov/cancer/breast/statistics/.

[146] *Prat. sp.* 65 (PG 87.2915–16); *Prat sp.* 176 (PG 87.3043–6).

[147] *Prat. sp.* 1 (PG 87.2851–4).

[148] *Prat. sp.* 40 (PG 87.2891–6).

[149] *Prat. sp.* 28, (PG 87.2875–6). There are a few "mystery" diseases in our day, such as fibromyalgia, a multi-system, idiopathic medical disorder that challenges characterization and understanding. S. Chakrabarty and R. Zoorob, "Fibromyalgia," AFP, Vol. 76, No. 2 (2007): 247–54. I am not suggesting that Abba Cyril had fibromyalgia.

[150] *Prat. sp.* 3 (PG 87.2853–4); *Prat. sp.* 204 (PG 87.3093–6); *Prat. sp.* 205 (PG 87.3095–8).

[151] *Prat. sp.* 142 (PG 87.3003–4); *Prat. sp.* 164 (PG 87.3031–2); *Prat. sp.* 207 (PG 87.3097–100); *Prat. sp.* 208 (PG 87.3099–102); 12, Nissen, "Unbekannte Erzählungen," 367–8. Known often as "accidie" among monastics, this is addressed in Andrew Crislip, "The Sin of Sloth or the Illness of the Demons? The Demon of Acedia in Early Christian Monasticism," HTR, Vol. 98, No. 2 (2005): 143–69.

snake bites all make an appearance as the primary maladies in *The Meadow*. As mentioned above, there does not appear to be hostility towards doctors in *The Meadow*, and although this is not the case for all hagiography in Moschos' tales, the work of physicians is not belittled. Several tales include doctors who operate in compassionate ways, even if they cannot always solve the problems at hand. Of this list, we will consider a beneficial tale that contains a fatal snake bite – or at least it is *initially* fatal.

"It seems," Galen wrote, "that there is nothing more dangerous in life than poisons, and [the bites] of noxious animals."[152] Although the snake was—in theory—associated with the healing god Asklepios and was celebrated by Greeks and Romans as a curative agent, not an agent of harm,[153] nevertheless it was also a reptile whose surprise attacks, resulting in either instant death or instant suffering, inspired great strides in toxicology.[154] Abba Zosimos, a Cilician monk living at Mount Sinai, relates to Moschos how 20 years previously, when he settled in the area of Porphyreôn with his disciple John, "a serpent"[155] struck John, who "immediately died, with blood flowing from all his parts."[156] Distressed, Zosimos went to some nearby anchorites, who, based on Zosimos' countenance, guessed immediately that John was dead. They went to the body, and

> they looked at him, stretched out there on the ground, then they said to me: "Do not be sorrowful, Abba Zosimos; God is helping." They called the brother, saying: "Brother John, arise; the elder has need of you." The brother got up from the ground at once. They looked for the snake, caught it and cut it into two before our eyes. Then they said to me: "Abba Zosimos, go to Sinai; it is the will of God to entrust you with the church of Babylon."[157]

I do not think that this is a beneficial tale about raising the dead, even though a man who "died immediately" got up when ordered to do so. Rather, I think it is a tale of obedience and discernment. This is not to suggest that either a snake bite or wounds significant enough to cause bleeding are any small matter, and I do not mean to diminish the anguish or pain that the snake surely inflicted upon the disciple. Of course this cannot be known definitively; John probably was

---

[152] Galen (ed. C.G. Kühn), XIV, 230–31, in John Scarborough, "Nicander's Toxicology I: Snakes," Pharm Hist, Vol. 19, No. 1 (1977): 3.

[153] Majno, *The Healing Hand*, 285.

[154] Scarborough, "Nicander's Toxicology I: Snakes," 4; Majno, *The Healing Hand*, 203, 283–5, 339, 381.

[155] "ὄφις," "serpent" or "snake."

[156] "καὶ εὐθὺς τέθνηκεν, αἱμορροήσας δι' ὅλων τῶν μορίων αὐτοῦ." *Prat. sp.* 124 (PG 87.2985–8).

[157] Ibid.; Wortley, *Spiritual Meadow*, 101. "Babylon" is Cairo.

bitten by a "*Cerastes cerastes*,"[158] one of the various types of venomous horned vipers indigenous to Northern Africa and Southwest Asia,[159] and there are reasons why the type of snake might be important to the interpretation of the tale. The *Cerastes cerastes* is a stout snake with small scales above the eyes reminiscent of horns, which contributes to a look more evil then the snake's probable intent. The *Cerastes cerastes*' venom is a noxious concoction, and it is painful but not potent; however, it does contain hemotoxins, an anti-coagulating agent, and this could explain the blood loss that John experiences. There are few deaths related to bites from this snake, but these are details that the abba probably did not have and, for all he knew, his disciple had died. The anchorites, on the other hand, were living in that area, and might have guessed that John's wound was not fatal. But for the abba, that John would get up from the ground when he is ordered to do so would seem an act of great obedience, and serves to underscore the important bond between a disciple and his elder.

Beyond this death-defying obedience, there are a few other elements that stand out in this tale. First, both the wound and the agent of the wound provide the opportunity to participate in the divine economy; the anchorites inform the elder that he is not to be sorrowful because "God helps."[160] In what way God is helping remains ambiguous. It is not clear if God is helping by having allowed the disciple to be wounded to begin with, or if God is helping in that the disciple is not going to die from the inflicted wound. Paucity of detail leaves this open to interpretation, and it is likely that if the question were put to Moschos we would receive the response that it makes no difference. God helps; end of discussion. Were those details important, we would have received them. Second, the disciple demonstrates that he is either risen from the dead or not dead to begin with when he responds to the anchorites' order: "Brother John, arise; the elder needs you."[161] That he does so offers the opportunity to consider the "monastic sick role," a component of the social world of the monastic, and one that will be explored more fully below. As outlined in Andrew Crislip's history of the hospital within the monastic milieu, unlike those in ill health in the pre-Christian empire, the ill within the monastic environment were guaranteed care, exception from traditional duties and neither blamed nor stigmatized for their ill health.[162] While ordering the disciple to "arise" does not indicate that the anchorites believed that the disciple was faking his injury, nevertheless, I suggest it provides an example of the aforementioned discernment

---

[158] Associated with "Horus," the *Cerastes cerastes* is identified as "fy" in hieroglyphics. John Nunn, *Ancient Egyptian Medicine* (University of Oklahoma Press, 2002): 183–9.

[159] Yuval Sterer, "A Mixed Litter of Horned and Hornless Horned Vipers: Cerastes Cerastes Cerastes (Ophidia: Viperidae)," Isr J Zool, Vol. 37 (1992): 247; *Venomous Snakes of the Middle East: Identification Guide* (Washington, DC: Defense Intelligence Agency, 1991): 17–21.

[160] "βοήθάει ὁ Θεός," *Prat. sp.* 124 (PG 87.2985–8).

[161] "Ἀδελφέ Ἰωάννη, ἐγείρου, ὁ γέρων δέεταί σου." *Prat. sp.* 124 (PG 87.2985–8).

[162] Crislip, *From Monastery to Hospital*, 70.

on their part: they have correctly discerned that he is not dead. Based on their knowledge of the terrain they inhabit, their years in the desert and their wisdom, they are able to see that the disciple has not sustained either a life-threatening injury or one that precludes special treatment.

Finally, it is worth considering the death and destruction of that snake. The reptile is caught and cut in half, and subsequently the abba and his disciple are informed that they are to leave for Sinai, for "God wants to entrust you with the church of Babylon,"[163] a prophetic utterance that, by the end of the beneficial tale, comes to fruition.[164] That an anchorite might have the gift of prophecy or discernment is not truly remarkable; it is a standard component of ascetic life. However, that the prophecy is announced after the snake is caught and cut up[165] suggests a unique divining method that points towards magical practices that will rise in favor in the later history of the Byzantine Empire, despite ecclesiastical condemnation.

Medical Management in Early Medieval Byzantium: Enduring

The body presents a problem. It houses a soul, for which it deserves recognition for such a noble task. But the needs and desires with which the body tempts the soul are contemptible. For Christians the problems of the body may be solved by the theology of the resurrection, but that theology is complicated by Paul's claim that "[f]lesh and blood cannot inherit the kingdom of God."[166] While the value of the body will be debated, that the soul is the superior of the two is hardly questioned. "At best," Temkin writes, "the body was thought to be the partner of the soul, and at worst it was despised as a degrading vehicle."[167]

As mentioned above, in texts from the *Meadow* that address ill health, curing of the "degrading vehicle" is the norm. There are more individuals (lay and religious) who suffer and are cured than there are those who endure their suffering because healing is neither available to them, nor granted nor desired. To that end, Diadocus of Photike's assurance that "[t]here is nothing to prevent us from calling a doctor when we are ill"[168] seems to be general wisdom in the *Pratum*. On the other hand, there are certainly some spectacular instances of support for the other position,

---

[163] *Prat. sp.* 124 (PG 87.2985–8).
[164] Ibid.
[165] Cicero, *De Divinatione*, 2.27, in Hans-Joseph Klauck, *The Religious Context of Early Christianity: A Guide to Graeco-Roman Religions* (Minneapolis, MN: Fortress Press, 2003): 180–82; David E. Aune, *Prophecy in Early Christianity and the Ancient Mediterranean World* (Grand Rapids, MI: William B. Eerdmans Publishing Company, 1983): 35–6.
[166] I Cor. 15.50.
[167] Temkin, *Hippocrates in a World of Pagans and Christians*, 138.
[168] "Διαδόχου ἐπισκόπου Φωτικῆς τῆς Ἠπείρου κεφάλαια γνωστικὰ ρ'," 53 (SC 5); des Places, 114–15; Palmer, Philip Sherrard and Kallistos Ware, 268.

including eye diseases,[169] spiritual diseases of faint-heartedness,[170] dehydration,[171] accidie,[172] malnutrition and ulcers.[173] Here we will see that many who live their lives as preparation for death would be inclined to agree with Gregory Nazianzus that the hospital was "the easiest way up to heaven."[174]

"The inner man flourished"

The first beneficial tale with a disease worth enduring is found in a *Meadow* tale of Barnabas, an anchorite of The Caves in Jordan, who failed to remove a sharp object which became embedded in his foot when he went down to the river.[175] He would not allow a doctor to examine it[176] and eventually his foot became septic[177] so that it "compelled him to seek assistance in the Towers."[178] Although we can presume that he received some kind of medical care, "[h]is foot became more and more infected and he used to say to everybody who called on him that the more the outer man suffered, the more the inner man flourished."[179] It is worth considering this tale alongside another, "The Life of Abba Myrogenes Who Had Dropsy."[180] It is interesting to note that the degree of severity of the abba's ill health is such that it defines who he is in the very title of the tale. Beyond that, there is nothing but a single paragraph, short enough to be worth quoting in full:

> At the Lavra of the Towers there was an elder named Myrogenes who had been so harsh in his treatment of himself that he developed dropsy. He would often say to the elders who came by to take care of him: "Pray for me fathers, so that I do not develop dropsy in my inner man. I pray to God that I may endure this sickness for a long time." When Eutychios, the Archbishop of Jerusalem, heard about his, he wanted to send Abba Myrogenes all that he needed; but he never

---

[169] *Prat. sp.* 77 (PG 87.2929–32); *Prat. sp.* 118 (PG 87.2981–4).
[170] *Prat. sp.* 164 (PG 87.3031–2).
[171] *Prat. sp.* 184 (PG 87.3055–8).
[172] *Prat. sp.* 142 (PG 87.3003–4).
[173] *Prat. sp.* 42 (PG 87.2895–6).
[174] Gregory Nazianzen, *Oratio*, 43.63 in Bernardi, *Grégoire de Nazianze*, 42–3, 262.
[175] *Prat. spir.* 10 (PG 87 2859–60).
[176] This is a nice reminder that a doctor would be available to an anchorite.
[177] "καὶ ἐσάπη ὁ ποῦς αὐτοῦ," *Prat. sp.* 10 (PG 87.2860).
[178] "καὶ ἠναγκάσθη λαβεῖν ἑαυτῷ πυργίον εἰς τὰ Τυργία." Ibid. Located close to Jericho and the Jordan River, Towers monastery was—in the sixth century—second in importance for desert monasticism in this area. Joseph Patrich, *Sabas, Leader of Palestinian Monasticism: A Comparative Study in Eastern Monasticism, Fourth to Seventh Centuries*, DOS (Washington, DC: Dumbarton Oaks, 1995): 118–21.
[179] *Prat. sp.* 10 (PG 87.2860); Wortley, *Spiritual Meadow*, 9. We do not know definitively that this infection killed Barnabas, but the remainder of the tale suggests that it might have.
[180] *Prat. sp.* 8 (PG 87.2857–8).

got anything back in reply to his offer other than: "Pray for me father, that I might be delivered from eternal torment."[181]

Taking all this together, we can conclude a few things about these individuals and their particular challenges. First, both interpret their diseases or wounds as part of their ascetic program, which brings two requirements of the ascetic life into tension and even potentially into conflict with one another: to endure a disciplined—even harsh—physical regime while being mindful of attending to the physical and spiritual needs of others.[182] Finding that balance is difficult within one's own body,[183] but illness provided the opportunity beyond the sick body for balance to be struck within the community as well. As a particular element of ill health became unmanageable for one ascetic, it provided the opportunity for another to engage in care for their ill brother, to the degree that they were medically able.

Although dropsy, or edema—fluid retention—is attributed in our day to malnutrition, liver disease, diabetes, blood clots, arthritis, heart or kidney failure,[184] in this beneficial tale Abba Myrogenes' dropsy is directly attributed to his harsh treatment of his body, and admirably so. In like manner, the sparse details of the "Life of Barnabas" seem to suggest that he intentionally leaves in place what is embedded in his foot for the purpose of fighting his body for the sake of his soul. Their decisions are clearly not based on the aforementioned more cautious claims of Basil, Diadocus of Photike, Evagrius and Amma Syncletica, but reflect instead a position along the lines of Macarius the Egyptian's harsh advice: "Know then, having searched yourself, [that] you must never bring the fleshly afflictions before mundane physicians, as if Christ, in whom you believe, were unable to cure you."[185] Macarius was not alone in this position, for Origen also distinguished between the spiritual status of those who relied on medicine and those who relied on prayer: "A man ought to use medical means to heal his body if he aims to live in that simple and ordinary way. If he wishes to live in a way superior to that of the multitude, he should do this by devotion to the supreme God and by praying to Him."[186] Second, in both cases, they are cared for by others. Barnabas refuses all care up to a certain point, but even he eventually recognizes that his injury has moved beyond the point of self-management. It is safe to conclude that he was in frequent contact with the brothers at the Towers who were in a position to take him there; were he not, he

---

[181] *Prat. sp.* 8 (PG 87.2857); Wortley, *Spiritual Meadow*, 8.

[182] Harvey, "Physicians and Ascetics in John of Ephesus," 89–90.

[183] Elizabeth A. Castelli, "Mortifying the Body, Curing the Soul: Beyond Ascetic Dualism in *The Life of Amma Synclectica*," *Differences*, Vol. 4, No. 2 (1992): 141.

[184] John E. Hall, *Guyton and Hall Textbook of Medical Physiology* (Philadelphia, PA: Saunders, 2010): 259–61; 285–302; 477–84.

[185] Macarius, *Homily* 48.1 (PG 34.807–10); in Temkin, *Hippocrates in a World of Pagans and Christians*, 157.

[186] Origen, *Contra Celsum* 8.60 (PG 11.1559–62); Chadwick, 498.

might have died from what was probably septicemia, or blood poisoning,[187] which he perhaps does anyway. This tells us something about his type of community: although he lives independent of the Towers he is constantly on their radar. Abba Myrogenes resides at the Towers, and it is clear that he is being cared for and attended, to the degree that his illness is known even beyond the walls of the lavra, for hierarchs wish to send him anything that he needs. Finally, both beneficial tales refer to the development of the "inner man," evidence that they understand their disease as a particular element of a daily martyrdom, representative in no subtle way of the sin each must battle for the sake of the soul's salvation. Beyond this notion of sin, however, I suggest that the "inner man" refers also to the interior world that must be constructed by a solitary ascetic who might struggle in their desire to be apart from people who consistently seek them out for healing, favors, teaching, advice and arbitration. By their nature, those drawn to the interior of the desert are those who seek solitude; ironically, this element alone seems automatically to draw others to them, others whom they are compelled to assist. The more that they are pursued, the greater their involvement in society, the more opportunity for the "inner man" to be accessed,[188] as we learn from Abba Myrogenes, who, as noted above, "would often say to the elders who came by to take care of him: 'Pray for me fathers, so that I do not develop dropsy in my inner man.'"[189] Moschos may well have been aware of a similar account shared by Palladius—who himself suffered from dropsy[190]—in his *Lausiac History* of blessed Benjamin, a renowned healer who became so bloated that Palladius, Bishop Dioscorus and Evagrius averted their eyes when they visited him. He suffered so greatly for most of one year that he could not lie down, had to be seated on a very large chair, and when he died the door and door jambs had to be torn down to get his swollen body out. And yet, although he suffers from a disease, he is not suffering from an illness, for he remains engaged in relationship with others: he continues to heal, asking only for his colleagues to "Pray, my children, that the inner man not contract dropsy; for this body did not help me when it was well, nor has it caused me harm when faring badly."[191] Painful though it sounds, Benjamin appears to have found that balance, the incorporation of endurance of ill health into his very healing practice, to the degree that he transcends the needs of the body at all.

---

[187] Gerald L. Mandell, John E. Bennet and Raphael Dolin, *Principles and Practice of Infectious Diseases* (Philadelphia, PA: Churchill Livingstone, 2004): ch. 70.

[188] Richard Valantasis, "Constructions of Power in Asceticism," JAAR, Vol. 63, No. 4 (1995): 807.

[189] *Prat. sp.* 8 (PG 87.2857); Wortley, *Spiritual Meadow*, 8.

[190] Palladius, "John of Lycopolis," *The Lausiac History*, 35.4–13, in Bartelink, *La Storia Lausiaca*, 168–77; *Palladius: The Lausiac History*, trans. Robert T. Meyer, ACW 34 (New York: Paulist Press, 1964): 102.

[191] Palladius, "Benjamin," *The Lausiac History*, 12.1–2, in Bartelink, *La Storia Lausiaca*, 54–7; in Meyer, *Palladius: The Lausiac History*, 47–8.

I would not argue that blood poisoning, edema, leprosy or fevers were ailments that ascetics actively sought. But the main characters in these tales fall victim to illnesses, accidents and injuries in the same way as anyone else. The very terrain in which they lived provided many opportunities: deserts have snakes; unwashed cuts will become septic; and sometimes one must pass through the rocks to get to the shore. Unless someone else with great discernment interfered, however, ill health was very often interpreted as a component of the ascetic project of the individual figure, and—as we see in the last case—the ascetic project might be very well carried out by a non-ascetic.

"Lord, ruin me!"

It is challenging to identify the second disease to be endured in *The Meadow*, for the actual sicknesses with which our characters are afflicted—leprosy and a fever—are merely substitutes for a particular disease of the monastic life: sexual temptation. I have selected these two tales because they include not only sexual temptation but the subsequent sicknesses that prevent action being taken on the part of the individual. The first tale is told to John and Sophronios by Abba Polychronios concerning a brother in the community of Penthoucla who was "exceedingly mindful and ascetic."[192] However, he did struggle with the problem of lustful thoughts and he eventually gave up:

> As he was not winning the battle, he left the monastery and went off to Jericho to satisfy his desires. Just as he was entering the den of fornication, he was suddenly afflicted with leprosy all over. When he saw himself in such a condition, he immediately returned to the monastery, giving thanks to God and saying, "God has stricken me with this terrible disease in order that my soul should be saved," and he glorified God exceedingly.[193]

The second tale is from one of the later collections, and most likely not part of John's original collection. The tale concerns an "attractive young woman"[194] who prayed loudly in one of the churches of Constantinople, and drew attention to herself by her prayer, "Lord, ruin me!"[195] When her prayers and tears were finished, a man who witnessed this display was concerned about her. He inquired about her level of despair and offered to help, and she told him the following: "My lord, I had a husband from the time I was a virgin, but he died some time ago leaving me a widow. Now, my body rises up against me in its desire for intercourse with a man. That is why I call upon God: to humble me, so that I do not have the

---

[192] "ἦν πάνυ προσέχων αὑτὸν, καὶ ἀσκητής." *Prat. sp.* 14 (PG 87.2861–2).
[193] *Prat. sp.* 14 (PG 87.2861); Wortley, *Spiritual Meadow*, 11.
[194] "γυνὴ εὔοπτος νεωτέρα," V, Mioni, "Il Pratum Spirituale de Giovanni Mosco," 86.
[195] "Κύριε, τάραξόν με." Ibid.

experience of a second husband."[196] After she departed, the man had his servant follow her and mark her door to be able to identify it in the future. The second time he sent his servant to check on her the servant found "her confined with a violent fever, lying in bed and moaning,"[197] which the man later attributed to her "chaste soul,"[198] for which "he glorified God."[199]

There are more differences between these two tales than similarities, yet they are worth treating together if for no other reason than to note how the latter tale of the woman, the much longer tale, probably represents the more developed and chronologically later version of the theme of affliction for the sake of the soul. First, neither wishes for the affliction of sexual temptation, but it is interesting to identify the distinction between their methods of problem solving: the brother plans to solve the problem of sexual temptation by giving in to the temptation for something that is not allowed within his community; on the other hand, the woman prays to God in church for humbling so that she does *not* give in to temptation for something that—in her context as laity—is allowed. He is going into a "den of fornication" but she is praying that she not have any desire for a second husband, which is neither immoral nor illegal. She does not seem to be saying that she wants simply to have sex, but sex within the marital bed. A second point worth noting is that while the woman prays for affliction, the brother simply is afflicted without having asked. Partly this might represent the development of the theme of disease as deterrent of sin, from simple acknowledgement of the affliction to the even more pious prayer for the actual affliction itself. As well, that the brother contracts a deadly disease while the woman struggles with fever might indicate that the woman is being shown a degree of charity befitting her piety, while he was already on his way into the den. As we identify socio-historical elements embedded in these beneficial tales we need not worry about the *deus ex machina* plot development whereby he becomes instantly afflicted with leprosy, a disease that seems historically to be a "place holder" for an unidentifiable skin rash, an allergic reaction or a sexually transmitted disease.[200] This terse beneficial tale prevents us from finding out the details of how he came to learn of his disease, and where the disease appeared. Perhaps he was prevented from entering when someone saw evidence on his face, neck or hands. But regardless, what is historically accurate in this account is that Palestinian monks contracted leprosy and Palestinian monasteries cared for social outcasts who contracted skin diseases, including the Monastery of St Theodosius where Moschos began his career.[201] Finally, let us

---

[196] Ibid.," in Wortley, *Spiritual Meadow*, 219–20.

[197] "ὗρεν αὐτὴν λάβρῳ πυρετῷ συνεχομένην κατακειμένην ἐπί κλίνην καὶ στενάζουσαν." V, Mioni, "Il Pratum Spirituale de Giovanni Mosco," 87.

[198] "ὥφρονα ψυχὴν." Ibid.

[199] "καὶ ἐδόξασε τὸν Θεόν." Ibid.

[200] Vilhelm Møller-Christiensen, "Evidence of Leprosy in Earlier Peoples," in *Diseases in Antiquity*, 304–35.

[201] Joseph Zias, "Was Byzantine Herodium a Leprosarium?" BA, Vol. 49, No. 3 (1986): 184.

consider the purpose of the physical affliction. The brother recognized that he was afflicted for the sake of his salvation, for the disease would have prevented him from entering the brothel, from engaging with a prostitute and from further relations with the public. Although, unlike Barnabas and Abba Myrogenes, our brother does not rejoice about his "inner man," he does acknowledge that the soul will benefit as a result of the deterioration of the body, consistent with the previous two accounts. The woman, however, does not mention salvation, nor is it mentioned in the text. We can conclude that salvation is not the issue for this woman, but the point of her desire for affliction is that she *not* be married a second time, which reveals a distinction between the state of her soul and the state of her being. Her soul, at present, is not the concern, nor really are her bodily desires; rather, her ultimate concern is that she does not wish for her marital status to change. This suggests to me that this woman is independent enough that she can live alone without need of the financial support of a male figure, unlike poor Mary identified above. Also unlike Mary, this woman wishes to avoid the marital bed for a reason, and that the servant of the illustrious citizen follows her to her house, and that she prays for the eradication of sexual desires indicates to me that there is a degree of autonomy that she does not wish to renounce, and a monastic lifestyle that she wishes to continue unabated. Her presence at the church, praying loudly and weeping openly, her desire to fight desire—even chaste, marital bed, desire—speaks loudly about her wish for the continent, hermitic life. According to the text, God grants that request in the form of a bone-wracking fever, not for the sake of the soul but the sake of that which cannot inherit the kingdom of God. On one hand, the infertile woman, the woman with breast cancer and the snake-bitten disciple were brought before holy ascetics with members of their communities hoping that by their prayers the diseased might be transformed from carriers of disease and shame to carries of grace and, in the process, be reincorporated into the body of community; on the other, Barnabas, Abba Myrogenes, the beautiful young woman and the brother willingly welcome—even invite—ill health for a different type of transformative purpose in their lives. Either way, they participate in the economy of salvation through distinct and highly individualistic, non-liturgical processes that honor the fragile clay jars that house the treasures.[202]

---

[202] II Corinthians 4.7.

Chapter 4
Mortality in *The Meadow*: Dying, Death and Predetermination[1]

Introduction

Early Christian theological claims about death and dying were dramatically shaped by the literary and political culture in which they emerged. The gospel accounts offer a stunning portrayal of passive suffering punctuated only by the most minimal expressions of anguish on Jesus' part.[2] This anguish will also be transformed in martyr accounts that model dying resolve on the earlier tradition of the sacrifice of the noble mother and her seven sons by Antiochus, who later boasted of the admirable resolve of this family to his military as he encouraged them to emulate their fortitude.[3] Even with the possibility of persecution eliminated after Galerius' Edict of Toleration in 311, a stoic death remains the model for classically trained patristic theologians, whose orations assure the Christian that the soul of the righteous will find rest in what Ambrose regarded as "a good death."[4] Despite trials that great ascetics will have with demons in the desert, hagiographic accounts depict them—the new martyrs—dying with composure and joy, their battles with demons complete. The dying words of St Antony to his disciples, according to Athanasius, pinpoint the sources of death and the sole source of life: "You know the treacherous demons—you know how savage they are, even though weakened in strength. Therefore, do not fear them, but rather draw inspiration from Christ always, and trust in him. And live as though dying daily."[5] Dormition tales depicting Mary as the model of serene dying[6] arise at the end of the fourth century to counter anxiety of the shifting imperial boundaries and bodies. Although the Cappadocian fathers will present refined treatments

---

[1] Material for this fourth chapter is drawn from Brenda Llewellyn Ihssen, "Forewarned is Forearmed: Predetermination in John Moschos' *Pratum Spirituale*" (paper presented at the annual national meeting of the North American Patristics Society, Chicago, Illinois, 26 May 2012).
[2] Matthew 27.46, Mark 15.34, Luke 23.34–43, John 19.26–8.
[3] IV Maccabees 17.23.
[4] Ambrose, *De bono mortis*, 4.14–15 (CSEL 32/1.715–17), 5.16 (CSEL 32/1.717–19), 8.31–3 (CSEL 32/1.730–33).
[5] Athanasius, *Vita S. Antoni*, 91 (PG 26.969–70): in Gregg, *Athanasius*, 97.
[6] Brian E. Daley, S.J., "'At the Hour of Our Death': Mary's Dormition and Christian Dying in Late Patristic and Early Byzantine Literature," DOP, Vol. 55 (2001): 73.

on proper attitudes towards dying,[7] in all, a great deal gets written on a subject concerning which we ultimately know very little, yet remains the fundamental common experience of all humanity. But as consistent as death itself, what beneficial tales lack in refinement they make up for in creativity, and the careful historian can uncover remarkable nuances in the beliefs that existed even within groups that identified themselves as doctrinally orthodox. This is particularly true in the case of tales that address death, dying and the activity of the dead, which reflect, for the most part, the imprecise eschatology of Byzantine Christianity, for which the mystery of salvation in the death of Christ and deification in the body of Christ was a mystery worth respecting and therefore doctrinal formulations were not required.[8] In a limited way, Wortley writes, this particular quality of Byzantine Christianity left the individual "free to form his or her own opinions about death, judgment, heavenly rewards, and infernal punishments."[9]

What were those opinions? What can Moschos' beneficial tales tell us about how monks and those who interacted with them faced and interpreted death? That the hour of a predetermined death might be known, that the dead might be left to rest in peace, and that death might not end our relationships and our interactions with one another are all topics that occupy several memorable beneficial tales. The first part of this chapter will consider how particular details of repentance, sacraments and burial from these passages on the final hours of a proper orthodox[10] life suggest a theology of predetermination in the lives of desert ascetics; the second part will consider to what degree beneficial tales that address the location of monastic bodies provide evidence of tension between the monastic community and the solitary ascetic; and the final part will consider the activity of those who occupy the "middle state"[11] of the soul, neither alive nor absent. Common to all three sections is a theme of struggle, but not necessarily the struggle against death. Embracing—as one must when living so precariously— the belief that wrestling with the tension between life and death is a component of monastic life, to what degree do *Meadow* tales addressing death, burial, dead bodies and the middle state of souls reflect the aforementioned tension between the established monastery and the more autonomous desert ascetic? Is it possible

---

[7] Gregory Nazianzus, *Oration* 7.21, in Daley, "At the Hour of Our Death," DOP, 74.

[8] John Meyendorff, *Byzantine Theology: Historical Trends and Doctrinal Themes* (New York: Fordham University Press, 1979): 221–2.

[9] John Wortley, "Death, Judgment, Heaven, and Hell in Byzantine 'Beneficial Tales,'" DOP, Vol. 55 (2001): 53–69; 56.

[10] "Orthodox" here means a Christian identified with Chalcedonian theology. See the Introduction for the theological distinctions of the day, and their implications.

[11] This is a reference to Lucian's satire of funeral rites: "Those (dead) of the middle way in life, and they are many, wander about in the meadows without their bodies, in the form of shadows that vanish like smoke in your fingers." *On Mourning* 9, in Jeffrey A. Trumbower, *Rescue for the Dead: The Posthumous Salvation of Non-Christians in Early Christianity*, OSHT (Oxford University Press: 2001): 17.

that death itself might be the last field upon which monastic figures struggled for social agency?

Predetermination: Forewarned is Forearmed

In an early tenth-century church of Saint Simeon the Stylite at Zilve, a Cappadocian monk named after the famous stylite labored to construct his own grave. The epitaph left behind on the wall reads: "While I live I dig this burial cave; receive me, O tomb, as you have the Stylite."[12] Conversely, in the early twenty-first century, we labor to avoid not only death itself, but knowledge of its impending arrival. In a country that currently invests more than $88 billion per year in anti-aging treatments,[13] the notion of a monk preparing his own burial place, carving his own epitaph, makes little sense to those who treat aging as a disease. But in the early Byzantine era, rife with disease, poverty, famine, shifting populations, political instability and violence, death was less easily avoided than in our day of careful health management.[14] Consequently, what was not avoided—what was sought, in fact, by a monk—was clear knowledge of death's approach. That one would die was certain. It was best to be prepared. On the other hand, to be struck down without warning, without preparation, that made little sense. In fact, it rather violated a common task of a monk to meditate daily on his death, at least according to John Climacus: "As thought comes before speech, so the remembrance of death and of sin comes before weeping and mourning ... This, then, is the sixth step. He who has climbed it will never sin."[15] In his *Ladder of Divine Ascent*, St John Climacus writes that God conceals the knowledge of the hour of death from humanity in order to save it; were it not for this, people would spend their lives in the depths of sin and depravity, seeking baptism and tonsure only on the verge of their demise.[16] And yet a considerable number of spiritually beneficial

---

[12] Natalia B. Teteriantnikov, "Burial Places in Cappadocian Churches," GOTR, Vol. 29, No. 2 (1984): 141–74 (155); Guillaume de Jerphanion, *Une Nouvelle Province de L'art Byzantin: Les Eglises Rupestres de Cappadoce* (Paris: P. Geuthner, 1934): 570–80; Spiro Kostof, *Caves of God: the monastic environment of Byzantine Cappadocia* (Cambridge, MA: MIT Press, 1972): 48. Lyn Rodley, *Cave Monasteries of Byzantine Cappadocia* (Cambridge University Press): 192.

[13] Arlene Weintraub, *Selling the Fountain of Youth: How the Anti-Aging Industry Made a Disease Out of Getting Old—And Made Billions* (New York: Basic Books, 2010): 3, 13–14.

[14] Statistics vary over the life of the empire, but in general terms, only three categories of the Byzantine population lived in conditions that allowed them life beyond the fourth decade: imperial figures, scholars and ascetics. Alice-Mary Talbot, "Old Age in Byzantium," BZ, Vol. 77 (1984): 267–78 (269).

[15] John Climacus *Scala Paradisi* (PG 88.793–8); John Climacus, *The Ladder of Divine Ascent*, trans. Colm Luibheid and Norman Russell (New York: Paulist Press): 135.

[16] John Climacus, *Scala Paradisi* (PG 88.793).

tales depict dedicated ascetics operating in such a way that suggests that they have been provided with precise knowledge of the moment of their death, a typical indication of their holiness (and perhaps God's confidence in their holiness), and a standard topos of hagiographic material.[17] Consequently, this first section of death and dying passages in select beneficial tales from John Moschos' *Meadow* will consider how particular details of repentance, sacraments and burial from passages on the final hours of a proper orthodox life suggest a theology of predetermination, a theology that necessitates a degree of social agency for desert ascetics.

There are two details worth noting at the outset. First, the brevity of spiritually beneficial tales means that the author has precious little time to convince the audience of the holiness of the elder or ascetic, and thus predetermination might also be operating as a literary device that signals to the reader or audience either the orthodoxy of the ascetic or the desire on their part for social agency—or both.[18] It is also worth noting that the term "predetermination (προορισμός)" does not actually appear in the texts with which I am concerned.[19] At the heart of the question of predetermination are issues of knowledge and fate, or the reconciliation of God's sovereignty and activity in salvation with personal human freedom and agency.[20] Questions inevitably linked to predetermination usually begin with: Does God fix a limit to one's life, and, if so, can it be known?[21] Further, if the limits of one's life are fixed and can be known, then how is salvation—or damnation—freely chosen if this particular knowledge is accessible to the human mind? And while

---

[17] In addition to foreknowledge of death, traditional topoi include crowds of mourners—lay and religious alike—deathbed scenes, final speeches by the dying and so on. Dorothy Abrahamse, "Rituals of Death in the Middle Byzantine Period," GOTR, Vol. 29, No. 2 (1984): 125–34 (127). To be fair, saints are not the only ones who sense death; patients with no previous history of heart problems have consulted physicians before death due to "a premonition that something was going to happen." T.R. VanDellen, "Sudden Death ... Premonition of Things to Come," IMJ, Vol. 141, No. 4 (1973): 392.

[18] I am grateful to Philip Rousseau's comments on the role of the author and theological construction as literary device.

[19] In an email correspondence, John Wortley notes, "προορᾶν"—a problematic verb—occurs once in the *Apophthegmata Patrum systématique* [*APsys*]: "Προοπώμην τὸν Κύριον ἐνώπιόν μου διαπαντὸς ὅτι ἐκ δεξιῶν μού ἐστιν ἵνα μὴ σαλευθῶ;" "Je voyais le Seigneur devant moi sans cesse"; *Les Apophtegmes Des Pères: Collection Systematique Chapitres X–XIV*, trans. Jean-Claude Guy, S.J.; *Sources Chrétiennes* 474 (Paris, 2003): 11.51.30; 166–7. "I have set the Lord always before me; because he is at my right hand I shall not be moved [Ps 16.8]." *The Book of the Elders: Sayings of the Desert Fathers, The Systematic Collection*, trans. John Wortley (Collegeville, MN: Cistercian Publications, 2012): 200.

[20] Joseph A. Munitiz, "The Predetermination of Death: The Contribution of Anastasios of Sinai and Nikephoros Blemmydes to a Perennial Byzantine Problem," DOP, Vol. 55 (2001): 9–20 (10–11).

[21] Questions grow more complicated when one considers the state of sin or purity in which one finds oneself at the moment of death. The classic example from the New Testament is that of Judas (Luke 22.3–6, John 6.64, 70–71; 13.2, 18).

predetermination is often classified as a distinctly "western" problem—due to the identification of predetermination with predestination and its greatest champion, John Calvin—this is a theological problem that intrigued eastern writers as well. Christian scriptures do not help, for they provide a range of views about divine providence, from the hardening of Pharaoh's heart[22] to Jesus' lament that he is unable to gather the children of Jerusalem "together as a hen gathers her brood under her wings" for they were not willing.[23]

A range of responses towards the topic is also found among apostolic and patristic theologians. Unwilling to accept that God is arbitrary, Origen denies literal interpretation of "the Lord hardened Pharaoh's heart." With perfect justice, he writes, a single action by God produces different results, dependent on the character of the individual: "Thus the marvelous works done by God are as it were the rain, while the differing wills of men are like the tilled and neglected land, though as land they are both one nature."[24] This is developed as well by John of Damascus, who writes that ultimately all depends on the actions taken by humans, and "if some things appear to many to be unjust, it is because of the unknowability and incomprehensibility of God's providence."[25] What is dependent on the human is known by God, but not determined by God: "Thus, [God] foreknows the things that depend upon us, but [God] does not predestine them—because neither does [God] will evil to be done nor does [God] force virtue."[26] In short, by the end of the seventh century, eastern theologians place salvation in the hands of those who are free to choose or not choose, as is their

---

[22] Exodus 4.21; 7.3, 13; 9.12; 10.1, 20, 27; 11.10; 14.4, 8. See also Irenaeus, *Adv. Haer.* 4.45; Origen, *Princ.* 3.1.8–11; *Comm. Rom.* 7.16; *Hom. Exod.* 4.2; Gregory of Nyssa, *De via Moysis*, II.73–88. See note 20. John of Damascus, *Expos.* 2.29 (PG 94.963–70), in Andrew Louth, *St. John Damascene: Tradition and Originality in Byzantine Theology* (Oxford University Press, 2005): 142.

[23] Matthew 23.37.

[24] *Princ.* 3.1.9–10. col. 118., in W.J.P. Boyd, "Origen on Pharaoh's Hardened Heart: A Study of Justification and Election in St. Paul and Origen," StP, Vol. 7 (Berlin: Akademie-Verlag, 1966): 439.

[25] "Properly speaking, all those things depend upon us which pertain to the soul and about which we deliberate." John of Damascus, *Expos.* 2.26 (PG 94.957–60); see also *Disp. Sar.* (PG 96.1336–7).

[26] John of Damascus, *Expos.* 2.30 (PG 94.969–80): in *St. John of Damascus: Writings*, trans. Frederic H. Chase, Jr, FC (Catholic University of America, 1958): 263. Use of inclusive language is my doing. See also Maximos the Confessor, who distinguishes *prognosis* (foreknowledge) from *proorizmos* (predetermination or predestination); like Moschos, Maximos insists that God does not predetermine acts but only foreknows them. Maximos the Confessor, *Disputatio Inter Maximum Et Theodosium, Episcopum Caesareae Bithyniae* 3 (CPG 7735); *Maximos the Confessor, Dispute at Bizya* 3, in Pauline Allen and Bronwen Neil, *Maximos the Confessor and His Companions*, OECT (Oxford University Press, 2004): 77–87. I thank Dr Richard Steele for directing me to this reference.

wont,[27] a view distinct from an Augustinian conception of human freedom limited by a frail nature, which renders one incapable of refraining from sin, even if one wishes to do so.[28]

A helpful theologian for thinking about predetermination in the beneficial tales of *The Meadow* is the sixth-century Pseudo-Dionysius the Areopagite. According to Andrew Louth, "providence casts a long shadow over Denys's thought,"[29] a sign of the theologian's affinity with Neoplatonism, which distinguishes providence from "fate" by the concept of procession. Specifically for Dionysius, procession allows for the possibility of a recognition of shared nature—albeit quite indistinctly—between higher and lower beings,[30] which leads to knowledge acquired appropriate to the human station: "That is, through the knowledge we have, which is geared to our facilities, we may be uplifted as far as possible to the Cause of everything."[31] According to Louth, "as far as possible" means that the individual experiencing this "uplifting" is one with God's will for them;[32] put simply, divine and human will are in as harmonious a state as they can experience and fulfill the will of the other in that moment.

Dionysius' theology is both beautiful and terrifying, and I suggest that we encounter traces of this sophisticated theology in Moschos' *Meadow*, if only as conceptual agreement on a critical theological issue. The first tale to consider is "The Life and Death of an Elder Who Would Not Be Higoumen of the Lavra of the Towers." A tale of repentance and reluctance, it is so brief that I include it in its entirety:

> There was an elder dwelling at the Lavra of the Towers and when the higoumen died, the priests and other brethren at the lavra wanted to make him higoumen because of his great virtue. The elder begged them [not to], saying: "Let me rather go and weep for my sins, fathers, for I am no fit man to undertake the care of souls. This is a task for great fathers [such as] those who were with Abba Anthony and the others". The brethren, however, would not permit this. Each day they came begging him [to accept], but he would not. When he saw that they were determined to make him change his mind, he said to them all: "Give me

---

[27] Andrew Louth, *St. John Damascene: Tradition and Originality in Byzantine Theology* (Oxford University Press: 2002): 140–44.

[28] Augustine, *On Man's Perfection in Righteousness*, 1; 2.3.

[29] Andrew Louth, *Denys the Areopagite* (Westport, CT: Continuum, 2002): 93.

[30] Ibid.

[31] Dionysius the Areopagite, *The Divine Names*, V.9.825A (PG 3.823–6); Pseudo-Dionysius, *The Complete Works*, trans. Colm Luibheid and Paul Rorem (New York: Paulist Press, 1987): 102.

[32] Louth, *Denys the Areopagite*, 94.

three days for prayer and I shall do whatever God wills[33] of me". This was on a Friday: He died on the Sunday morning.[34]

Anyone who has ever unwillingly assumed a leadership position that they truly did not want probably hears this tale with no little amusement; the elder prefers *death* to a position to which he does not believe that he is legitimately called by God. It is, of course, customary for a holy person initially to refuse leadership; this demonstrates humility and, subsequently, endears the community of followers to them. St Antony repeatedly turned away those who attempted to attend to his needs while engaged in the spiritual warfare of the desert.[35] As well, Cyril of Scythopolis writes of Euthymius that he "did not want to make his place a cenobitic house or even a laura; when people came to him wishing to renounce the world, he would send them to the blessed Theoctistus in the monastery below."[36] Eventually, however, the holy person is pressed into a service at which they naturally excel. Not our *Meadow* elder. Rather than honor their press for his leadership, he maintains the virtue of humility that they so value and admire, "the quality held in highest esteem by the Desert Fathers," Wortley writes, "the very foundation on which all else rested."[37]

Although the tale is characteristically bereft of detail, Moschos presents for his audience an example of an elder fully determined to deny himself (and them!), an elder aware of and in alignment with whatever God wills for him; further, what God wills for the elder—likewise what the elder wills for himself—is expressed in the perfect knowledge that death provides an opportunity to maintain his autonomy, here identified as "whatever God wills of me."[38] Though neither acknowledged as saintly nor even named, this discerning elder's humility in the face of those determined to elevate him is the key to his salvation from their insistence on his authority, and his subsequent death affirms his orthodoxy by demonstrating his alignment with God's will. Was it predetermined that the elder would *not* be the leader of this community? The tale suggests that he dies precisely because he is aware that this is not to be, that he is not predetermined to join ranks in a company that includes the great Abba Antony.

With respect to predetermination and sacraments, I highlight a tale told to Moschos by a monk who visited the monastery of Abba Theodosius, regarding the relationship between the monastery and an anchorite:

---

[33] I prefer "wills" rather than "requires," because θέλει (from τό θέλημα) also includes in its definition a "faculty of will," or the "act of willing."

[34] *Prat. sp.* 7 (PG 87.2857); Wortley, *Spiritual Meadow*, 8.

[35] Athanasius, *Vita S. Antonii* (PG 26.835–976), in Gregg, *Athanasius*, 98.

[36] 16.25,15. Cyril of Scythopolis, *Life of Our Father Saint Euthymius*, in *Lives of the Monks of Palestine. Kyrillos von Skythopolis*, trans. Eduard Schwartz (Leipzig, 1939), 21.

[37] Wortley, "What the Desert Fathers meant," 322–43 (295).

[38] "καὶ εἴ τι θέλει ὁ Θεὸς ποιῆσαι ἔχω," *Prat. sp.* 7 (PG 87.2857).

112   John Moschos' Spiritual Meadow

> On the holy Lord's Day [an anchorite] would come and partake of the holy mysteries. On one occasion [he] came and something offended him; so, for five weeks he did not make his customary appearance at the monastery—which saddened those who lived there. Then ... he came one Sunday and the fathers ... rejoiced at the sight of him. They made an act of obeisance[39] before him and he did likewise to them—and thus there was peace between them. He partook of the holy body and blood of our Lord Jesus Christ, placed himself in the midst of the church and promptly died, without knowing a moment's illness[40]... the fathers of the monastery realised that the anchorite had known of his impending death. It was because of this that he had come, so that he would not have anything against anybody when he went to the Lord.[41]

As in the previous tale, despite the paucity of detail the audience still manages to learn a great deal: first, something offends our ascetic in a monastery to which he is linked solely through the sacrament.[42] What or who offends him is not clear; what is clear is that whatever or whoever offends him is considerably less important than the fact that he was offended at all. Second, those who live in the monastery are saddened when the ascetic fails to appear and rejoice when they see him, so we know that he is beloved by them and considered part of the body of believers.[43] Third, both parties recognize the importance of humility ("ταπεινοφροσύνη") before one another in the face of offense, a factor that appears to have been given greater weight than blame, explanation and apology, none of which are even addressed as prerequisites before unity is restored. Fourth, when peace is restored, the sacrament is taken. Finally, reconciliation with the body *of* Christ (the community) and the body *in* Christ (the community in the act of the sacrament) achieved through humility of all parties, our ascetic "promptly died, without knowing a moment's illness."[44] Our grazer might not have known "a moment's illness,"[45] but he knew something, and I would argue that the progression of events once he returns to the community suggests a model of the end of a proper, orthodox life, in which one can catch a glimpse of the will of the individual in alignment with the activity of providence. The condition into which the grazer and the community had fallen might be accurately defined

---

[39] "*prostratique*" (Ltn); "ἔβαλον," (Gr.); quite plainly, "threw themselves down."

[40] Dying "without knowing a moment's illness" does not mean that he was not ill; in the hard life of the professional desert ascetic, bodily discomfort and illnesses were recognized, interpreted and experienced in multiple ways, but most often as something that was known in a completely different way than common folk would know. See Chapter 3.

[41] *Prat. sp.* 86 (PG 87.2944); Wortley, *Spiritual Meadow*, 69–70.

[42] "καὶ ἤρχετο κατὰ ἁγίαν Κυριανκῇω, καὶ μετελάμβανεν τῶν ἁγίων μυστηρίων." *Prat. sp.* 86 (PG 87.2944); grazers did not live independent of community or one another. See Chapter 2.

[43] *Prat. sp.* 86 (PG 87.2944).

[44] "καὶ εὐθὺς ἐτελειώθη, μὴ ἀσθενήσας τὸ σύνολον," ibid.

[45] Ibid.

as a state of schism, which by virtue of its brokenness could only be considered unnatural; once this was restored to its proper and natural state of unity, which culminated in participation in the Eucharist, the grazer—having aligned his will with God's will by providing the opportunity for the community to experience true peace—dies. His reward? Not "a moment's illness."[46] While the grazer acted out of free will, his actions were in accordance with and in alignment with the will of the "Preexistent," which, Dionysius' claims, "is the Source and the end of all things."[47] The grazer's action of returning to the community so that right relations could be restored through humility meant that the sacrament was observed properly. Because they had made peace through humility, none of them partook in an unworthy manner and thus did not eat and drink in judgment against themselves,[48] a fact that the fathers of the monastery recognize: "that the anchorite had known of his death, and on account of this he came, in order that he not have anything against [anybody] when he to the Lord."[49] By acquiescing to the needs of the community and by denying himself, he allowed the community the opportunity to exist—at least briefly—as an earthly image of the prototype of worship in the divine realm, an icon of the multitude before the throne.[50] It is worth noting that this is supported in John of Damascus' *Against Those Who Attack the Divine Images*; referencing Dionysius, he writes that

> [t]here are also in God images and paradigms of what [God] is going to bring about, that is [God's] will that is before eternity and thus eternal. For the divine is in every respect unchanging, and there is in it no change or shadow of turning. Saint Dionysius, who had great insight in matters divine, what belongs to God and what may be said about God, says that these are images and paradigms and predeterminations. For in [God's] will everything is predetermined by [God], that will unfailingly come to pass, is designated and depicted before it comes to be, just as, if one wants to build a house, its form is described and depicted first in mind.[51]

---

[46] Ibid.

[47] Dionysius the Areopagite, *The Divine Names*, V.10.825B (PG 3.825–6); Rorem, 102.

[48] I Cor 11.27–9.

[49] "Ἔγνῳσαν οὖν οἱ Πατέρες τοῦ μοναστηρίου, ὅτι προέγνω τὴν τελευτὴν αὐτοῦ ὁ ἀναχωρητὴς, καὶ διά τοῦτε ἦλθεν, ἵνα μὴ ἔχων κατά τινος, ἀπέλθῃ πρὸς Κύριον." *Prat. sp.* 86 (PG 87.2944).

[50] Revelation 7.9.

[51] John of Damascus, *First Apology Against Those Who Attack the Divine Images* 1.10, *Die Schriften des Johannes von Damaskos* (Berlin: de Gruyter, 1969–88): 84) in *St. John of Damascus On the Divine Images*, trans. David Anderson and Andrew Louth (Crestwood, NY: St Vladimir's Seminary Press, 2003): 25–6. Alteration of the masculine pronoun to "God" or "God's" is my doing.

But like the icon of which John writes, the ideal earthly community is ephemeral, a shadow of a more true reality that exists in the cosmic realm. Perhaps the closest that one might come to the true reality is within the context of the communing body, and that might look in one tale like a cenobitic environment free from strife, or it might be the accomplishment of the sacrament itself, as a cap on an ascetic life that moves with success towards perfection. In this latter case, a second, slightly longer beneficial tale that demonstrates knowledge of death connected to sacraments is found in an account of Abba Gregory, who lived also as a grazer in the mountains near the monastery of Abba Theodosius with his disciple. When his disciple died, the abba, owning nothing, was required to descend from the mountain to enlist help to bury the body. One of the sailors who helped him—Thalilaios—remained as his new disciple. After three years and six months living successfully as a grazer, Thalilaios begged the elder to take him to Jerusalem to venerate the holy sites because he "knew beforehand"[52] of his death. They worshipped in Jerusalem, they were baptized in the Jordan River and three days later Thalilaios died.

The final passage considered concerns predetermination and the burial of a body. This theme of burial is very rich, with multiple tales that support predetermination.[53] However, the one I wish to highlight is *Meadow* tale 123.[54] In his youth, Abba Zosimos traveled to "Ἀμμωνιακήν"; while staying in a cell he met an elder who, rather than greeting him, identifies Zosimos by name, aggressively questions his reasons for being there and informs him that he cannot stay. Puzzled, Zosimos throws himself down[55] before him, which only causes the elder to verbally abuse him, fall silent and walk away. After hours in prayer, the elder returns, kisses Zosimos, and informs him that "'Naturally, child, you are welcome. For God brought you here in order for you to bury my body.'… And with that," Zosimos relates, "the servant of the Lord lay down and fell asleep, and I dug a grave for him and buried him, and after two days I departed, glorifying God."[56]

This is one of the more interesting of *The Meadow* tales because this poor elder does not represent the average righteous ascetic in possession of the knowledge of his death. Rather than embrace this knowledge with perfect *apatheia* or even gentle resistance, the elder resists by trying to chase off the omen of his looming demise, a man innocent of the significance of his own arrival and therefore puzzled by the odd reception he receives. "A perfect sense of death is free from fear,"[57] John Climacus writes, and I do not think that what we have in this text is a perfect sense of death. I believe that this elder is fearful and resentful, and his desire to restrain the

---

[52] "προέγνω," *Prat. sp.* 91 (PG 87.2947–50).

[53] See, for example, *Prat. sp..* 84 (PG 87. 2941–2); *Prat. sp.* 90 (PG 87.2947–8); *Prat. sp.* 93 (PG 87.2951–2); *Prat. sp.* 170 (PG 87.3035–8).

[54] *Prat. sp.* 123 (PG 87.2935).

[55] "*prostravi*" (Ltn); "βάλλω," (Gk).

[56] "καὶ ταῦτα εἰπὼν ἔθηκεν ἑατὸν, καὶ ἀνεπαύσατο ὁ δοῦλος τοῦ Θεοῦ. Ἐγὼ δὲ ὀρύξας ἔθαφα αὐτὸν, καὶ μετὰ δύο ἡμέρας ἀνεχώρησα δοξάζων τὸν Θεόν." *Prat. sp.* 123 (PG 87.2935).

[57] John Climacus, *Scala Paradisi* 6 (PG 88.796); Luibheid and Russell, 133.

inevitable, his outburst, his silent reflection and peaceful reconciliation are all that makes this tale one of the more endearing accounts. It is a touching reminder of the human frailty of even the hardiest desert ascetic who—like all of us—does not wish to yield to that which age demands. Although the elder is not dying *at that moment*, his initial resistance and then acceptance of the predetermined will of God for the end of his life and in a manner that curbs his independence suggests a struggle of the soul, a bitterly painful type of deathbed scene that could be considered his "most dangerous hour."[58] In their study of rural Greek peasantry, anthropologists Richard and Eva Maria Blum discovered that the inevitability of death prompted fatalistic behaviors that greatly varied: some—like the elder and the grazer—either willingly or passively accepted their situation; others—like the Ἀμμωνιακ elder—attempted to forestall the inevitable.[59] I mention this study because it reveals a particular truism for twentieth-century Greece as well as seventh-century Palestine: death is mysterious and frightening, and one's particular degree of sanctity does not and can not sanitize it. Further, I suggest that this particular tale affirms the aforementioned delightful variety that one encounters among beneficial tales that address death and dying,[60] a variety that highlights their appeal to common sentiments.

Despite his process it is clear that the Ἀμμωνιακ elder has been granted this knowledge because he has met the criteria of right belief, for when answering Zosimos' inquiry regarding how many years he has been there with a reply that will link this ascetic to the death of nearly every saint, Zosimos notes that "it appeared to me as if his face were of fire."[61] Zosimos' vision is not unprecedented. Well rooted in Athanasius' account of the death of Antony the Great, whose face as he lay dying "seemed bright"[62] to his disciples, this topos will—like foreknowledge of death—accompany the deaths of many saints.[63]

---

[58] Abrahamse, *"Rituals of Death,"* 128.

[59] Richard H. Blum and Eva Maria Blum, *The Dangerous Hour: The Lore of Crisis and Mystery in Rural Greece* (New York: Scribner, 1970): 313. Worth noting is a Byzantine service to ease a dying person: "Order for letting the soul break loose." D. Placido de Meester, *Liturgia Bizantina*, ii, *Part* vi: *Rituale-Benedizionale Bizantino* (Rome, 1929): 74, in Paul Fedwick, "Death and Dying in Byzantine Liturgical Traditions," *Eastern Churches Review*, Vol. 8, No. 2 (1976): 153.

[60] Wortley, "Death, Judgment, Heaven, and Hell," 56. In another tale, while carrying a dead brother's items to storage, a steward weeps. Asked why, he says, "after two days others [shall carry] mine" ("καὶ μετὰ δύο ἡμέρας ἄλλοι τὰ ἐμά"), which proves true. *Prat. sp.* 5 (PG 87.2857).

[61] "καὶ ἐφάνη μοι τὸ πρόσωπον αὐτοῦ ὡς πῦρ." *Prat. sp.* 123 (PG 87.2935).

[62] Athanasius, *Vita S. Antonii* 92 (PG 26.971–2); Gregg, *Athanasius*, 98; referencing St Antony; see "Sisoes, 14," (PG 65.395B) in *Apalph*, in Ward, *Sayings of the Desert Fathers*, 214–15. One of the accounts of St Simeon the Stylite reports that one full day after dying his face was "bright, completely like light;" *Life and Daily Mode of Living of Blessed Simeon*, 29.6–8, in H. Lietzmann, *Das Leben des heiligen Symeon Stylites*, in Doran, *Lives of Simeon Stylites*, 98.

[63] Abba Pambo's face was like "lightning," Abba Silvanus' whole body and face would shine angelically, and Arsenius—like Zosimos—was seen by a brother to be entirely

But these few topoi aside, spiritually beneficial tales in general and Moschos' *Meadow* in particular are *not* accompanied by traditional evidence of a holy life that one finds in the lives of saints, primarily by virtue of their brevity. What can the historian do in the absence of detail? Can history be found? I suggest that history is found in the absence. I suggest that the anonymity of the elders and abbas who die in these tales, the absence of crowds that do not stream to the bedside of the dying ascetic, the absence of funeral processions, laments, grieving brothers and sisters, laity fighting over body parts, hair and clothing and sometimes the complete absence not only of tombs but also of bodies, are closer to the reality of death in the desert and death in community that the common monks experienced. Further, they are a testament to the success of the ascetics to live a life of humility, right belief and relative anonymity, for unlike saintly superstars of lengthier hagiography, these humble figures live out the doctrine of orthodox Christianity in a life sometimes defined only by a few simple lines about their death. In this, the historian can be reasonably sure that spiritually beneficial tales are able to provide something distinct from traditional topoi of the saints' lives.

Orthodox Christians are not the only ones dying in Moschos' *Meadow*, and a few tales remain to affirm that there are implications for dying outside of the limits of the faith. One heretic, for example, is featured in an account that has him dying head-down in the toilet.[64] The death of a heretic implicates not only their body and their memory, but the space where they die as well. Confirmation of the sanctity of space occupied by a holy person is seen in reverse in tale 177.[65] The tale, not much longer than the title, concludes with a poor Egyptian monk found having strangled himself after inhabiting the cell where Evagrios had been led astray by a demon who reportedly lived there.

To conclude, although these three accounts suggest predetermination through sacramental activity, the priority of repentance or the reality of burial, they hold two pieces in common: there is a clearly predetermined death and this death is linked to the relationship of two important parties. One party is either a solitary desert ascetic or a somewhat independent elder, the charismatic figure who carries authority in a way that is recognized as unconstrained by the community. The second party is a member, or members, of a monastic institution; in this case, he or they represent institutional authority, even if they are not necessarily the hegumen. Both parties are required in order for the tale to be told. Both parties also appear to be wrangling for some degree of control over their circumstances, and in each case the answer to the question "Who is in charge?" remains unclear. One elder dies before allowing a community to elevate him; another capitulates to the group's need for his physical presence; and a third struggles with the arrival of the representative of an exterior institution, clearly one charged with bringing

---

aflame. *Apophthegmata Patrum Alphabetikon* 12 (PG 65.372A), 12 (PG 65.411C) and 27 (PG 65.80D), respectively.

[64] *Prat. sp.* 43 (PG 87. 2896–8).

[65] *Prat. sp.* 177 (PG 87.3048).

his autonomous ways to an end. And so I close with a question that will guide the analysis of Moschos' beneficial tales in the following two sections of this chapter: could death be another field upon which the struggle between charismatic and institutional authority works itself out? If the moment of death expresses the very limit of power, the most private and personal expression of being,[66] does a theology of predetermination in the *Meadow* tales suggest a challenge to the dominant paradigm of control in the monastic world?[67] These are not holy men who function as a locus of power or a rural patron of a community that depends on them for wisdom and strength. Largely unknown and anonymous in the desert, they carry little Christian collective memory, facilitate nothing in the realms of religious or political change,[68] and what little they say is rarely poetic. Max Weber would be disappointed by these ascetics, whose disciples often number no more than one, and who, after burying their beloved elder, merely lie down and die.[69] And, while evading administrative authority, pressure for the distribution of the sacrament or controlling the location of peripatetic monks is sometimes beyond the control of a desert elder, forearmed with foreknowledge of God's intention and will, lying down and dying is not.

Conflict and the Corpse

In his extensive work on the subject of asceticism, Richard Valantasis has constructed several typologies,[70] two of which are useful for thinking about death and dying as a topic that offers evidence that monastic figures might be concerned with social agency. The first is identified as the "combative subject."[71] Typified in the figure of St Antony the Great, the combative subject engages in ascetic trials

---

[66] Michel Foucault, *The History of Sexuality, Volume I: An Introduction*, trans. Robert Hurley (New York: Random House, 1980): 138.

[67] David Brakke, *Athanasius and Asceticism* (Baltimore, MD: Johns Hopkins University Press, 1995): 245ff.; David Brakke, "Shenoute, Weber, and the Monastic Prophet: Ancient and Modern Articulations of Ascetic Authority," in A. Camplani and G. Filoram (eds), *Foundations of Power and Conflicts of Authority in Late-Antique Monasticism*, OLA 157 (Leuven: Uitgeverij Peeters, 2007): 47.

[68] Peter Brown, "The Rise and Function of the Holy Man in Late Antiquity," JRS, Vol. 61 (1971): 80–101. Peter Brown, "The Saint as Exemplar in Late Antiquity," *Representations*, No. 2 (1983): 1–25. Peter Brown, "Arbiters of the Holy: The Christian Holy Man in Late Antiquity," *Authority and the Sacred: Aspects of the Christianisation of the Roman World* (Cambridge University Press, 1995): 57–78.

[69] Max Weber, *The Sociology of Religion*, trans. Ephraim Fischoff (Boston, MA: Beacon Press, 1963): 78–9.

[70] Valantasis' additional typologies are the "educative model" and the "pilgrim." Valantasis, "Constructions of Power," 803–4.

[71] Ibid.: 802–3.

and, in the process of moving from one identity to another, becomes a powerful individual largely due to the fact that their transformation includes spiritual warfare or demonic battles.[72] Not all ascetics emerge with titles such as "St" or "the Great," nor do they become great miracle workers, but I would point out that in the process of redefining the "self" the combative subject does emerge—like Antony—as self-governing, which may be perceived as threatening to systems that are suspicious of individuals venturing out to do spiritual combat armed only with lentils, or those whose ascetic endeavors seek to move beyond the expectations of group.[73] Although ascetics who adapt combative models are rarely concerned with the transformation of identity beyond their own, nevertheless they threaten to redefine for larger bodies to what expectations the group might be held (either collectively or individually), and thus they are potentially divisive figures. The second type of model that Valantasis proposes is the "integrative" subject, in which the subject—through ascetic activity—is transformed *within* the system. Unlike that of the "combative subject," the activity of the "integrative subject" fosters "a transformation or enlightenment that enhances and enriches the subject's life within the dominant culture."[74] According to Valantasis, the integrative model presents a lengthier process, and does not require a conflict between the new and old identities so much as a gradual transformation.[75] I would contend that the potential for conflict is introduced when a figure of authority or community attempts to impose an integrative model on an individual who wishes to be transformed and shaped by the combative model, reflecting the unresolved variance between a stationary ecclesiastical hierarchy in the figure of an abbot, and a charismatic figure in the form of an anchorite, who exists beyond the boundaries of the monastery. This conflict can even be witnessed when the anchorite has passed.

To return to the conflicts identified above—evading administrative authority, capitulation to pressure for distribution of the sacrament, population control around peripatetic monks—I would make the case that if an individual is acting in compliance with God's foreknown will, dying is not unreasonable, and die they did. Disciples, dedicated to the care of their teachers, were subsequently left with bodies to bury, then either die themselves or depart. This portion of the chapter will continue to address to what degree Moschos' beneficial tales provide evidence of tension between the monastic community and the solitary figure, and will conclude by asking how Valantasis' models might assist us in an analysis of anchorite/abbot tension. In these cases, the anchorites are dead.

Through death Christianity revealed itself to the Roman Empire. In the tradition of the gospel claim regarding the disciples' continued relationship with

---

[72] Ibid.: 802.

[73] Simeon the Stylite is expelled when he deviates from monastery rule with ascetic endeavors that repulse the community. *The Life & Daily Mode of Living of the Blessed Simeon the Stylite by Antonios*, 6–9, in Doran, *The Lives of Simeon Stylites*, 89–91.

[74] Valantasis, "Constructions of Power," 803.

[75] Ibid.

Jesus beyond death,[76] Christian belief in bodily resurrection and the additional inherited Roman refusal to release active relationship with those who died[77] forced the issue theologically. The desire to bury the dead in the manner of Jesus' burial forced the issue socially,[78] while architecturally the Christian dead made themselves known through localized funerary monuments, chapels and churches.[79] In a return to a less expensive, more ancient and traditional method of burial practice of interment,[80] Christian inhumation meant that the dead moved in; in doing so, they claimed space for the religion and were themselves claimed by the space. In the colonization of Roman public and private space by the Christian dead, Christian churches functioned first as sites of localized cults of the martyred dead—"martyries,"—and second, as Christianity grew in size and organization, as sites of worship and administration. In monasteries, as well, the dead played an important role in the life of a community for they contributed to the esteem of a monastery as a spiritual center or pilgrimage site. The body of a dead anchorite or holy person was a sacred object infused with *energia* which continued to inhere in the mortal remains of the deceased. In the network of sanctity any church or monastery that shared and participated in the protection of that which had cooperated in the sanctifying graces of God (which do not themselves die) was honored and esteemed by virtue of possession of that body, as easily as the esteem of a renowned spiritual father conferred esteem on their disciple.

Therefore it makes sense, when we encounter tales that stress the desire of monasteries to control the location of bodies of dead anchorites, to "integrate" them into their own environment. For example, a grazer died in a small cave and no one knew, having imagined that he had left the area. Abba Julian, however, was told in a dream by the dead anchorite to gather some men "to take me from the place where I am sleeping, on the landmark called The Deer."[81] The abba

---

[76] Matthew, 28.9ff.; Mark 16.9ff.; Luke 24.13ff.; John 20.11ff.

[77] According to Harlow and Laurence, one was not born into a family, but into a structure of ancestry associated with a particular site. Mary Harlow and Ray Laurence, *Growing Up and Growing Old in Ancient Rome: A Life Course Approach* (London: Routledge, 2002): 133.

[78] Acts 5.6; 5.10; 8.2.

[79] Jon Davies, *Death, Burial and Rebirth in the Religions of Antiquity* (London: Routledge, 1999): 193.

[80] Cicero (*De leg.* Ii, 22, 56) and Pliny (*Hist. Nat.* vii, 187). Interment provided for the needs of the soul and body *post mortem* and was simpler, at least in the case of the poor. Alfred Rush, *Death and Burial in Christian Antiquity* (Catholic University of America Press, 1941): 236–73; J.M.C. Toynbee, *Death and Burial in the Roman World* (Cornell University Press, 1971): 39; Ian Morris, *Death-Ritual And Social Structure in Classical Antiquity* (Cambridge University Press, 1992): 31–69; Caroline Walker Bynum, *The Resurrection of the Body in Western Christianity, 200–1336* (Columbia University Press, 1995): 51–8.

[81] "Δάβε τινὰς, καὶ δεῦπρ ἔπαρον με ἐκ τοῦ τόπου ὅπου καῖμαι, εἰς τὸ ὄρος τὸ λεγόμενον ἡ Ἔλαφος," *Prat. Sp.* 84 (PG 87.2941).

complied, but after looking for many hours could not find the body. Just as he was about to depart, a deer appeared and indicated with her hoof the site of the body. Found intact, the body of the grazer was carried to the monastery and buried. Did the grazer—a man who lived without communication for so long and so well that he successfully evaded attention even beyond the grave—desire integration into the community such that he made himself known through a vision and miracle, or does this tale successfully create that opportunity for relationship and integration on behalf of Abba Julian? Clearly the grazer was beyond contact, care and control of the community, and had accomplished this so well that not only did no one know that he died there, they did not even know that he had been living there. Abba Julian wields physical power over the corpse, which he forces into relationship with him. The corpse, on the other hand, is itself powerless to object to its removal or burial, and even points the way. According to Foucault, power is a relationship that creates types of subjects;[82] such power may be violent, oppressive, fearful or pastoral,[83] to which subjects respond. Regardless of the type of power, intrinsic to the relationship that power creates is the possibility of resistance to that power. In relation to our study of beneficial tales, it is not uncommon for the dead in hagiography to assert their power when they resist attempts to move them. But the grazer—being dead—is unable to offer any resistance. With forced reintegration into community, power is integrated over him through the figure of Abba Julian, who presumably relates this tale to the fathers of the monastery, who tell the tale, in turn, to John and Sophronios.

In addition to integration back into the community and forced relationship over an anchorite, pride in the acquisition of a body is transparent when John and Sophronios are visiting two elders who live together on an estate. They are shown some gravestones, and the elders announce: "In this tomb, Christians, lies a great anchorite."[84] When asked how the elders knew, they relate that seven years previously they were continuously beckoned to the summit of the mountain by a mysterious light. Exploration of the area provided no evidence of an actual fire, and yet for months the light burned. Finally, one evening they went up with a posse and stayed until the dawn light revealed the entrance of a cave, in which they found the body of the anchorite John the Humble. A hand-written sign with time of death indicated his name and that he had been dead for about seven years, and yet the body was in such a condition that it appeared he had died only just that day. He was carried down and buried in the church on the estate. The appropriation of the corpse of John the Humble is only one of several interesting elements in this brief tale. First, the monastic couple are living on a fairly remote estate, on the property

---

[82] Michel Foucault, "The Subject and Power," in Hubert L. Dreyfes and Paul Rabinow (eds), *Michel Foucault: Beyond Structuralism and Hermeneutics* (University of Chicago Press, 1983): 212.

[83] Ibid.: 213–16.

[84] "Ἐν τούτο τῷ μνημείῳ, Χριστιανοί, μέγας αναχωρητὴς κεῖται." *Prat. sp.* 87 (PG 87.2943–4).

of which is their own church, which reminds us of the diversity of monastic practices. Second, like the hunt for the grazer on the hill, a great deal of effort, time and labor goes into locating the source of the light. Third, in the process of the hunt for the source—again like the tale of the grazer—miraculous activity has a role to play, in this case a light rather than an animal. Finally, there is no discussion about the suitability of removing the body; he is removed and buried in their church. Unlike Abba Julian, this anchorite does not appeal to the elders to be found, and so the suitability of their integration of the body could be questioned. And yet the tale provides the argument in anticipation of any necessary defense, that the light is the divine communication of the dead to the living, evidence that John the Humble wishes them to find him and integrate him into their environment. Historically, a body or even a relic is not going to go where the will of God or the will of the saint does not allow.[85] The tomb is shown to John and Sophronios in what appears to be a natural element of monastic hospitality ("Here is our body"), which Peter Brown might identify as the "privatization of the holy," one way in which the influential layperson could claim a martyr (or in this case an anchorite) "and so bring the holy grave, either directly or by implication, out of the Christian community as a whole into the orbit of a single family."[86] In similar fashion, by bringing the body of the anchorite into the possession of the monastery or the elder's estate, the monastic community operates as the influential layperson who claims control over the care of a martyr who—along with other dead holy persons—is believed on a popular level to remain connected in some way to the site or shrine in which they are housed.[87]

Integrative control and care that a monastic community might provide for the body of an anchorite is seen as a marker of authority for that site and, one can assume, for the abba. That they might be entrusted to the care of their spiritual "kin" demonstrates their devotion to the body of Christ, and marks the site as holy.[88] Further, the social value of the site is enhanced by active association with

---

[85] In earlier ages, Delehaye writes, the translation of objects associated with heroes was most often accompanied by divine approval or command. Hippolyte Delehaye, *Les légendes hagiographiques* (Bruxelles: Société des Bollandistes, 1927): 154. See also Pierre Saintyves, *Les Saints, Successeurs Des Dieux* (Paris: E. Nourry, 1907): 41–3. One of the most colorful examples is that of St Nicholas, who berated his "liberators" for not acting more quickly on his behalf: "Why are you so slothful in performing your duty? It is my will that I leave here with you." Nicephorus, "The Translation of Saint Nicholas, Confessor," in *Saint Nicholas of Myra, Bari, and Manhattan: Biography of a Legend* (University of Chicago Press, 1978): 180.

[86] Peter Brown, *The Cult of the Saints: Its Rise and Function in Late Antiquity* (University of Chicago Press, 1981): 34.

[87] Stephen Wilson, "Introduction," in Stephen Wilson (ed.), *Saints and Their Cults: Studies in Religious Sociology, Folklore and History* (Cambridge University Press, 1983): 11.

[88] Patrick Geary, "Sacred Commodities: the Circulation of Medieval Relics," in Arjun Appadurai (ed.), *The Social Life of Things: Commodities in Cultural Perspective* (Cambridge University Press, 1986): 176.

the memory of the dead. But it also diminishes the combative authority of the body of the individual anchorite, and shifts the social location of power from the inner reality of their own private authority to the outer realities constructed by the cenobite, whose life is constructed alongside a dominant society whose authority remains above them. When John and Sophronios visit with the archimandrite of their own monastery of St Theodosios, they are told that while Abba George was in the process of building a church at Phasaelis, an anchorite appeared to him in his dream and inquired gently, "Abba George, did it seem just to you, sir, after so many labors and so much training, to leave me out of the church you are building?"[89] When Abba George awoke he enlarged the plan of the building, and in doing so unearthed the body, which was later interred in the right-hand aisle, complete with a "beautiful monument."[90] Again, is a solitary—an individual who has dedicated their living and dying to the practice of negation and humility to the extent that they live, die and are buried in a completely anonymous fashion—anxious about reintegration into the very community they endeavored greatly to avoid? Or, does the construction of the church and the subsequent unearthing of a body provide the opportunity to bring a self-governing figure into line? I suspect that the account betrays Abba George's desire to enhance the prestige of the space[91] under his charge and bring a "combative" anchorite into compliance with the group.

That an anchorite might successfully evade integration into community after death is borne out by a previously noted beneficial tale.[92] When the elder anchorite died, his disciple buried him, then descended the mountain and found a farmer who agreed to assist him. While the disciple stood in prayer,[93] the farmer unearthed the elder, after which the disciple stepped into the grave, lay down on the body, embraced his elder and "surrendered his soul."[94] The farmer filled in the grave and descended the mountain, and although he returned to the site to get a blessing from "the holy ones,"[95] he could not find evidence of a grave. Worth noting first is that the farmer was going to return to get a blessing from two dead men, which indicates either that he was planning to unearth the grave a second time or merely

---

[89] "Εἰπὲ, κῦρι ἀββα Γεώργιε, ἁπλῶς ἐδοξέν σοι μετὰ τοσούτους κόπους καὶ τοσαύτην ἄσκησιν ἔξω με ἐασαι οὗ κτίζεις ναου;" *Prat. sp.* 92 (PG 87. 2949–50).

[90] "μνημεῖον κάλλιστον," *Prat. sp.* 92 (PG 87.2951–2).

[91] Wilson, *Saints and Their Cults*, 28.

[92] *Prat. sp.* 90 (PG 87.2947–48).

[93] Davies claims "[w]e have no 'formal' Christian burial liturgy until about the year 900, though there are pieces of one in various forms." Davies, *Death, Burial and Rebirth*, 191.That there are no forms of liturgy performed for those buried possibly indicates either the absence of a liturgical tradition within the context of the death of an ascetic or to the brevity of the beneficial tale. Although the oldest Byzantine funeral witness to a funeral rite is dated to the eighth century, nevertheless elements of the rite speak to an ancient origin, and prayers for the dead are deeply embedded in Eucharistic prayer; to what degree such prayers would be readily on the lips of the disciple of a grazer, we cannot know.

[94] "καὶ παρέδωκεν τὴν ψυχήν," *Prat. sp.* 90 (PG 87.2947–8).

[95] "τῶν ἁγίων," ibid.

communicate through prayer. This is a good reminder of close relationships between laity and monastics: this farmer knew nothing of these two other than that they were dead, but the efficiency of their blessing is unquestioned. However he intended to get a blessing, he was not able to accomplish his purpose because he could not find where he had buried them. Although this man is but a peasant and does not represent a community of monastics, nevertheless his failure to find the site is no slight on his intelligence or spiritual life. Instead, it is affirmation that the bodies of the anchorite and his disciple are to be abandoned to the earth; they are not to become a focal point for devotion or cultic practices.

No true saint wants the focus of attention to end with them. It is a consistent mark of holiness that it is God's activity working through the disciplined flesh of an ascetic figure that makes possible healing, reconciliation or abundance, even as they function "as Christ" in the world.[96] That an anchorite would wish not to have their burial site or their body become a focus of cultic attention is seen in one of the earliest Christian novels, Athanasius' *Vita Antonii*.[97] Concerned as Antony—or Athanasius, actually—might have been over Egyptian burial practices,[98] he refused the invitation of the monks of the outer mountain to remain with him and die, and instructed his disciples to "perform the rites for me yourselves, and bury my body in the earth. And let my word be kept secret by you, so that no one knows the place but you alone."[99] While Athanasius' main purpose in this passage is to use Antony's words and actions to encourage Egyptian Christians to practice inhumation rather than embalming, a secondary concern is to prevent Antony's body from being disturbed. Thus Athanasius quotes Antony's words, "In the resurrection of the dead I shall receive my body incorruptible once again from the Savior."[100]

What can we learn from these select beneficial tales about the importance of the dead body of the combative anchorite in the early medieval Byzantine period, and its relationship to the integrative monastic community? I would argue that in addition to traditional elements often associated with dead or dying desert anchorites that demonstrate links of care and collegiality between themselves and their disciples, one also finds such care between ascetic "colleagues." For example, Abba Julian, a stylite, asked his disciples to burn incense but not at the customary hour; when questioned, he replied that his fellow stylite—Brother Symeon of Ægaion—had been struck by lightning and his soul was departing.[101]

---

[96] Brown, "The Saint as Exemplar in Late Antiquity," 15–19.

[97] Athanasius, *Vita Antonii*, 90 (PG 26.967–70); in Gregg, *Life of Antony*, 96.

[98] Egyptian Christian *martyria* featured bodies that enjoyed benefits of advanced embalming practices; they had no reason to discontinue the practice. John Wortley, "The Origins of Christian Veneration of Body Parts," RHR, Vol. 1 (2006): 21–8.

[99] Athanasius, *Vita Antonii*, 91 (PG.969–72); in Gregg, *Life of Antony*, 97.

[100] Ibid.

[101] *Prat. sp.* 57 (PG 87.2911–12). This tale is a reminder of the very real dangers that stylites especially would have faced, such as lightning storms, or other types of severe weather.

In addition to the aforementioned predetermination of one's impending death, select beneficial tales in Moschos' *Meadow* provide—even if not intentionally—evidence of post-mortem tension between the monastic community and the solitary. Acquisition of the corpse of an anchorite was not traditionally considered theft, *per se*, and boundaries between theft and acquisition were historically quite notoriously thin.[102] If the abba or monks were led to the body in a vision, dream or through some other type of miraculous activity, it was evident that the anchorite was casting about to be found, dissatisfied with their current state. If bodies were transported to the monasteries, it was only because anchorites allowed themselves to be transported. Referencing Saintyves and Delehaye in his essay on the cult of St Besse, Hertz writes that "[n]othing is more common in this literature than the theme of the theft of relics or the episode of a translation interrupted by a prodigious resistance put up by the holy corpse itself."[103] Of course, this is a convenient theological and anthropological excuse for grasping at the body of one who has eluded relationship with another during the course of a lifetime. According to Valantasis, ascetic social relations always introduce tension, because different types of ascetic lives interpret power differently.[104] That one person might contain power *over* themselves and *within* themselves is challenging for someone of the same profession who interprets asceticism and its behaviors in a distinct way. The notion of the contemplative monk engaged in peaceful prayer is romantic, but such an image does not do justice to the subtext; beneficial tales from Moschos' *Meadow* suggest that living, dying, dead or buried, monasteries and anchorites struggled for control in a cosmically pitched battle not always against evil, but sometimes against each other.

A "Middle Way" in *The Meadow*: Night of the Living Dead

A generation or two before John Moschos' travels, Bishop Jacob of Serugh encouraged Christians not to "call upon the deceased at their grave, because he does not hear you since he is not there. Rather seek him in the house of mercy."[105] Although they buried their dead and kept their memories alive as pagans had done before them, Christians did not—as some religious of antiquity did—indulge in the belief that those who were dead lived on, but under ground.[106] And yet, despite proto-orthodox patristic eschatology that concerned itself with the post-mortem

---

[102] Holger A. Klein, "Eastern Objects and Western Desires: Relics and Reliquaries between Byzantium and the West," DOP, Vol. 58 (2004): 283–314.

[103] Robert Hertz, "St. Besse: A Study of an Alpine Cult," in Wilson, *Saints and Their Cults*, 69, notes 42 and 43. See also Saintyves, *Les Saints, Successeurs Des Dieux*, 35.

[104] Valantasis, "Constructions of Power," 810.

[105] Rush, *Death and Burial in Christian Antiquity*, 246.

[106] Ibid.

stage of existence as one *not* centered in the earth,[107] the bishop's caution suggests that Christians of that era shared several responses to death: deep physical connection between the living and those who had passed, a corresponding link with the earthy site of their burial and the belief that those who passed remained—though in some limited way—actively involved in the affairs of those weighed down with this mortal coil. Continued dedication to these elements shaped Christian cultic practices, which, in turn, shaped the construction of a theological anthropology around the dead that included high appreciation for memory, visions and dreams, the connection of the soul of a holy person with their body and relics such as fragments of bone or clothing, and the community that housed that body.[108] Through mystical encounters, through bodies, portions of bodies and the very sites themselves, Christians continued in various stages of relationship with the dead, whose liminal arena of existence, this "middle way," was never clearly defined.

Variety existed initially in the construction of an eschatological theology; the Byzantines had, it seemed, no "'system' around the last things,"[109] nor were they terribly interested in imposing any systematic definition on the topic until confronted with the Latin doctrine of purgatory at medieval western councils.[110] Surely this lack of precision was linked, in some way, with two inheritances: first, an appreciation for the "irrational," manifest in Greek society through the practice of "θεουργία," which provided for some as reasonable a road to salvation as philosophy did for those who took comfort in the intellectual culture;[111] second, the ambiguity of the term "Hades" ("ᾅδης"), which makes an appearance in Greek poetry, mythology, the Septuagint, the New Testament and in select patristic writings.[112] Combined with these Hellenistic inheritances, however, were Christian and Jewish scriptures, both of which provided authoritative texts[113] that

---

[107] See Irenaeus, in *Adv. Haer.*, 5.31–2; Clement of Alexandria, *Strom.* 6.6.44.5–47; Origen's eschatology is complex, from a residing of all souls in Hades for punishment or rest—*De princ.* 4.3.10—to righteous souls in paradise—*Hom. Luc.*, frg. 253. Conversely, see Origen, *Comm. Matt.* 15.35 and *Comm. Jo.* 13.58. For an intellectual shift, see Nicholas Constas, "'To Sleep, Perchance to Dream': The Middle State of Souls in Patristic and Byzantine Literature," DOP, Vol. 55 (2001): 97–9; Brian Daley, S.J., *The Hope of the Early Church: A Handbook of Patristic Eschatology* (Grand Rapids, MI: Baker Academic, 1991): 44–66.

[108] Constas, "The Middle State of Souls," 91–4.

[109] Ibid.: 124.

[110] The concern of Byzantine theologians was repentance rather than retribution. George Every, "Toll Gates on the Air Way," ECR, Vol. 8, No. 2 (1976): 140.

[111] E.R. Dodds, *The Greeks and the Irrational* (University of California Press, 1963): 287–9.

[112] Prestige Leonard, "Hades in the Greek Fathers: Lexicon of Patristic Greek," JTS, 24 (1923): 476.

[113] Constas, "The Middle State of Souls," 93. Perhaps most influential is "Lazarus and the Rich Man," in which sins of the dead rich man are recalled for him by Abraham. Luke 16.19–31.

would significantly impact views that Christians held on the afterlife. In addition, Constas claims, liturgical and cultic practices that Christians composed in the face of their dying and rising savior assumed over time the status of theological conviction that the soul of the dead individual remained in relationship with the body (in whatever form it assumed, broken or otherwise), the earth that housed it and those who cared for it and the site. The remainder of this chapter will consider passages from select beneficial tales that address individuals who have passed, and will highlight four types of tales in Moschos' *Meadow*: the dutiful dead, the displeased dead, some combative corpses and even one comical corpse.

The Dutiful Dead

As we learned in the section on predetermination and death, the individual who was in compliance with God's will for their life and was forewarned about their impending demise was certainly provided with an opportunity to bring any unresolved business to a conclusion. The business of dying has long been understood in stages, one of which is the process of preparation for the actual moment of death. Even those in seemingly perfect health are represented as taking leave in proper stages, such as Alkestis, in Euripides' play of the same title, whose maidservant relates that she bathed, dressed herself nobly in gems and wept with her children and husband.[114] Likewise, Socrates bathed and chatted with friends before downing hemlock,[115] and Oedipus' daughters bathed their father while he lamented that everything was at an end.[116] Having engaged in these requisite activities, there is no need to go in any direction but forward to death. And while necessary preparations for death bled into Christian accounts as well,[117] in select beneficial tales we discover that the process of dying does not necessarily abide by a canon of ritual baths, settling affairs or taking leave of loved ones.[118] However, one can observe shadows of these when, in the course of dying, they are ignored. This is most apparent around the topic of "leave taking," the principal ritual that recognizes relationship. For example, one of the brothers dies, his body is laid in the church and the sêmantron is struck to signal all to come and mourn together.[119] Abba Hagiodoulos arrives, grieving; he approaches the body and orders the brother to rise and embrace him. Naturally, the good dead brother complies, and "he rose

---

[114] Euripides, *Alcestis*, in *Euripides, Cyclops, Alcestis, Medea*, trans. David Kovacs (Harvard University Press, 1994): 177–201.
[115] Plato, *Phaedo*, 63.E, trans. Harold North Fowler (Harvard University Press, 1914): 393.
[116] Sophokles, *Oedipus at Kolonos*, 1585–665.
[117] Consider the elaborate leave-taking of St Macrina. St Gregory of Nyssa, *Vita Sanctae Macrinae*, ed. V. Woods Callahan, in Werner Jaeger, J.-P. Cavernos and V. Woods Callahan (eds), *Gregorii Nysseni Opera Ascetica* (Leiden, 1952): 347–414.
[118] Robert Garland, *The Greek Way of Death* (Cornell University Press, 1985): 16.
[119] *Prat. sp.* 11 (PG 87.2859–62).

and greeted the elder."[120] It is never the task of the historian to ask "Do dead men rise?" but, rather, to ask a different set of questions altogether: what makes this story compelling to those who told it, those who preserved it and those who heard or read it? With that in mind, it is difficult to assess if the brother obeys the abba out of love or obedience, both of which are central to cenobitic monasticism.[121] Although the motive is not clear, what is clear in this most intimate and tender moment is that the relationship between the two transcends and continues beyond the chasm that death places before them. Even on the other side of life the brother obeys the abba, and thus his death—or at least the second and final death—is an expression of his obedience to the authority of the elder. Although the tendency might be to marvel at the power of an elder whose very word causes a dead man to sit up, it is worth noting the virtue of the brother who obeys the word of his elder.[122] In this, the tale is beneficial in a variety of ways: theologically it hints at an eschatology that includes the notion of rest prior to resurrection, and socially it reveals the extent to which a great elder can (or should) inspire love and obedience from his or her charge, as well as the extent to which a disciple can (or should) be willing to obey her or his elder. Foucault might have been writing about this very beneficial tale (although I am quite sure he was not) when he wrote in *Technologies of the Self* that "The monk must have the permission of his director to do anything, even die."[123]

The elder–disciple bond that Abba Hagiodoulos represents is not necessarily limited to those within the cloister; one consistent benefit of beneficial tales is that they remind their audience that charity, love, humility and other monastic virtues are in no way limited to monastic figures, but can be glimpsed in the actions of laity as well. In a text that will later be attached to *The Meadow* tradition, an unnamed tale of a "Christ-loving man Christopher"[124] tells of an official who operates as a member of the "Regiment of the Protectors" by day and as a secret philanthropist by night. After each day of working and fasting, "Christopher" would eat a simple meal of bread, vegetables and water, collect funds from a money-dealer[125] and spend the remainder of the night distributing alms to those in need, primarily in prisons and in the arcades. In this tale, when he encountered

---

[120] "Ὁ δὲ ἀναστὰς ἠσπάσατο τὸν γέροντα." Ibid.

[121] Philip Rousseau, *Ascetics, Authority and the Church in the Age of Jerome and Cassian* (Oxford University Press, 1978): 19–32.

[122] Graham Gould, *The Desert Fathers on Monastic Community* (Oxford: Clarendon Press, 1993): 27.

[123] Michel Foucault, *The Essential Foucault: Selections from The Essential Works of Foucault 1954–1984*, ed. Paul Rabinou and Nikolas Rose (New York: The New Press, 2003): 165.

[124] "Ἦν τις ἀνὴρ φιλόχριστος, Χριστόφορος," Naturally there is no need to point out what is implied by the choice of name. III Mioni, "Il Pratum Spirituale de Giovanni Mosco," 84.

[125] The text does not say—or does not care to say—why Christopher receives money from this person. It is interesting to think, however, that this individual engaged in one of the most despised professions—money-lending—might be a saint in disguise.

a dead man, he washed the body and dressed it in a burial shroud, appropriate clothing and footwear. He purchased candles and set a gold coin on the man's chest for those who would bury him, and then requested that the brother "Rise up, brother, and give me Christian love."[126] The dead man complied: sat up, embraced him, then lay down and "fell asleep."[127] All of this terrified the shopkeeper who provided the candles, water and clothing and later spread the tale. This would be a terrifying thing to see, but while most would be terrified by these events, few would have been surprised in a world in which mystery had value, and moments of cosmic activity were recognized and welcomed. In this tale, the virtuous conduct of "Christopher" functions in two ways, depending on the audience: for a monastic, it is a reminder of the hidden sanctity, charity and care exercised in the world by the laity, or those whose lay-monastic life might be concealed. For the laity, it is a reminder that they are no less responsible for the care of their brethren than those whose vocation is defined by a rule that demands professional virtue. And for either audience, it is affirmation of the close relationship between the marginal members of society and the activity of a loving God who can be interpreted back into the beneficial tale either as the deliverer of tender mercies *to* those languishing in prisons and dying in the arcades, or *as* the imprisoned and dying, identified in the gospels as the "least of these."[128]

The Displeased Dead

The importance of proper burial is a common theme throughout Greek, Roman and Jewish literary traditions; respectable interment of a body in this world—and all of the details surrounding that—was understood as having a direct impact on the ability of the soul to rest in the other.[129] Once a body was buried, the spirit of a pagan funeral was defined by the *vale*, the taking leave or "farewell" that occurred at the burning or burying of the body; this would often be accompanied by wishes such as "May the earth lie lightly upon thee."[130] In several *Meadow* tales, the earth rested too lightly, for the dead continued to interact unabated with those on the earth, rather than under it, highlighting the unbreakable commitment to asceticism of the monastic, and the ultimate inability to completely hide one's

---

[126] "Ἐγείρου, ἀδελφέ, καὶ δός μοι τὴν ἐν Χριστῷ ἀγάπην." III Mioni, "Il Pratum Spirituale de Giovanni Mosco," 85.

[127] "ἐκοιμήθη." Ibid.

[128] Matthew 25.40.

[129] Jeffrey A. Trumbower, *Rescue For the Dead: The Posthumous Salvation of Non-Christians in Early Christianity* (Oxford University Press, 2001): 19–23. Keith Hopkins, *Death and Renewal*. Sociological Studies in Roman History Volume 2 (Cambridge University Press, 1983): 213. J.M.C. Toynbee, *Death and Burial in the Roman World* (Cornell University Press, 1971): 61–2.

[130] CIL 14, 1896; J. Orellius, Inscriptionum Latinarum Selectarum Amplissima Collectio III, 7396, in Rush, *Death and Burial in Christian Antiquity*, 255. See also Morris, *Death-Ritual And Social Structure*, 42.

level of orthodoxy (or pronounce on someone else's). In a disturbing tale that speaks more to church politics than piety, one Abba Cosmas the Eunuch dies while visiting Theoupolis, and the patriarch buries him next to a bishop.[131] Three days later, Abba Basil, when visiting the remains of Abba Cosmas, is informed by a former paralytic that not only was he cured at the site of the dead abba, but that the abba called out at night: "Do not touch me; stay there; do not come near me, you heretic and enemy of truth, and of the holy Catholic Church of God."[132] When this is reported to the patriarch, he expresses pleasure that this post-mortem pronouncement has revealed the true doctrine of the dead bishop, who is strangely silent in all of this. It is easy to be distracted by the activity and words of the paralytic, whose cure infers healings in the gospel.[133] In addition to noting the importance of scripture for anchoring a tale, several elements highlight what mattered to people who valued this tale: first, beyond antiquity into (at minimum) the early middle Byzantine period, tales such as this provide evidence that Christianity continued to take seriously the imperial charge to bury those without wealth, status or guild.[134] Rather than deposit the stranger in a pauper's grave, the patriarch, wanting to honor him for reasons not revealed, buries the body next to a bishop. Second, the "heresy" of the bishop is revealed through the dead man's cries, although precisely what the heresy might be we cannot know. Third, this use of "Μὴ ἅψη μου," also translated as a simple "stop touching me," might suggest that in death they could confirm what was suspected in life, that the dead bishop engaged in unrighteous "touching," however one wishes to interpret "touch." Third, to what degree might this tale reflect an opportunity for a slighted party to besmirch the reputation of an individual who is completely powerless to enter into dialogue or defense about their alleged "heresy"? Rivalry did exist between monasteries and holy sites; one cannot help but wonder at the opportunity that was presented by the death of an unpopular bishop, even for the author of the tale. Finally, that the abba finds the paralytic keeping house on the tomb of the recently buried Abba Cosmas indicates that at least into the late sixth century individuals continued to engage in the activity of entering into a dream state (*enkoimesis*) at

---

[131] *Prat. sp.* 40 (PG 87.2891–6).

[132] "Μὴ ἅψη μου (*"noli me tangere,"* Ltn) ˙ παρ' ἐκεῖ˙ μὴ ἐγγίσῃς μου, αἱρετικὲ καὶ ἐχθρὲ τῆς ἀληθείας, καὶ τῆς ἁγίας τοῦ Θεοῦ καθολικῆς Ἐκκλησίας." *Prat. sp.* 40 (PG 87.2893–4). Use of this phrase traditionally signifies that someone impure (or living or in the flesh) is attempting to touch or hold onto someone who is not in that same state. John 20.17.

[133] Matthew 9.1–2; Mark 2.1–12; Luke 5.17–26; John 5.1–18.

[134] Trumbower, *Rescue For the Dead*, 21; Hopkins, "III. Burial Clubs and Collective Tombs," *Death and Renewal*, 211–17; Éric Rebillard, "Les formes de l'assistance funéraire dans l'Empire romain et leur évolution dans l'Antiquité tardive," *Antiquite tardive*, VII (1999): 276.

sites noted for healing, a medical method known in ancient Greece more than a thousand years earlier.[135]

While in Antioch, John and Sophronios learn of a steward named Thomas who died while in the city attending to monastery business and—as he was unknown—was buried in the foreigner's burial-ground.[136] According to Evagrius, who also includes this account, Thomas was an *apocrisarius*, the individual charged with collecting the annual stipend.[137] Evagrius notes some interesting details that *The Meadow* does not include: that Thomas predicts his own death after a violent reaction of Anastasius, the distributor of the money, who strikes Thomas because he is tired of Thomas "constantly pestering him." However he died, the next day, according to *The Meadow*, a woman was buried on top of him and within a matter of hours, "the earth raised her."[138] Though reburied, by morning she was again unearthed, so she was buried elsewhere. When a second woman was buried over the monk and was again unearthed, the monk was pulled from the tomb with great fanfare and buried in the cemetery alongside the relics of holy martyrs. The evidence that Thomas is a holy man is that even in death he does not allow the body of a woman to lie above him. Though potentially offensive to modern sentiments, this statement suggests a memory of Thomas as one marked by chastity and renunciation of opposite-gender relationships or opposite-gender touching. Strong support for the idea that Thomas would continue in his ascetic life beyond life can be found in Dorotheos of Gaza, who writes:

> [a]s the Fathers tell us, the souls of the dead remember everything that happened here—thoughts, words, desires—and nothing can be forgotten ... what he did against virtue or against his evil passions, he remembers, and nothing of it is lost. And if a man helped someone or was helped by someone else, this is remembered as is the person concerned, all this is remembered. In fact, the soul

---

[135] Helen Askitopoulou, Eleni Konsolaki, Ioanna A. Ramoutsaki and Maria Anastassaki, "Surgical Cures Under Sleep Induction in the Asclepieion of Epidauros," Int. Congr. Ser., 1242 (2002): 12; Audrey Cruse, *Roman Medicine* (Stroud, UK: Tempus Publishing Ltd, 2004): 15–32.

[136] *Prat. sp.* 88 (PG 87.2945–6).

[137] *Hist.eccl.* IV.35, in Whitby, *Ecclesiastical History*, 240.

[138] "καὶ περὶ ὥραν ἐννάτην ἀνέβασε αὐτὴν ἡ γῆ," *Prat. sp.* 88 (PG 87.2915). Evagrius, *Ecclesiastical History*, IV.35; in Whitby, *Ecclesiastical History*, 240. Allen and Peters note that the prophecy is not recorded in the other sources that contain this tale (*The Meadow* and the *Vita* of St Martha), but the common theme of bodies ejected from the earth is present. "Vers l'année 603 ou peu après cette date, Jean Moschus se trouvait de passage à Antioche. Un prêtre de l'église lui raconta l'histoire de Thomas, avec certaines variantes qui s'écartent en quelques points de la version d'Évagrius et la complètent en plusieurs autres." Paul Peeters, "Saint Thomas d'Emese et la Vie de Sainte Marthe," AnBoll, Vol. 45 (1927): 264. Pauline Allen, *Evagrius Scholasticus: The Church Historian*, Spicilegium sacrum Lovaniense, Etudes et documents, fasc. 41 (Leuven: Spicilegium sacrum Lovaniense, 1981): 200.

loses nothing that it did in this world but clearly remembers everything at its exit from this body more clearly and distinctly once freed from the earthliness of the body.[139]

Dorotheos points to the importance of social context and memory in the historical construction of a person's life, distinct from liturgical commemoration,[140] and suggests that the remembrance of death provides the opportunity for the collective memory[141] of those who create, who tell and who hear the tale; all parties participate in the process, and support the meaning-making of a lifetime of choices over virtues and vices by Thomas. Flesh has to move out of the way for that to take place.

Together, all of these parties participate in the remembrance, and therefore the historical construction, of Thomas's ascetic life. For Thomas, here identified—or collectively remembered?—as a chaste man in life, could one not expect that he would remain that way in death? For those who passed on the story of Thomas's death and participated in this way in the historical construction of his life, surely remembrance of him as a modest monk influenced the degree to which his body would continue to model that modesty; for the audience of this beneficial tale, the activity of Thomas's corpse is affirmation that death is not an escape from the obligations, vows or promises that are held in this life, and both soul and body continue to work together to protect the identity and integrity of the deceased individual. According to Constas, the relationship of body and soul will intrigue the imaginations of middle Byzantine theologians. "For all parties," he writes, "the body was increasingly seen as foundational to the nature of human identity."[142] The elevation of the integrity of components of bone and blood, dirt and cave, murder weapon or girdle surely played a critical role in the continuity of mortal and post-mortem relationship, adding to the overall value of the individual *qua* individual.

Combative Corpses

Taken to its logical conclusion, body and soul identification will move beyond affirmation of love and obedience, or proof of orthodoxy or heterodoxy; in protest against physical violation or theft, the dead body and its relationship to the living body in select beneficial tales will serve as moral and theological exemplars for those exterior and interior to the ascetic profession, as Moschos and Sophronios

---

[139] Dorotheos of Gaza, "Fear of the Punishment to Come and the Need for Never Neglecting One's Salvation" (PG 88.1747–62) in *Dorotheos of Gaza: Discourses and Sayings*, trans. Eric P. Wheeler (Kalamazoo, MI: Cistercian Publications, 1977): 185.

[140] Megan McLaughlin, *Consorting with Saints: Prayer for the Dead in Early Medieval France* (Cornell University Press, 1994): 55–101.

[141] Amos Funkenstein, "Collective Memory and Historical Consciousness," HM, Vol. I, No. 1 (1999): 6.

[142] Constas, "The Middle State of Souls," 99.

attest. While waiting in Alexandria for Stephan the Sophist to awake from his nap, they wait at the Tetrapylon, abandoned at that time of day but for the presence of three blind men who take it in turn to answer the question: "How in fact did you lose your sight?"[143] One reports that he developed ophthalmia,[144] the second was exposed to fire at length through his trade as a glass-blower and the third—identified as a prodigal[145]—sustained a work-related accident. He was a grave-robber by trade, and while his most recent corpse-victim was content to let the robber take his clothes, the corpse drew the line at the burial shroud, and sat up and clawed at the prodigal's face and eyes, blinding him.[146] Highly disturbed by what they have heard, Moschos and Sophronios leave, after deciding that they will not engage in any more business for the day, for they have gained much from this encounter. They do, however, write down the tale and state the moral so that there may be no ambiguity, "in order that you, hearing these things might benefit. For it is true, no one who does evil can escape notice of God."[147] There is no accounting for the community of the grave-robber in this account; the prodigal does not return as a repentant son. This is quite unlike the second beneficial tale I wish to highlight, in which a man appears at a monastery in a state of extreme distress. When questioned, he informs the abba that he had been a grave-robber and heard of the death of a daughter of a high-ranking official. He went at night to her sepulchre and after he had stripped the corpse and left her naked she sat up and grabbed his hand, and chastised him most vigorously and at length:

> Oh man, did you have to strip me naked? Have you fear of God? Ought you not have had pity on me in death? Should you not respect my sex? How can you, as a Christian, condemn me to presenting myself naked before Christ because you had so little respect for my sex? Is mine not the sex which gave you birth? Do you not outrage your own mother in so using me? Wretched man, what sort of defence will you offer for this crime against me when you come to the terrifying judgment seat of Christ? As long as I lived, no strange man ever saw my face; and now, after death and burial, you have stripped me and looked upon my naked body. What is there to be said for humanity when it can stoop to such depths? What a heart, what hands you are going to have when you come to receive the all-holy body and blood of our Lord Jesus Christ![148]

---

[143] "Ὄντως σοι πῶς γέγονας τυφλός;" *Prat. sp.* 77 (PG. 87.2932).

[144] "οφθαλμιάσις."

[145] "ἄσωτος;" surely an intentional allusion to the prodigal son, Luke 15.11–32.

[146] *Prat. sp.* 77 (PG. 87.2932).

[147] "ἵνα καὶ ὑμεῖς ἀκούοντες ταῦτα ὠφεληθῆτες. Ἀληθῶς γὰρ, ὅτι οὐδεὶς ποιῶν κακὸν, λανθάνει Θεόν'." *Prat. sp.* 77 (PG. 87. 2929–32).

[148] *Prat. sp.* 78 (PG. 87.2933–6); Wortley, *Spiritual Meadow*, 59. A shorter—but considerably much less dramatic—version of the account is found in the *Bibliotheca Hagiographica Graeca*, 1450i, Huber 14 (W034): "de iuvene qui mortuam exspoliavit." http://home.cc.umanitoba.ca/~wortley/main1-99.html#w034.

Begging release, he promised to renounce his ways. Unconvinced, she threatened him with torture and death, to live forever together with her in a shared Infernal Revenue Service: "This tomb will be shared by the two of us."[149] Only after much weeping and begging on his part does she relent, and only on the condition that he renounce his career and spend the remainder of his days repenting in a monastery, which he promises to do. After he restores her to her previous clothed state, she lies down, dead. That he would spend the remainder of his days living a life of repentance hardly seems a punishment, but it is consistent with Byzantine tradition, which preferred exile or confinement to prison or mutilation; there was always the hope that, given time for reflection, a criminal might repent and a soul would be saved.

Clearly these are folktales designed to both entertain and function as a Christian security system against those who would attempt to rob the dead of that with which remains rightfully theirs even in the afterlife, and here I refer not to a shroud or jewels, but to the dignity that should be afforded to all bodies, living or dead. For eastern Christianity, even in death the body remains in the image of God, for God—in Christ—was, at one point, a dead body. If violence done to a living body is an offense to the image of God who shares in the humanity of God's creation, then violence done to a dead body would share in that same offence. Told from the point of view of those who suffer or survive the activity of combative corpses, the tales reveal several socio-historical details of interest. First, we learn how people suffered: in the first tale one of the three blind men suffers from ophthalmia, a disease mentioned in several beneficial tales and other ancient sources.[150] We learn something of the types of injuries that individuals sustained in workplace settings, as well as the fact that one injured in such a way is no longer working, as both the former sailor and former glass-blower are sitting in a public space in the middle of the day. That individuals who are otherwise able-bodied are rendered unemployed by the loss of their eyes speaks also to the importance of sight in this society, traditionally regarded as the most noble of the human senses.[151] In addition, we learn that grave-robbing is a lucrative trade, and desecration of a corpse was serious enough to require a lifetime of repentance or a lifetime of blindness. Though not quite of the *genre* of apocalyptic literature, tales of combative corpses share with apocalypses a cosmic message that has earthly implications—in other words, to raise the theological consciousness of individuals in order that they might behave in a way that is—like the tales—"beneficial."

---

[149] *Prat. sp.* 78 (PG. 87.2929–32); Wortley, *Spiritual Meadow*, 59–60.

[150] *Prat. sp.* 163 (PG 87.3029–30); J. Fronimopoulos and J. Lascaratos, "'Eye injuries' by the Byzantine writer Aetios Amidinos," *Doc Ophthalmol*, Vol. 1–2 (1988): 121–4; Richard J. Durling, "Medicine in Plutarch's *Moralia*," *Traditio*, Vol. 50 (1995): 311–14.

[151] Anthony Synnot, "Puzzling Over the Sense: From Plato to Marx," in David Howes, *The Varieties of Sensory Experience: A Sourcebook in the Anthropology of the Senses* (University of Toronto Press, 1991): 63–5.

The Comical Corpse

The final section of this study of death in *The Meadow* addresses one single tale,[152] and represents a genre of writing quite understudied in Byzantine literature: the apocalypse. Jane Baun's review of secondary literature on Byzantine apocryphal texts, particularly medieval apocalyptic texts, reveals that literature of "otherworld" experiences has much to teach about the religious formation of those "far from theology" (*Theologiefern*).[153] Such types of literature, she deftly notes, both accurately reflect and shift our modern cliché from "Think globally, act locally" to "Think cosmically, act locally." In other words, as multiscalar Christian ecological ethics teaches, because all things earthly and heavenly are intimately connected, decisions about behaviors, practices, habits and choices have to be made and understood at multiple levels; thinking "globally"—or "cosmically"—does not mean that the immediate details may be neglected.[154] Further, the multiscalar dimension of Christian salvation is that it requires the prayers and activity of more than the individual alone, both during life *and* beyond.[155] This is, to wit, the goal of beneficial tales: as they highlight significant virtues to emulate and vices to eschew, they encourage moral activism, raise consciousness and (ideally) change behaviors.

Our final tale goes thus: while in the Thebaïd, John and Sophronios are told of a great elder who has lived outside the city with a small group of disciples for over 70 years. One of the disciples was very lax, and less concerned about the state of his soul than the elder would like. No amount of cajoling could alter his careless ways. Many times the elder disciplined him with threats, saying "Brother, be mindful of your own soul, for death awaits, and you will be cast into punishment."[156] The elder was distressed for the soul of the disciple, fearful because despite his warnings the young man failed to exhibit the characteristics of faith. The disciple remained unconcerned, and died. The elder, saddened by this, prayed that Jesus might reveal the ultimate state of the young man's soul. In a trance, the elder saw "a crowd in a river of fire, and in the midst the brother, submerged to his neck."[157]

---

[152] *Prat. sp.* 44 (PG 87.2897–900).

[153] Hans-Georg Beck, *Die Byzantiner und ihr Jenseits: zur Entstehungsgeschichte einer Mentalität* (München: Verlag der Bayerischen Akademie der Wissenschaften, 1979): 50, in Jane Baun, *Tales from Another Byzantium: Celestial Journey and Local Community in the Medieval Greek Apocrypha* (Cambridge University Press, 2007): 27–8.

[154] "Christians should ... continually make scalar choices, shifting between different levels of attention to develop a truly multiscalar ethics." Kevin J. O'Brien, *An Ethics of Biodiversity: Christianity, Ecology, and the Variety of Life* (Georgetown University Press, 2010): 92.

[155] Every, "Toll Gates on the Air Way," 150.

[156] "Ἀδελφὲ, φρόντεζε τῆς ἑαυτοῦ ψυχῆς, ἔχεις ἀποθανεῖν, καὶ εἰς κόλασιν ἀπελθεῖν." *Prat. sp.* 44 (PG 87.2897–8).

[157] "καὶ πλῆθος ἐν αὐτῷ τῷ πυρί, καὶ μέσον τὸν ἀδελφὸν βεβαπτισμένον ἕως τραχήλου." *Prat. sp.* 44 (PG 87.2899–900).

Not able to resist, the elder chides him, asking him to confirm that he had warned him of this fate. Surprisingly, the disciple assures the elder that his prayers for his soul had been useful: "I thank God, father, that I have indulgence for my head; for on account of your prayers I am standing on the head of a bishop."[158]

This unique tale is beneficial in ways that are practical, theological and comical. It operates—and succeeds—on many levels: the standard "Tours of Hell" element assures careless disciples, negligent spouses and naughty children that a river of fire awaits to punish them if they are not mindful of the state of their souls, and therefore it encourages virtuous living through reference to an allusion common in Byzantine apocalypses.[159] On a practical level it reinforces the bond that exists between the disciple and the elder, a bond so strong that communication—and clearly affection and responsibility—live long after death has separated them. Finally, it is humorous, and that matters too. Derek Krueger, in his study of Leontius of Neapolis' *Life and Conduct of Abba Symeon Called the Fool for the Sake of Christ*, notes that a particular feature of the holy-fool genre is the use of what might be considered "comedic" elements; this leads him to ask: "Is it possible that early Christians had a sense of humor?"[160] He answers his own question later in the text in the affirmative,[161] the same affirmative conclusion that I draw here about Moschos' tale, even as the roughly contemporary hagiographers are not using humor in the same way. And while it seems as if analysis of this enjoyable tale is a break from the above considered passages on death, yet the theme of "control" remains common through to the end. Jokes and the use of humor suggest that levity—with its flashes of joy, sometimes unrestrained—is one way in which individuals transcend systems that keep these experiences at bay. In her anthropological study of jokes, Mary Douglas employs the work of Bergson and Freud to conclude that humor allows individuals to break free from models encrusted with tedium, a freedom made all the more joyful in its thwarting of the authority that creates or controls those models. "For both," she writes, "the essence of the joke is that something formal is attacked by something informal, something organized and controlled, by something vital, energetic, an upsurge of life …"[162] Behind the levity of the tale we find a deeply seriously and often prudently suppressed contempt that monastics held for hierarchs.[163]

Were John and Sophronios told this tale when they arrived in the Thebaïd, to relax them after their journey? Did the elder who greeted them with this tale spend

---

[158] "Εὐχαριστῶ τῷ Θεῷ, Πάτερ, ὅτι κἂν ἡ κεφαλή μου ἄνεσιν ἔχει. Κατὰ γὰρ εὐχάς σου ἐπάνω κορυφῆς ἵσταμαι ἐπισκόπου." Ibid.

[159] Baun, *Tales from Another Byzantium*, 85.

[160] Krueger, *Symeon the Holy Fool*, 2.

[161] Ibid., 126.

[162] Mary Douglas, *Implicit Meanings: Essays in Anthropology* (London: Routledge & Paul, 1975): 95.

[163] James C. Scott, *Domination and the Arts of Resistance: Hidden Transcripts* (Yale University Press, 1992): 192. I thank Dr Richard Steele for directing me to this source.

hours searching his memory for a tale that would delight and amuse them? Did the laughter of these men echo briefly before they clasped their own hands over their mouths, so that they might not cause scandal to those in prayer? It is easy to forget that monks laugh too, but in the development of community humor is important: it invites trust and creates bonds of affection built through participation in a joyful moment, the pleasurable memory lingering long after the laughter has ceased. This is probably a favorite tale that would be recited or read not on sombre feast days, but surely in evenings when sleep was elusive, as an accompaniment to a rare honeyed treat, or when tension needed to be dissolved. Here *The Meadow* continues to engage us as we learn more of what we share with Christians of an earlier age. Knowing that monks laugh (maybe even when they are not supposed to) is a delightful addition to what we already know and share of their experiences of suffering, poverty, hunger, illness and death.

Conclusion

As noted in the Introduction, the beneficial tales of John Moschos invite the modern reader to consider how these texts address issues of agency and providence, the autonomy and independence of the individual (ascetic and lay) as they are represented in the literary evidence. In doing so, we can learn further about the types of lives that laity and monastic figures led in the centuries at the end of antiquity, the early Byzantine era.

In the first chapter I sought to explore relationships that existed between monastic and lay figures for the purpose of considering what these relations might teach us about liminal boundaries that existed in the early Byzantine era between the secular and the religious. First, in both beneficial tales we learn that the wisdom of the elder is accessible to the novice in moments and in places where the novice might not initially expect to find it. This particular characteristic of Moschos' work is one that he shares with his contemporary Bishop Leontios of Neapolis, whose work also highlights intimate relationships of the ascetic with humdrum happenings of secular life, hinting at the activity of God in places where piety denies it, in startling moments, in shadowy places. Thus the social dimension of spiritual formation is expanded beyond desert, cell and monastery; here field and home operate as a site for monasticism in miniature, which allows us to consider how early Byzantine monastics might have understood sacred space. Further, we learn that it is possible that someone exterior to a conventional ascetic relationship might intentionally or unintentionally direct a monk's training in obedience, endurance and chastity. An abba traditionally aims for spiritual self-sufficiency in the training of a disciple, an objective that pre-dates monastic rules.[1] This is attained only by obedience to sometimes harsh and sometimes gentle training that a discerning elder imposes on a novice, in imitation of a hierarchy rooted in the relationship between Jesus and God. In Theodore's case, Moschos' tale demonstrates that there is room at the table for those who learn from an elder who all but enslaved him. Still, Theodore interprets these circumstances to the benefit of his soul and his social standing among the grazers. If we think about how this tale might have operated among its intended recipients, surely it would have promoted a generous attitude towards those whose life circumstances did not allow them to commit themselves to a more formal ascetic program. I dare imagine that there were more individuals than our Theodore who fell into that category; that we can identify the "threshold monk" in this tale might encourage us to continue to look carefully at texts that suggest divisions between worlds

---

[1] Rousseau, "The Desert Fathers and their Broader Audience," 122–9.

that might very well not be divided. In the lascivious monk's case, Moschos' tale demonstrates that the sexual arrogance of male monks can be curbed by the very individuals who might otherwise be accused of instigating their impure thoughts. If we consider how this tale might have operated among its intended recipients, we can delight in the positive qualities that these women possess, which suggest that spiritual training and the role of "elder" is not limited to men. Finally, these tales affirm a longstanding relationship between monks and laity:[2] although they reverse more traditional interactions, they still support the claim that the ascetic life was neither apart from nor in opposition to the broader culture that contained it. One might conclude that wisdom gained at the feet of a lay Christian—even a bad one—could be superior to attempting to cultivate the virtues of the angelic life on one's own,[3] as evidence in the tales betrays social practices distinct from a particular theory of engagement with the secular world.[4] Characterized by ambiguity and competition, the integrity of the inner life was best and consistently tested by engagement. Consequently, the texts argue on behalf of a theory of disengagement that ascetics themselves do not put into practice, which suggests precisely the opposite: engagement with a world they are seeking to transcend.[5]

The goal of Chapter 2 was to consider what beneficial tales might reveal to us about how wealth and poverty affected people in the early Byzantine era. Obviously there are moralistic tales that stress the importance of giving, that Christian charity is superior to the profit of a secular economy,[6] and that bishops—and angels—can be deceptive if need be, for they know better the state of one's soul and how that soul is affected by the presence or absence of money and honor. But in addition to these factors are theological claims that clearly reflect the historical reality of the effects of a shifting economic system: the body of the poor is the body of Christ; giving to the poor is giving to God; and investing in God is investing in salvation, and investing in salvation might mean "in the here and now" or it might mean celestial salvation. And of course, hard realities are present in *The Meadow*, and they coexist with miraculous activity. Side by side with fish coughing up gems and murderous angel-monks, we learn, among other things, that people will make decisions to prostitute themselves because they are hungry; creditors will drive people into jails or to suicide; sexual predators stalk the marginalized; fear of hunger and poverty will drive the best of people to hoard; theft can equal death; it is difficult to be generous; the public reduction of

---

[2] Ibid.,102.

[3] This is seen in the following anonymous *apothegm*: "If you see a young man climbing up to heaven by his own will, grab his foot and pull him down, for this is good for him." *APanon* 244, ROC, in Gould, *The Desert Fathers on Monastic Community*, 29.

[4] Rousseau, "The Desert Fathers and their Broader Audience," 107; Rousseau, "The Desert Fathers, Antony and Pachomius," in Cheslyn Jones, Goeffrey Wainwright and Edward Yarnold, S.J. (eds), *The Study of Spirituality* (Oxford University Press, 1986): 120.

[5] Rousseau, "The Desert Fathers and their Broader Audience," 107.

[6] Laiou, "Trade, Profit and Salvation," in Holman (ed.), *Wealth and Poverty*, 244.

status is humiliating. In the end, these are things that we know about ourselves. It can be either a comfort that we share the trials of the past, or a great sadness that we have not eradicated them from society.

In addition to recognition of these simple human traits, the overarching structure of this chapter considered Moschos' treatment of money in select beneficial tales in a larger conversation, to seek and identify connections between wealth, poverty and soteriology, and to consider how select tales suggest that cultural values such as honor, shame, personal agency and humility factor into the social intercourse of giving and receiving. The first theme considered the married lending team, Evagrios and the righteous man; in all cases Christ *as* the poor is explicit in the texts through claims that Christians make, through Jesus's own claims, or—in one case—the claims of a heavenly document. This theology is present in the sermons of Gregory of Nyssa, John Chrysostom and Basil of Caesarea, each of whom highlights that charity is a paramount obligation of a Christian life, relieving the body of the suffering poor in the present by identifying them with the body of the suffering Jesus, who rewards such activity with eternal life. The second theme considered activities of thieves, an Alexandrine girl, and an angel-monk; in these cases, poverty for the sake of salvation is demonstrated through extreme almsgiving and even murder, which is not encouraged in patristic texts; nevertheless, renunciation of that which stands between sinner and salvation is, an activity demonstrated in all cases. The final theme of almsgiving demonstrated that this activity, rooted in sacrifice, was used to maintain or shift status among disparate populations, to represent God's character to those deserving of reward or punishment, and in ways directly connected to salvation. I noted above that many of these tales provide affirmation of creative and compassionate economic practices in times of social unrest, which might have contributed to the spread of Christianity in the Byzantine Empire. In several accounts, charity and philanthropy certainly provided effective methods of evangelism, as conversions took place not in the wake of violence or fear, but in the wake of merciful actions in an age of great instability: the husband, the thieves and the Alexandrine girl were led into Christianity as a result of direct experiences with people crushed by debt; the righteous man had his faith "perfected" by Jesus *as* the poor; the unnamed saved had their faith preserved intact due to the clever—or cruel?—activity of an angel-monk, and Evagrios provided post-mortem confirmation to the gathered witnesses that money lent to the poor was, in fact, lent to God. The public nature of many of the revelations might have influenced unnamed witnesses in the accounts; of them we can know nothing.

But why do they matter, these stories about poor people? Analysis of these texts helps with a bigger question: how are economic inequities addressed in Moschos' *Meadow*? The amount of tales that depict lay people aiding lay people indicates that charity and philanthropy were not limited to social programs of the church, monasteries or monks. A recent study by UC Berkeley researcher Paul K. Piff reveals to us that during times of financial stress there is increased compassion among the poor relative to the rich, that the poor are more inclined towards charity. "According to our conceptualization," Piff writes, "acts of generosity and benevolence among lower class people are a means to build relationships and strengthen social bonds."[7] Philanthropy in a time of shifting boundaries demonstrates that true charity has no boundaries. Analysis of Moschos' *Meadow* proves theologically what Piff proves scientifically: shared humanity impels us to be humane.

The central question for Chapter 3 was: how did medical and spiritual management contribute to the construction of religious and social identity in the early medieval Byzantine Empire? Despite the presence of female monastics and ascetics in monasteries and in the deserts, the nameless, voiceless woman with breast cancer is given no language in the text to ask for healing—if she wants it—and no voice to reject it—if she feels compelled to suffer. To what degree does this healing actually diminish her religious identity? It seems that her experience as a possibly unwilling participant in a healing casts her in a different light than if we were to interpret this passage as merely a tale of God's mercy and John's obedience and discernment, which it was surely intended to be within the context of its construction. If healing is her desire, and coincides with the divine economy, then the placing of John's hand on her breast is a tender gesture that reaffirms the value of created matter, and ultimately upholds the two-natured Christology that Moschos holds dear as infinite and finite meet at the site of disease. We might identify this healing as a moment of compassion by a person who "sees" her and her husband's need, or we might see it as the reining in of an undisciplined wife, a wanna-be ascetic whose behavior needs to be brought into line, or even the tempering of a heretical tendency to reject created matter and thus scorn the norms and hierarchies upon which people once believed societies were built.[8]

For the infertile woman, whether or not this woman wanted a child, Abba Daniel aids in the transformation of all her relationships with his prayer for God to grant her a child. She is no longer just the daughter of her father and the wife of her husband; she is now also the mother of a son. This is a good thing, if in fact this woman wanted this child and wanted to preserve a marriage to a man who would be free to divorce her if she did not produce a family for him or if the baby were proven to have been the son of another father.[9] Pregnancy, childbirth, nursing, parenting, recognition of biological links with a family line, each of these elements changes all of her relationships, both familial and civic, but again, we

---

[7] "The Rich are Different from You and Me: They are More Selfish," *The Economist*, 31 July 2010, 64. See http://www.economist.com/node/16690659. Paul K. Piff, Michael W. Kraus, Stéphane Côté et al., "Having Less, Giving More: The Influence of Social Class on Prosocial Behavior," JPSP, Vol. 99, No. 5 (2010): 771–84.

[8] Patlagean, "Birth Control in the Early Byzantine Empire," 12–13. Although she does not provide a comprehensive list, Patlagean notes that those who pushed against social norms with respect to behavior and appearance were visible and scandalous affronts to hierarchies established by church and society.

[9] Gardner, "Aristophanes and Male Anxiety," 147, 150–51.

cannot know if she was in any way an agent in any of these changes because, like the woman with breast cancer, her voice is also absent from the tale.

With respect to the snake-bitten disciple, I recognize that we must consider carefully what is being cured, for there is no mention in the account of the application of any pharmaceuticals.[10] The anchorites do not "cure" the disciple as much as they discern that he was not dead, and, beyond that, they instigated the process of discerning why the disciple was suffering. Was the purpose of the serpent attack to reinforce that they were not residing in the place that God intended for them? If so, perhaps what was suffering from ill health was *not* the body of the disciple but the relationship between the abba and his disciple, as well as the vision of the abba. For two things are revealed in the process of "curing" the disciple: first, like the man at the pool of Bethesda[11] who takes up his mat and walks, the disciple becomes obedient to his elder Abba Zosimos and gets up from the ground not with difficulty, not with pain or in a state of suffering, but "at once." So the religious identity of the disciple is transformed in that he learns the extent of proper discipleship, and socially his relationship with his elder will have to change. Second, the abba had hoped "to settle" in Porphyreôn, and did remain there for two years, near two anchorites. But what is also revealed through the curing of the disciple is that they are not to remain in that particular site; thus the abba's social location is transformed by the suffering of his disciple and recognition of the superior vision and discernment process of the anchorites.

As we turn to enduring, I would not claim that either Barnabas and Abba Myrogenes—or Palladius, for that matter—seek out their illnesses, nor is there evidence that they enjoy them; but either they or their biographers recognize in the disease a unique opportunity to employ bodily sickness for the sake of the soul. By at least initially rejecting medical treatment they participate in what Andrew Crislip identifies as the "utility of illness," which requires that they cast their faith in God's ability to heal as preferential to any medical treatment that might be afforded from an individual or doctor.[12] To a certain degree this quality of endurance humanizes those who practice the angelic life. Further, it empowers individual ascetics who are able to maintain some degree of autonomy as long as they can control their own bodies, wracked though they may be with pain. It is worth considering also how the ascetics might have inherited Greek attitudes about rights that one has over one's own body in the face of a stranger's advice. Ludwig Edelstein points to the discontinuity between the modern patient and the ancient patient *vis-à-vis* their relationship to the physician:

> Moreover, it always remained strange to the ancients that man should renounce his rights over himself and should obey the physician, who reigns over him as

---

[10] They certainly existed, and for this purpose, and can be dated from the third century BCE. Scarborough, "Nicander's Toxicology I: Snakes," 3.

[11] John 5.1–18.

[12] Crislip, *From Monastery to Hospital*, 26.

the king reigns over his subjects, to borrow a phrase of Galen. To accept such a rule again seemed unnatural, for the body is our own; we are its masters, and no one else.[13]

It is true that those in this chapter who "endured" probably died from their diseases, but the entirety of an ascetic program is preparation for death. Dying from a disease did not mean that the body lost; it meant that the soul triumphed. As Peregrine Horden notes:

> the holy man was often the best judge of the state of his own soul and his physical condition. He often foresaw his own death. He knew which illness he might seek to ameliorate, which one should be endured because it was a sign of moral failure or a test of nerve, and which should be faced in the confidence that his work was done and his end was approaching.[14]

To return to our ascetics, both beneficial tales of Barnabas and Abba Myrogenes demonstrate that what matters in the ascetic program is not what disease they survived (for both appear *not* to have survived their diseases); rather, the purpose of these beneficial tales is to celebrate what they suffered, or—to use the language of this section—what they endured. Consequently, pain contributed to the development of the "sick self."[15] In a state of ill health, the ascetic is provided an opportunity to "know" the body in a different way, not just to transcend the normal needs of the body such as hunger, desire and so forth. The endurance, then, of their sickness empowers them spiritually even as it weakens them physically, which forces them to become more and more bodily dependent on a larger community. This type of ascetic regime is no rejection of the body, Judith Perkins writes, but is an investing of the body "with new significance," and therefore the "body's pains were profitable"[16] for the individual, for the community who cared for them, and for those who interacted with them. Within the monastic community ill health compels the community to embrace the body of the sick as Jesus did the ill brought to him, or as the Good Samaritan[17] embraced the broken stranger on the road. As a disease allows the sick ascetic an opportunity to discern their body differently from those who are not sick, the sick body also operates as "an object of knowledge" for others,[18] surely a challenge to the identity of a hermit.

---

[13] Edelstein, "The Relation of Ancient Philosophy to Medicine," in Temkin and Temkin (eds), *Ancient Medicine*, 363.

[14] Peregrine Horden, "The Death of Ascetics: Sickness and Monasticism in the Early Byzantine Middle East," in W.J. Shiels (ed.), *Monks: Hermits and the Ascetic Tradition: Papers Read at the 1984 Summer Meeting and The 1985 Winter Meeting of the Ecclesiastical History Society* (Oxford: Basil Blackwell, 1985): 50.

[15] Judith Perkins, *The Suffering Self*, 155.

[16] Ibid., 142.

[17] Luke 10.25–37.

[18] Samellas writes, rather poignantly, that "[t]he afflicted soul provided the most fertile soil for the growth of knowledge." Samellas, *Death in the Eastern Mediterranean*, 70.

What has this consideration of medical care in *The Meadow* revealed to us about early Byzantine society? What assumptions can we make from just a brief study of only a few beneficial tales? First, the tales stress the importance of the charismatic healer; while physicians present prognosis over the state of a disease, ascetics discern the soul of the patient. Dominic Monteserrat, in his treatment of Christian healing shrines, writes that at these sites "sick pilgrims found themselves the focus of attention in the public places and religious rituals, where ill health and human physical imperfection were, for once, placed in an exalted position as vessels for the spiritual power which brings the heavenly down to earth."[19]

Second, the tales stress the way in which medical issues bound and altered relationships between the laity and the professional religious. According to the texts, healing at the hands of ascetic figures kept families intact, demonstrated recognition of pain and suffering, and stopped the outflow of cash to physicians who did not discern, heal or see who was before them. In a few cases, as we saw, healing of women by male ascetics was also done without comment on the appropriate or inappropriateness of that interaction. As we also saw, women did not have a voice in these particular tales to express whether or not they wanted healing. But although we might not agree with *how* Moschos writes about women, we can concede that for Moschos, women are worth writing about. Finally, let us return to Abba Joseph of Thebes, who announced that of the methods of ascesis available, "I have chosen sickness." It is clear that, like the abba, many others in Moschos' *Meadow* made the same choice, and it was a choice that they medically managed well. To die from the sickness that they chose was irrelevant. A rational choice for sickness in the body displayed unequivocally a healthy soul.

Like the Byzantine liturgy, the beneficial tales of *The Meadow* do not offer any coherent view of how death might be understood. Death is a mystery that eludes any opportunity to fully—or even partially—understand it. Rather, beneficial tales that we considered in Chapter 4 that address death and dying teach us not about death, but about the character of those who faced death, those who remained and even those on the other side of death. Nicholas Constas' comments regarding the middle state of souls might very well apply to all of these categories, for the act of dying and our approaches to death and the dead body are "often a phase of self-discovery, or of being self-discovered, in which one's true character is uncovered and revealed."[20]

In addition to something of the character of individuals, what is also uncovered and revealed in these tales is that death provides an opportunity. For some—the grazer, anchorite or author of the tale—it provides an opportunity for maintaining or attempting to maintain one's autonomous status; for others—the community, the abbot with a building program, the thief—it provides an opportunity to reclaim that which brings prestige, to assert control over one who previously avoided such control, or the opportunity to grasp something that does not belong to that person

---

[19] Monteserrat, "Carrying On the Work of The Earlier Firm," 241–2.
[20] Constas, "The Middle State of Souls," 91.

(clothing, jewels or even the body itself). Further, there are other dimensions to consider: theologically, the tales support the value of human existence, rest for the frail body, hope for continued relationship in the joy of the resurrected body, and affirmation of the goodness of the created order. Anthropologically, things are more problematic: the body of the dead person still presents a thorny issue, not for the disciple—who buries, mourns, prays and then dies—but for the community that seeks, unearths, grasps, transfers and thus claims the body for its own. In this way, the ecclesiastical hierarchy ultimately forces the self-regulating movement of the ascetic to an end easily as much as death itself, and the control over the dead body is a potent witness that no one is a Christian outside of the *ekklesia*, whether they want to be, or not.

Despite the evidence above, I fear slightly making the claim that within *The Spiritual Meadow* one finds tale after tale that supports the will of the individual Christian. In part I am concerned that it will be misinterpreted, as if I am suggesting that *The Meadow* is a collection of tales that depict an authoritative church hierarchy eager to keep malcontent monks in line. But I will make the claim anyway, and risk being misunderstood. I believe that within tales that demonstrate the social history of this era—in which mundane activities such as talking to a woman, buying food, being robbed, fighting a fever or dying of old age form the central plot—one finds *neither* arrogant, overweening pride *nor* subversion, but a beneficial message of the validity of the individual, trust in the understanding of the "self" as capable of making a decision before God and with God, even if that decision is neither upheld nor respected by those around them. This is consistent with a religion that traces its most ancient roots to Abraham's response to God's order to flout tribal convention and "Go from your country and your kindred and your father's house to the land that I will show you."[21] Consequently, it should come as no surprise that at the end of antiquity we find the validity of each unique person as seeds planted deeply in the soil of communal Palestinian/Egyptian monasticism, fertilized with their ascetic choices. The result, Moschos claims, is a radiant blooming of "roses," "lilies" and "violets"[22] to adorn God's *Meadow*.

---

[21] Gen. 12.1.
[22] "ῥόδων, κρίνοις» and «ἴων," *Prat. sp.* PG 87.2851–2.

Bibliography

Primary Sources

All biblical passages are taken from:
The New Oxford Annotated Bible with Apocrypha: New Revised Standard Version. Edited by Michael D. Coogan, Marc Z. Brettler, Carol A. Newsom and Pheme Perkins. Oxford University Press, 2010.

Aetios of Amida. English translation in *Aetios of Amida: The Gynaecology and Obstetrics of the VIth Century, A.D.* Translated by James V. Ricci. Philadelphia: The Blakiston Company, 1950.

Ambrose, *De Tobia.* Patrologia latina. Edited by J.-P. Migne. 217 vols. Paris, 1844–64. English translation in *S. Ambrosii, De Tobia: A Commentary, with an Introduction and Translation.* Translated by Lois Miles Zucker. Washington, DC: Catholic University of America, 1933.

Ambrose, *De bono mortis. Corpus scriptorium ecclesiasticorum latinorum 32.*

Anastasios the Sinaite. *S. P. N. Anastasii, cognomento Sinaïtae, Patriarchae Antiocheni, Opera omnia, quae supersunt.* Edited by Frédéric Nau. "Le texte grec du moine Anastase sur les saints pères du Sinaï," Oriens Christianus 2, 1902.

Anastasius, *Saint Anastase le Perse: et l'histoire de la Palestine au début du VIIe siècle.* Editions du Centre National de la Recherche Scientifique, Paris, 1992.

Anonymous Apophthegmata. Patrologia graeca. Edited by J.-P. Migne. 162 vols. Paris, 1857–86. Edited by Frédéric Nau. "Histoires des solitaires égyptiens," *Revue de l'Orient Chrétien* 12 (1907) through 18 (1913).

Anonymous. *Der Heilige Tychon.* Edited by H. Usener. Leipzig and Berlin. 1907.

Anonymous. *Historia monachorum in Æepypto.* Patrologia graeca. Edited by J.-P. Migne. 162 vols. Paris, 1857–86. André-Jean Festugière, *Subsidia Hagiographica* n° 53. Brussels, 1971. French translation in André-Jean Festugière, *Enquête sur les Moines d'Egypte*, in *Les Moines d'Orient* IV/1. Paris: Éditions du Cerf, 1961–65. English translation in *The Lives of the Desert Fathers.* Translated by Norman Russell. Oxford: Cistercian Publications, 1980.

Antonios. *The Life & Daily Mode of Living of the Blessed Simeon the Stylite by Antonios.* H. Leitzmann, *Das Leben des heiligen Symeon Sytlites*, Texte und Untersuchung zur Geschichte der altchristlichen Literatur 32.4. Leipzig: Hinrichs, 1908. English translation in *The Lives of Simeon Stylites.* Translated by Robert Doran. Kalamazoo, MI: Cistercian Publications, 1992.

Apophthegmata Patrum, collectio alphabetica. Patrologia graeca. Edited by J.-P. Migne. 162 vols. Paris, 1857–86. "Histoires des solitaires égyptiens." *Revue de l'Orient Chrétien* 12–18. Edited by F. Nau, 1907–13. English translation in *The Sayings of the Desert Fathers: The Alphabetical Collection*. Translated by Benedicta Ward, SLG. Kalamazoo, Ml: Cistercian Publications, 1975.

Apophthegmata Patrum, collectio systematica. Patrologia graeca. Edited by J.-P. Migne. 162 vols. Paris, 1857–86. French translation in *Apophtegmes des Pères: Collection Systematique Chapitres*. Translated by Jean-Claude Guy, S.J.; *Sources Chrétiennes* 474 (Paris, 2003). English translation in *The Book of the Elders: Sayings of the Desert Fathers, The Systematic Collection*, Translated by John Wortley. Collegeville, MN: Cistercian Publications, 2012.

Apophthegmata Patrum. Ethiopian Collection [Eth. Coll.]. Edited with Latin translation by Victor Arras. *Collectico Monastica.* Corpus Scriptorum Christianorum Orientalium 238–9. Louvain: Secrétariat du Corpus SCO, 1973–74. In Daniel Caner. *Wandering, Begging Monks: Spiritual Authority and the Promotion of Monasticism in Late Antiquity.* Berkeley, CA: University of California Press, 2002.

The Apostolic Fathers, Volume I: I Clement. II Clement. Ignatius. Polycarp. Didache. 1998. Translated by Kirsopp Lake. LCL. Cambridge, MA: Harvard University Press.

The Apostolic Fathers: Volume II. Shepherd of Hermas. Martyrdom of Polycarp. Epistle to Diogentus 1997. Translated by Kirsopp Lake. LCL. Cambridge, MA: Harvard University Press.

Aristotle. *Nicomachean Ethics*. Translated by J.A.K. Thompson. London: Penguin, 1955.

Athanasis. *De incarnatione verbi.* Patrologia graeca. Edited by J.-P. Migne. 162 vols. Paris, 1857–86. English translation in *On the Incarnation.* Translated by A Religious of C.S.M.V. Crestwood, NY: St Vladimir's Seminary Press, 1996.

———. *Vita Antonii.* Patrologia graeca. Edited by J.-P. Migne. 162 vols. Paris, 1857–86. English translation of *The Life and Affairs of Our Holy Father Antony* in *Athanasius: The Life of Antony and the Letter To Marcellinus.* Translated by Robert C. Gregg. Mahwah, NJ: Paulist Press, 1979.

Athanasius, Pseudo. *Vie de Sainte Syncletique.* Translated by Sr Odile Benedicte Bernard. Spirituale Orientale n° 9. Abbaye De Bellefontaine, 1972. English translation in *The Life and Activity of the Holy and Blessed Teacher Syclectica.* Translated by Elizabeth A. Castelli. *Ascetic Behavior in Greco-Roman Antiquity: A Sourcebook.* Edited by Vincent L. Wimbush. Minneapolis, MN: Fortress Press, 1998.

Augustine. *De opera monachorum* 23.28. Patrolgina latina. Edited by J.-P. Migne. 217 vols. Paris, 1844–64. In *Fathers of the Church, A New Translation: St Augustine: Treatise on Various Subjects.* Edited by Roy J. Defferari. New York: Cima Publications, 1952.

———. *Perfectione justitiae hominis, De.* Patrolgina latina. Edited by J.-P. Migne. 217 vols. Paris, 1844–64.

Babrius and Phaedrus. 1975 Translated by Ben Edwin Perry. LCL. Cambridge, MA: Harvard University Press.

Basil of Caesarea. *Homilia in illud: Destruam horrea mea*. French translation in *Saint Baisle: Homélies sur la richesse: Edition critique et exégétique*. Edited and translated by Yves Courtonne. Paris: Firmin-Didot, 1935. English translation in *The Sunday Sermons of the Great Fathers*. Translated by M.F. Toal. Chicago, IL: Henry Regnery, 1959.

_____. *Regulae fusius tractatae*. Patrologia graeca. Edited by J.-P. Migne. 162 vols. Paris, 1857–86. In *Saint Basil: Ascetical Works*. Translated by Sr M. Monica Wagner. Washington, DC: Catholic University of America Press, 1962.

_____. *Homilia in psalmum 14*. Patrologia graeca. Edited by J.-P. Migne. 162 vols. Paris, 1857–86. English translation in *Saint Basil: Exegetic Homilies*. Translated by Agnes Clair Way. Fathers of the Church 46. Catholic University Press, 1963.

_____. *Saint Basil: The Letters*. 1994. Translated by Roy J. Deferrari. 3 vols. LCL. Cambridge, MA: Harvard University Press.

_____. *Homilia dicta tempore famis et siccitatis*. Clavis Patrum Graecorum. 2852. English translation in *The Hungry are Dying: Beggars and Bishops in Roman Cappadocia*. Oxford Studies in Historical Theology. Translated by Susan R. Holman. Oxford University Press, 2001.

_____. *An Ascetical Discourse*. Patrologia graeca. Edited by J.-P. Migne. 162 vols. Paris, 1857–86. English translation in *Saint Basil: Ascetical Works*. Translated by Sr M. Monica Wagner. Washington, DC: Catholic University of America Press, 1962. English translation in *The Asketikon of St. Basil the Great*. Translated by Anna M. Silvas. Oxford University Press, 2005.

Besa. *Letters and Sermons of Besa*. Translated by K.H. Kuhn. *Corpus Scriptorum Christianorum Orientalium* 157. Louvain: Imprimerie Orientaliste, 1956.

Cassien, Jean, *Conférences*. Sources Chrétiennes 64. Translated by Dom E. Pichery. Paris: Les Éditions du Cerf, 1959.

Cicero. *De Divinatione*. In *The Religious Context of Early Christianity: A Guide to Graeco-Roman Religions*. Hans-Joseph Klauck, Minneapolis, MN: Fortress Press, 2003.

_____. *Tusculan Disputations*. Translated in English in Martha C. Nussbaum, *The Therapy of Desire: Theory and Practice in Hellenistic Ethics*. Princeton University Press, 1994.

_____. *De legibus*. *Cicero: De re Publica (On the Republic), De Legibus (On the Laws)*. Translated by Clinton W. Keyes. LCL. Cambridge, MA: Harvard University Press, 1928.

Clement of Alexandria. *Stromata*. Patrologia graeca. Edited by J.-P. Migne. 162 vols. Paris, 1857–86. English translation in vol. 2 of *The Ante-Nicene Fathers*. Edited by Alexander Roberts and James Donaldson. 1886–89. 10 vols. Peabody, MA: Hendrickson, 1994.

Codex Theodosianus. English translation in *The Theodosian Code and Novels*. Translated by Clyde Pharr. Princeton University Press, 1952.

Corpus juris civilis. English translation in *The Civil Law: Including the Twelve Tables, the Institutes of Gaius, the Rules of Ulpian, the Opinions of Paulus, the Enactments of Justinian, and the Constitutions*. Translated by Samuel Parsons Scott. New York: The Lawbook Exchange, Ltd, 1973.

Cyril of Jerusalem. *Catechesis*. Patrologia graeca. Edited by J.-P. Migne. 162 vols. Paris, 1857–86.

Cyril of Scythopolis. *Lives of the Monks of Palestine*. Patrologia graeca. Edited by J.-P. Migne. 162 vols. Paris, 1857–86. *Kyrillos von Skythopolis*. Edited by E. Schwartz. Texte und Untersuchungen zur Geschichte der altchristlichen Literatur, 4. Leipzig, J.C. Hinrichs, 1939. *Vita S. Theodosii a Cyrillo Scythopolitano Scripta*. Edited by H. Usener. Bonn: Typis C. Gergi University, 1890. English translation in *The Lives of the Monks of Palestine*. Translated by R.M. Price. Cistercian Studies. Kalamazoo, MI: Cistercian Publications, 1991.

Diadoque de Photice. *Œuvres Spirituelles*. Edited by Édouard des Places. *Sources Chrétiennes*, 5. Paris: Éditions du Cerf, 1955.

Dionysius the Areopagite. *The Divine Names*. Patrologia graeca. Edited by J.-P. Migne. 162 vols. Paris, 1857–86. English translation in *Pseudo Dionysius: The Complete Works*. Translated by Paul Rorem. Classics of Western Spirituality. New York: Paulist Press, 1987.

Dionysius, Pseudo. Patrologia graeca. Edited by J.-P. Migne. 162 vols. Paris, 1857–86. English translation in *Pseudo Dionysius: The Complete Works*. Translated by Colm Luibheid and Paul Rorem. Classics of Western Spirituality. New York: Paulist Press, 1987.

Dorotheos of Gaza. "Fear of the Punishment to Come and the Need for Never Neglecting One's Salvation." Patrologia graeca. Edited by J.-P. Migne. 162 vols. Paris, 1857–86. In *Dorotheos of Gaza: Discourses and Sayings*. Translated by Eric P. Wheeler. Kalamazoo, MI: Cistercian Publications, 1977.

Epictetus. *Dissertationes*. English translation in Ludwig Edelstein, *Ancient Medicine; Selected Papers of Ludwig Edelstein*. Baltimore, MD: Johns Hopkins University Press, 1967.

Euripides. *Euripides, Cyclops, Alcestis, Medea*. 1994. Translated by David Kovacs. LCL. Cambridge, MA: Harvard University Press.

Evagrius Ponticus. *Praktikos*. Clavis patum latinorum 2430. English translation in *Evagrius Ponticus. The Praktikos. Chapters on Prayer.* Translated by John Eudes Bamberger, OCSO. Kalamazoo, MI: Cistercian Publications, 2006.

Evagrius Scholasticus. *Historia ecclesiastica.* Patrologia graeca. Edited by J.-P. Migne. 162 vols. Paris, 1857–86. English translation in *Ecclesiastical History of Evagrius Scholasticus*. Translated by Michael Whitby. Liverpool University Press, 2001.

First Greek Life. F. Halkin, *Sancti Pachomii Vitae Graecae, Subsidia hagiographica* 19. Brussels, 1932. English translation in *Pachomian Koinonia: The Life of St. Pachomius and His Disciples*, vol. I. Translated by Armand Villeux. Kalamazoo, MI: Cistercian Publications, 1980.

Georgios, ho Eleusios. *Vie de Theodore de Sykeon.* Edited by A.-J. Festugière. Subsidia hagiographica 48. Bruxelles: Société des Bollandistes, 1970. English translation in *Three Byzantine Saints: Contemporary Biographies of St. Daniel the Stylite, St. Theodore of Sykeon and St. John the Almsgiver.* Translated by Elizabeth Dawes and Norman H. Baynes. Crestwood, NY: St Vladimir's Seminary Press, 1996.

Galen. *XIV.* Edited by C.G. Kühn. In John Scarborough, "Nicander's Toxicology I: Snakes," *Pharmacy in History* 19, No. 1 (1977).

Gospel According to Thomas. Edited and translated by Bart D. Ehrman and Zlatko Pleše. *Apocryphal Gospels: Texts and Translations.* Oxford University Press, 2011.

Gregory Nazianzus. *Oration* 7. Patrologia graeca. Edited by J.-P. Migne. 162 vols. Paris, 1857–86.

———. *Oration* 14. *On the Love of the Poor and Those Afflicted with Leprosy.* Patrologia graeca. Edited by J.-P. Migne. 162 vols. Paris, 1857–86. English translation in *St. Gregory of Nazianzus: Select Orations.* Translated by Martha Vinson; The Fathers of the Church 107. Washington, DC: The Catholic University of America Press, 1963.

———. *Oration* 17. Patrologia graeca. Edited by J.-P. Migne. 162 vols. Paris, 1857–86.

———. *Oration* 18. Patrologia graeca. Edited by J.-P. Migne. 162 vols. Paris, 1857–86.

———. *Oration* 33. Patrologia graeca. Edited by J.-P. Migne. 162 vols. Paris, 1857–86.

———. *Oration* 34. Patrologia graeca. Edited by J.-P. Migne. 162 vols. Paris, 1857–86.

———. *Oration* 38. Patrologia graeca. Edited by J.-P. Migne. 162 vols. Paris, 1857–86.

———. *Oration* 40. Patrologia graeca. Edited by J.-P. Migne. 162 vols. Paris, 1857–86.

———. *Oration* 43. Patrologia graeca. Edited by J.-P. Migne. 162 vols. Paris, 1857–86. French translation in *Saint Grégoire de Nazianze: Le Theologien et son temps, 330–390.* Translated by Jean Bernardi. Initiations aux Pères de l'Eglise. Paris: Editions du Cerf, 1995.

Gregory of Nyssa. *Gregorii Nysseni Opera Ascetica.* Edited by W. Jaeger, John P. Cavarnos and Virginia Woods Callahan. Leiden, 1952.

———. *De deitate Filii et Spiritus sancti.* Gregorii Nysseni Opera, edited by Werner Jaeger. Berolini, apud Weidmannos, 1921–.

———. *Contra Usurarios.* Gregorii Nysseni Opera, edited by Werner Jaeger. Berolini, apud Weidmannos, 1921–. English translation in "Against Those Who Practice Usury." Translated by Casimir McCambley. *Greek Orthodox Theological Review* 36 (1991): 287–302.

———. *De via Moysis. Gregorii Nysseni De Vita Moysis.* Gregorii Nysseni Opera. Edited by Herbertus Musurillo. Leiden: Brill Academic Publishers, 1991.

_____. *Vita Sanctae Macrinae.* Edited by M. Pierre Maraval, *Vie de sainte Macrine. Sources Chrétiennes* 178. Paris, 1971. English translation in *Handmaids of the Lord: Holy Women in Late Antiquity & The Early Middle Ages.* Translation by Joan M. Peterson. Kalamazoo, MI: Cistercian Publications, 1996.

_____. *In illud: Quatenus uni ex his fecistis mihi fecistis.* Gregorii Nysseni Opera, edited by Werner Jaeger. Berolini, apud Weidmannos, 1921–. *On the Love of the Poor* English translation in *The Hungry are Dying: Beggars and Bishops in Roman Cappadocia.* Oxford Studies in Historical Theology. Translated by Susan R. Holman. Oxford University Press, 2001.

_____. *To Philagrius* (Letter 31). *Gregorii Nysseni Epistulae.* Gregorii Nysseni Opera. Edited by Georgius Pasquali. English translation in *Gregory of Nazianzus.* Translated by Brian E. Daley. The Early Church Fathers. London: Routledge, 2006.

Gregory the Presbyter, *Vita S. Patris Nostri Gregorii.* Patrologia graeca. Edited by J.-P. Migne. 162 vols. Paris, 1857–86.

Irenaeus, *Adversus Haereses.* Patrologia graeca. Edited by J.-P. Migne. 162 vols. Paris, 1857–86. English translation in *St. Irenaeus of Lyons: Against the Heresies Book 1.* Translated by Dominic J. Unger. Ancient Christian Writers. New York: Paulist Press, 1991.

Jerome. *Epistulae. Hieronymus.* Edited by Isidorus Hilberg. Corpus Scriptorum Ecclesiasticorum Latinorum, Hilberg. vol. LIV. Wien: VÖAW, 1996. English translation in *Select letters of St. Jerome.* 1963. Translated by F.A. Wright. LCL. Cambridge, MA: Harvard University Press.

John Chrysostom. *Homiliae in Matthaeum.* Patrologia graeca. Edited by J.-P. Migne. 162 vols. Paris, 1857–86.

_____. *Homiliae in Acta apostolorum.* Patrologia graeca. Edited by J.-P. Migne. 162 vols. Paris, 1857–86.

_____. *Ad populum Antiochenum de statuis.* Patrologia graeca. Edited by J.-P. Migne. 162 vols. Paris, 1857–86. English translation in vol. 9 of *The Nicne and Post-Nicene Fathers*, Series 1. Edited by Philip Schaff. 1886–89. 14 vols. Peabody, MA: Hendrickson, 1994.

_____. "Sixth Sermon on Lazarus and the Rich Man/On the Earthquake." Patrologia graeca. Edited by J.-P. Migne. 162 vols. Paris, 1857–86. English translation in *Saint John Chrysostom: On Wealth and Poverty.* Edited and translated by Catherine P. Roth. New York: St Vladimir's Seminary Press, 1984.

_____. *Homiliae in Genesim.* Patrologia graeca. Edited by J.-P. Migne. 162 vols. Paris, 1857–86.

_____. *De eleemosyna.* Patrologia graeca. Edited by J.-P. Migne. 162 vols. Paris, 1857–86. English translation in *St. John Chrysostom on Repentance and Almsgiving.* Translated by Gus George Christo. The Fathers of the Church. Washington, DC: Catholic University of Amer Press, 1997.

_____. *Homiliae in epistulum ii ad Corinthios.* Patrologia graeca. Edited by J.-P. Migne. 162 vols. Paris, 1857–86. English translation in "The Advocacy of Empty Bellies." Translated by M.J. De Vinne. UMI Dissertation Services, 1995.

_____. *Homiliae in Joannem.* Patrologia graeca. Edited by J.-P. Migne. 162 vols. Paris, 1857–86.
John Climacus. *Scala Paradisi.* Patrologia graeca. Edited by J.-P. Migne. 162 vols. Paris, 1857–86. English translation in *The Ladder of Divine Ascent.* Translated by Colm Luibheid and Norman Russell. Classics of Western Spirituality. New York: Paulist Press, 1988.
Johannes Des Mildthätigen, Erzbischofs Von Alexandreia. *Der Heilige Tychon. (Leben und Wunder Des Heiligen Tychon Von Der Hand Johannes Des Mildthätigen, Erzbischofs Von Alexandreia.* Edited by A. Brinkmann and Hermann Usener. Leipzig and Berlin, 1907.
John of Damascus, *First Apology Against Those Who Attack the Divine Images. Die Schriften des Johannes von Damaskos.* Berlin: de Gruyter, 1969–88. English translation in *St. John of Damascus On the Divine Images.* Translated by Andrew Louth. Crestwood, NY: St Vladimir's Seminary Press, 2003.
_____. *Expos.* 2. Patrologia graeca. Edited by J.-P. Migne. 162 vols. Paris, 1857–86. English translation in *St. John of Damascus: Writings.* Edited by Joseph Deferrari and translated by Frederic Hathaway Chase. The Fathers of the Church: a new translation, Vol. 37. Washington, DC: Catholic University of America Press, 1958. English translation *St. John Damascene Tradition and Originality in Byzantine Theology.* Translated by Andrew Louth, Oxford University Press, 2005.
_____. *Disputatio Saraceni et Christiani.* Patrologia graeca. Edited by J.-P. Migne. 162 vols. Paris, 1857–86.
John of Ephesus, *Lives of the Eastern Saints.* Patrologia orientalis. Edited and translated by E.W. Brooks X. Vols 17–19. Paris, Firmin-Didot, 1923–26.
John Moschos. *Pratum spirituale.* Patrologia graeca. Edited by J.-P. Migne. 162 vols. Paris, 1857–86. French translation *Le Pré Spirituel.* Translated by M.-J. Rouët de Journel. Sources Chrétiennes 12, 1946. Italian Translation in *Giovanni Mosco, Il Prato.* Translation by Riccardo Maisano. Naples: D'Auria M., 1982. English translation in *The Spiritual Meadow.* Translated by John Wortley. Cistercian Studies. Kalamazoo, MI: Cistercian Publications, 1992. "Il Pratum Spirituale de Giovanni Mosco, gli episodi inediti del Cod. Marciano greco II.21." Translated by Elpidio Mioni. *Orientalia Christiana Periodica* 17 (1951): 61–94. "Unbekannte Erzählungen aus dem Pratum Spirituale." Translated by Theodore Nissen. *Byzantinische Zeitschrift* 38 (1938): 351–76.
Justinian. *Novellae.* Edited by Paul Krueger, Theodor Mommsen and Rudolf Schöll. *Corpus Iuris Civilis: Novellae.* New Jersey: The Lawbook Exchange, Ltd, 2010.
Leontius. *A Supplement to the Life of John the Almsgiver, our saintly father and Archbishop of Alexandria, written by Leontius, Bishop of Neapolis in the Island of Cyprus.* Patrologia graeca. Edited by J.-P. Migne. 162 vols. Paris, 1857–86. English translation in *Three Byzantine Saints: Contemporary Biographies of St. Daniel the Stylite, St. Theodore of Sykeon and St. John the Almsgiver.* Translated by Elizabeth Dawes and Norman H. Baynes. Crestwood, NY: St Vladimir's Seminary Press, 1996.

Lucian. *On Mourning*. Translated in *Lucian Volume IV*. Translated by A.M. Harmon. LCL. Cambridge, MA: Harvard University Press, 1965. In Jeffrey A. Trumbower, *Rescue for the Dead: The Posthumous Salvation of Non-Christians in Early Christianity*. Oxford Studies in Historical Theology. Oxford University Press, 2001.

Macarius, Aegyptius. *Homily* 48. *Die 50 geistlichen Homilien des Makarios*. Edited by *Hermann Dörries; Erich Klostermann; Matthias Kroeger*. Patristische Texte und Studien, Bd. 4. Berlin: de Gruyter, 1964. In Owsei Temkin, *Hippocrates in a World of Pagans and Christians*. Baltimore, MD: Johns Hopkins University Press, 1991.

Macarius, Pseudo. *Liber Graduum. Book of Steps* in Daniel Caner. *Wandering, Begging Monks: Spiritual Authority and the Promotion of Monasticism in Late Antiquity.* Berkeley, CA: University of California Press, 2002.

Maximos the Confessor. *Disputatio Inter Maximum Et Theodosium, Episcopum Caesareae Bithyniae 3*. Patrologia graeca. Edited by J.-P. Migne. 162 vols. Paris, 1857–86. Clavis partum latinorum 7735. English translation in *Maximos the Confessor and His Companions*. Edited and translated by Pauline Allen and Bronwen Neil. Oxford Early Christian Texts. Oxford University Press, 2004.

Meretricis. *Vita Sanctae Pelagiae*. Patrolgina latina. Edited by J.-P. Migne. 217 vols. Paris, 1844–64. English translation in *Harlots of the Desert: A Study of Repentance in Early Monastic Sources.* Translated by Benedicta Ward, SLG. Kalamazoo, MI: Cistercian Publications, 1987.

Nicephorus. "The Translation of Saint Nicholas, Confessor." English translation in *Saint Nicholas of Myra, Bari, and Manhattan: Biography of a Legend.* Chicago, IL: University of Chicago Press, 1978.

Orellius. *Inscriptionum latinarum selectarum amplissima collectio: ad illustrandam romanae antiquitatis disciplinam accommodata ac magnarum collectionum supplementa complura emendationesque exhibens*. Johann Kaspar von Orelli; Wilhelm Henzen, Turici 1828–56.

Origen. *Contra Celsum*. Patrologia graeca. Edited by J.-P. Migne. 162 vols. Paris, 1857–86. English translation in *Origen. Contra Celsum.* Translated by Henry Chadwick. Cambridge University Press, 1953.

———. *De principiis.* Patrologia graeca. Edited by J.-P. Migne. 162 vols. Paris, 1857–86.

———. *Commentarii inRomanos*. Patrologia graeca. Edited by J.-P. Migne. 162 vols. Paris, 1857–86.

———. *Homiliae in Exodum.* Patrologia graeca. Edited by J.-P. Migne. 162 vols. Paris, 1857–86.

———. *Homiliae in Lucam.* Patrologia graeca. Edited by J.-P. Migne. 162 vols. Paris, 1857–86.

———. *Commentarii in evangelium Matthaei.* Patrologia graeca. Edited by J.-P. Migne. 162 vols. Paris, 1857–86.

———. *Commentarii in evangelium Joannis.* Patrologia graeca. Edited by J.-P. Migne. 162 vols. Paris, 1857–86.

_____. *Esplanatio super psalmum tricesimum septimum, Homily I.* Patrologia graeca. Edited by J.-P. Migne. 162 vols. Paris, 1857–86.

_____. *Adnotations in librum III regum* 15.23. Patrologia graeca. Edited by J.-P. Migne. 162 vols. Paris, 1857–86. In Gary B. Ferngren, *Medicine & Health Care in Early Christianity.* Baltimore, MD: Johns Hopkins University Press, 2009.

Palladius, *Historia Lausiaca.* Patrologia graeca. Edited by J.-P. Migne. 162 vols. Paris, 1857–86. *Historia Lausiaca.* Edited by Cuthbert Butler, in *The Lausiac History of Palladius, Introduction and Text.* Cambridge University Press, 1898, 1904. *Palladius: The Lausiac History.* Edited by G.J.M. Bartelink, translated by Marion Barchiesi. *Palladio, La Storia Lausiaca. Fondazione Lorenza Valla*, 1974. English translation by Robert T. Meyer. Ancient Church Writers 34. New York: Paulist Press, 1964.

Paul of Monembasia, and other authors. *Bibliotheca Hagiographica Graeca.* Edited by François Halkin, 5 vols. Brussels, 1957–84. *Spiritually Beneficial Tales of Paul, Bishop of Monembasia and of Other Authors.* Edited and translated in English by John Wortley. Kalamazoo, MI: Cistercian Publications, 1996.

Photius. *The Bibliotheca. Clavis partum latinorum. Photius: The Bibliotheca.* Edited by N.G. Wilson. London: Duckworth Publishing, 1994.

Plato. *Euthyphro. Apology. Crito. Phaedo. Phaedrus.* 1914. Translated by Harold North Fowler. LCL. Cambridge, MA: Harvard University Press.

_____. *Laws.* 1926. Translated by R.G. Bury. 6 vols. LCL. Cambridge, MA: Harvard University Press.

Pliny. *Letters.* Translated by William Melmoth. London, W. Heinemann: 1914.

_____. *Naturalis historia. Pliny: Natural History, Volume VII, Books 24–27.* Translated by W.H.S. Jones and A.C. Andrews. LCL. Cambridge, MA: Harvard University Press, 1956.

Procopius, *History of the Wars.* 1914. Translated by H.B. Dewing. 7 vols, LCL. Cambridge, MA: Harvard University Press.

_____. *The Secret History.* 1935. English translation in *Procopius: The Anecdota or Secret History.* Translated by H.B. Dewing. LCL. Cambridge, MA: Harvard University Press.

Saint Daniel of Sketis: A Group of Hagiographic Texts. Studia Byzantina Upsaliensia. Translated by Britt Dahlman. Uppsala Universitet, 2007.

Sebeos. *Patmut'iwn Sebeosi.* Edited by G.V. Abgaryan, Erevan, 1979. *The Armenian History Attributed to Sebeos*, English translation in *The Armenian History Attributed to Sebeos.* Translated by R.W. Thompson. 2 vols. Liverpool University Press, 1999.

Sophocles. *Oedipus at Colonus.* Translated by Eamon Grennan and Rachel Kitzinger. Greek Tragedy in New Translations. Oxford University Press, 2013.

Sophronios, *The Life of Mary of Egypt.* Patrologia graeca. Edited by J.-P. Migne. 162 vols. Paris, 1857–86. English translation in *Holy Women of Byzantium: Ten Saints' Lives in English Translation.* Translated by by Maria Kouli. Washington, DC: Dumbarton Oaks, 1996.

_____. *Sophrone de Jérusalem: Vie Monastique et Confession Dogmatique.* Edited by Christoph von Schönborn. Théologie historique 20. Paris: Beauchesne, 1972.

Sophronius and John Moschos. *The Life of Our holy Father, John the Almsgiver Miracula S. Artemii.* Papadopoulos-Keremeus, *Varia Graeca sacra,* 1–75 (BHG 173); English translation in *The Miracles of St. Artemios: A Collection of Miracle Stories by an Anonymous Author of Seventh-Century Byzantium.* Translated with commentary by Virgil S. Crisafulli and John W. Nesbitt. Supplemented by a Reprinted Greek Text and an Essay by John F. Haldon. *The Medieval Mediterranean: Peoples, Economies, and Cultures, 400–1453*, Vol. 13. Leiden: E.J. Brill, 1997.

Sozomen, *The Ecclesiastical History.* Patrologia graeca. Edited by J.-P. Migne. 162 vols. Paris, 1857–86. English translation in vol. 2 in *The Nicene and Post-Nicene Fathers.* Series 2. Edited by Philip Schaff. 1886–89. 14 vols. Peabody, MA: Hendrickson, 1994.

Tatian. *Oratio ad Graecos.* In Owsei Temkin, *Hippocrates in a World of Pagans and Christians.* Baltimore, MD: Johns Hopkins University Press, 1995.

Theodoret of Cyrrhus. *Philotheos Historia [Historia Religiosa].* Patrologia graeca. Edited by J.-P. Migne. 162 vols. Paris, 1857–86. *Bibliotecha veterum partum,* cod. 199. Paris, 1624. Edited and translated by Paul Canivet and Alice Leroy-Molinghen, *Histoire des moines de Syrie. Sources Chrétiennes* 257. Paris, Éditions du Cerf, 1977, 1979. English translation in *A History of the Monks of Syria.* Translated by R.M. Price. Kalamazoo, MI: Cistercian Publications, 1985.

Theodorus, Bishop of Petra and Cyril of Scythopolis. *Life of Theodosius.* Edited by H. Usener. *Der heilige Theodosius, Schriften des Theodoros und Kyrillos.* Leipzig: Teubner, 1890.

Theophanes the Confessor. *The Chronicle of Theophanes: Anni mundi 6095–6305 (A.D. 602–813).* Edited and translated Harry Turtledove. University of Pennsylvania Press, 1982.

Theophylact Simocatta. *History.* English translation in *The History of Theophylact Simocatta: An English Translation with Introduction.* Translated by Michael and Mary Whitby. Oxford University Press, 1986.

Multiple Authors

A Répertoire of Byzantine Beneficial Tales. Abstracts and index of nearly one thousand "spiritually beneficial tales" (*narrationes animae utiles*). Maintained by John Wortley. http://home.cc.umanitoba.ca/~wortley.

Abba Daniel of Scetis. Vie et récits de l'abbé Daniel le Scétiote (VIe siècle). Edited by L.Clugnet, *Revue de l'Orient Chrétien* 5 (1900). English translation in *Witness to Holiness: Abba Daniel of Scetis.* Edited by Tim Vivian, multiple translators. Kalamazoo, MI: Cistercian Publications, 2008.

Acta Concilii. Mansi. English translation in *Readings in Christianity.* Wadsworth, 2001.

Byzantine Monastic Foundation Documents: A Complete Translation of the Surviving Founders' Typika and Testaments. Edited and translated by John Thomas, Angela Constantinides Hero and Giles Constable. Washington, DC: Dumbarton Oaks, 2000.

Philokalia. English translation in *The Philokalia: The Complete Text Complied by St. Nikodemos of the Holy Mountain and St. Makarios of Corinth*, vol. 1. Translated and edited by G.E.H. Palmer, Philip Sherrard and Kallistos Ware. London: Faber and Faber, 1983.

The Seven Ecumenical Councils. In Vol. 14 of *The Nicene and Post-Nicene Fathers*, Series 2. Edited by Philip Schaff. 1886–89. Cambridge, MA: Hendrickson Publishers, 1999.

Secondary Sources

Abrahamse, Dorothy. "Rituals of Death in the Middle Byzantine Period." *Greek Orthodox Theological Review* 29, No. 2 (1984): 125–34.

Albright, W.F. and C.S. Mann. *Matthew: A New Translation*. The Anchor Yale Bible 26. Yale University Press, 2011.

Allbutt, Thomas Clifford. *Greek Medicine in Rome: The Fitzpatrick Lectures on the History of Medicine Delivered at the Royal College of Physicians of London in 1909–1910; With Other Essays*. New York: B. Blom, 1970.

Allen, Pauline. "The 'Justinianic' Plague." *Byzantion* 49 (1979): 5–20.

———. *Evagrius Scholasticus: The Church Historian*. Etudes et documents, fasc. 41. Leuven: Spicilegium sacrum Lovaniense, 1981.

Amundsen, Darrel W. *Medicine, Society, and Faith in the Ancient and Medieval Worlds*. Johns Hopkins University Press, 2000.

Anonymous, "What Price A Baby?" *Journal of Psychosocial Nursing & Mental Health Services* 37, No. 5 (1999): 7.

Arbesmann, Rudolph. "The Concept of 'Christus Medicus' in St. Augustine." *Traditio* 10 (1954): 1–28.

Askitopoulou, Helen. Eleni Konsolaki, Ioanna A. Ramoutsaki and Maria Anastassaki. "Surgical Cures Under Sleep Induction in the Asclepieion of Epidauros." International Congress Series 1242 (2002): 11–17.

Aune, David E. *Prophecy in Early Christianity and the Ancient Mediterranean World.* Grand Rapids, MI: William B. Eerdmans Publishing Company, 1983.

Avalos, Hector. *Health Care and the Rise of Christianity*. Grand Rapids, MI: Baker Academic, 2010.

Baldwin, Barry. "Beyond the House Call: Doctors in Early Byzantine History and Politics."*Dumbarton Oaks Papers* 38 Symposium on Byzantine Medicine (1984): 15–19.

Barnish, S. "The Transformation of Classical Cities and the Pirenne Debate," *Journal of Roman Archaeology* 2 (1989): 385–400.

Bauckham, Richard. *The Miracles of Jesus*. Edited by David Wenham and Craig Blomberg. Vol. 6. Sheffield: JSOT Press, 1986.

Baun, Jane. *Tales from Another Byzantium: Celestial Journey and Local Community in the Medieval Greek Apocrypha*. Cambridge University Press, 2007.

Baxter, Vern and A.V. Margavio. "Honor, Status and Aggression in Economic Exchange." *Sociological Theory* 18, No. 3 (2000): 399–416.

Baynes, Norman H. "The Pratum Spirituale" *Byzantine Studies and Other Essays*. University of London: The Athlone Press, 1955, 261–70.

Beck, Hans-Georg. *Die Byzantiner und ihr Jenseits: zur Entstehungsgeschichte einer Mentalität*. München: Verlag der Bayerischen Akademie der Wissenschaften, 1979.

Binns, John. *Ascetics and Ambassadors of Christ: The Monasteries of Palestine 314–631*. Oxford Early Christian Texts Oxford: Oxford University Press, 1996.

Biraben, Jean-Noël. *Les Hommes et la peste en France et dans les pays européens et méditerranéens: Tome I: La peste dans l'histoire*. Civilisations et Sociétés 35. Paris: Mouton, 1976.

Bitton-Ashkelony, Brouria. *Encountering the Sacred: The Debate on Christian Pilgrimage in Late Antiquity*. University of California Press, 2005.

Blum, Richard H. and Eva Maria Blum. *The Dangerous Hour: The Lore of Crisis and Mystery in Rural Greece*. New York: Scribner, 1970.

Bolkestein, Hendrik. *Wohltätigkeit und Armenpflege im vorchristlichen Altertum; ein Beitrag zum Problem "Moral und Gesellschaft."* Utrecht: A. Oosthoek Verlag, 1939.

Booth, Phil. "Saints and Soteriology in Sophronius Sophista's *Miracles of Cyrus and John*." *Studies in Church History* 45 (2009): 52–63.

_____. *Moschus, Sophronius, Maximus: Asceticism, Sacrament and Dissent at the End of Empire*. Transformation of the Classical Heritage. Berkeley, CA: University of California Press, forthcoming.

Bourbou, Chryssi. *Health and Disease in Byzantine Crete (7th–12th Centuries AD)*. Medicine in the Medieval Mediterranean. Farnham, UK: Ashgate, 2010.

Boyd, W.J.P. "Origen on Pharaoh's Hardened Heart: A Study of Justification and Election in St. Paul and Origen." *Studia Patristica* 7. Berlin: Akademie-Verlag, 1966: 434–42.

Bradshaw, Matt and Christopher G. Ellison. "Financial hardship and psychological distress: Exploring the buffering effects of religion." *Social Science & Medicine* 71, No. 1 (2010): 196–204.

Brakke, David. *Athanasius and Asceticism*. Johns Hopkins University Press, 1995.

_____. "Shenoute, Weber, and the Monastic Prophet: Ancient and Modern Articulations of Ascetic Authority," *Foundations of Power and Conflicts of Authority in Late-Antique Monasticism*, Orientalia Lovaniensia Analecta, Vol. 157. Edited by A. Camplani and G. Filoram. Leuven: Uitgeverij Peeters, 2007, 47–73.

_____. "Care for the Poor, Fear of Poverty, and Love of Money: Evagrius Ponticus on the Monk's Economic Vulnerability." *Wealth and Poverty in Early Church and Society*. Edited by Susan R. Holman. Ada, Michigan: Baker Academic, 2008, 76–87.

Brändle, Rudolph. *Matth. 25,31–46 im Werk des Johannes Chrysostomos*. Tübingen, Mohr Siebeck, 1979.

_____. "This Sweetest Passage: Matthew 25:31-46 and Assistance to the Poor in the Homilies of John Chrysostom." *Wealth and Poverty in Early Church and Society*. Edited by Susan R. Holman. Ada, MI: Baker Academic, 2008, 127–39.

Brothwell, Don. *Diseases in Antiquity: A Survey of the Diseases, Injuries and Surgery of Early Populations*. Edited by Don Brothwell and A.T. Sandison. Springfield, IL: Charles C. Thomas, 1967.

Brown, Peter. "The Rise and Function of the Holy Man in Late Antiquity." *Journal of Roman Studies* 61 (1971): 80-101.

_____. *The Cult of the Saints: It's Rise and Function in Late Antiquity*. University of Chicago Press, 1981.

_____. "The Saint as Exemplar in Late Antiquity," *Representations* 2 (1983): 1–25.

_____. *The Body and Society: Men, Women, and Sexual Renunciation in Early Christianity*. Columbia University Press, 1988.

_____. *Society and the Holy in Late Antiquity*. University of California Press, 1989.

_____. *Authority and the Sacred: Aspects of the Christianisation of the Roman World*. Cambridge University Press, 1995.

_____. *Poverty and Leadership in the Later Roman Empire*. Brandeis University Press, 2002.

_____. "The Rise and Function of the Holy Man in Late Antiquity," in Peter Brown, *Society and the Holy in Late Antiquity*. University of California Press, 1989, 103–52.

Bryer, Anthony. *The Oxford Handbook of Byzantine Studies*. Edited by Elizabeth Jeffreys, John Haldon and Robin Cormack. Oxford University Press, 2008.

Bultmann, Rudolf. *The History of the Synoptic Tradition*. Translated by John March. Oxford: Basil Blackwell, 1968.

Burton-Christie, Douglas. *The Word in the Desert: Scripture and the Quest for Holiness in Early Christian Monasticism*. Oxford University Press, 1993.

Bynum, Caroline Walker. *The Resurrection of the Body in Western Christianity, 200–1336*. Columbia University Press, 1995.

Cameron, Averil. *Christianity and the Rhetoric of Empire: The Development of Christian Discourse*. Berkeley, CA: University of California Press, 1991.

_____. "New Themes and Styles in Greek Literature: Seventh-Eighth Centuries." *The Byzantine and Early Islamic Near East: Problems in the Literary Source Materials*. Studies in Late Antiquity and Early Islam, No. 1. Edited by Averil Cameron, Lawrence I. Conrad and John Haldon. Princeton, NJ: Darwin Press, 1992, 81–105.

Cameron, Averil and Lawrence I. Conrad (eds). *The Byzantine and Early Islamic Near East: Elites Old and New*. Studies in Late Antiquity and Early Islam. Princeton, NJ: Darwin Press, 2004.

Caner, Daniel. *Wandering, Begging Monks: Spiritual Authority and the Promotion of Monasticism in Late Antiquity.* Berkeley, CA: University of California Press, 2002.

———. "Towards a Miraculous Economy: Christian Gifts and Material 'Blessings' in Late Antiquity." *Journal of Early Christian Studies* 14, No. 3 (2006): 329–77.

Castelli, Elizabeth Anne. "Mortifying the Body, Curing the Soul: Beyond Ascetic Dualism in *The Life of Amma Synclectica*." *Differences* 4, No. 2 (1992): 134–53.

———. "Gender, Theory, and The Rise of Christianity: A Response to Rodney Stark." *Journal of Early Christian Studies* 6, No. 2 (1998): 227–57.

Centers for Disease Control and Prevention, http://www.cdc.gov/cancer/breast/statistics/.

Chadwick, Henry. "John Moschus and His Friend Sophronius the Sophist." *Journal of Theological Studies* 25 (1974): 41–74.

Chakrabarty, S. and R. Zoorob. "Fibromyalgia." *American Family Physician* 76, No. 2 (2007): 247–54.

Charanis, Peter. "The Monk as an Element of Byzantine Society." *Dumbarton Oaks Papers* 25 (1971): 63–84.

Chitty, Derwas J. *The Desert a City: An Introduction to the Study of Egyptian and Palestinian Monasticism Under the Christian Empire.* Crestwood, NY: St Vladimir's Seminary Press, 1995.

Clark, Elizabeth A. "Antifamilial Tendencies in Ancient Christianity," *Journal of the History of Sexuality* 5, No. 3 (1995): 356–80.

———. "The Lady Vanishes: Dilemmas of a Feminist Historian after the 'Linguistic Turn,'" *Church History* 67, No. 1 (1998): 1–31.

———. "Holy Women, Holy Words: Early Christian Women, Social History and the 'Linguistic Turn.'" *Journal of Early Christian Studies* 6 (1998): 413–30.

Clark, Gillian. *Women in Late Antiquity: Pagan and Christian Lifestyles.* Oxford University Press, 1993.

———. *Women in Antiquity*, Greece and Rome Studies, Vol. 3. Edited by Ian McAuslan and Peter Walcot. Oxford University Press, 1996.

Cloke, Gillian. *This Female Man of God: Women and Spiritual Power in the Patristic Age, AD 350–450.* London: Routledge, 1995.

Connolly, Mark P., William Ledger and Maarten J. Postma, "Economics of Assisted Reproduction: Access to Fertility Treatments and Valuing Live Births in Economic Terms," *Human Fertility* 13, No. 1 (2010): 13–18.

Connor, Carolyn L. *Women of Byzantium*. Yale University Press, 2007.

Conrad, L. "Epidemic Disease in Central Syria in the Late Sixth Century: Some New Insights from the Verse of Hassán ibn Thábit," *Byzantine and Modern Greek Studies* 18 (1994): 12–58.

Constantelos, Demetrios J. "Physician-Priests in the Medieval Greek Church." *Greek Orthodox Theological Review* 12, No. 1 (1967): 141–53.

_____. *Byzantine Philanthropy and Social Welfare*. Rutger's University Press, 1968.

_____. "Clerics and Secular Professions in the Byzantine Church." *Βυζαντινά Θεσσαλονίκη*, Vol. 13 (1985): 375–90.

Constas, Nicholas. "'To Sleep, Perchance to Dream': The Middle State of Souls in Patristic and Byzantine Literature." *Dumbarton Oaks Papers* 55 Byzantine Eschatology: Views on Death and the Last Things, 8th to 15th Centuries (2001): 91–124.

Conybeare, Frederick C. "Notes and Documents: Antiochus Strategos' Account of the Sack of Jerusalem in A.D. 614," *The English Historical Review* 25, No. 99 (1910): 502–17.

Countryman, William. *The Rich Christian in the Church of the Early Empire*. New York: Edwin Mellon Press, 1980.

Crislip, Andrew. *From Monastery to Hospital: Christian Monasticism & The Transformation of Health Care in Late Antiquity*. University of Michigan Press, 2005.

_____. "The Sin of Sloth or the Illness of the Demons? The Demon of Acedia in Early Christian Monasticism," *Harvard Theological Review* 98, No. 2 (2005): 143–69.

_____. "'I Have Chosen Sickness'" The Controversial Function of Sickness in Early Christian Ascetic Practice." *Asceticism and Its Critics: Historical Accounts and Comparative Perspectives*. American Academy of Religion Cultural Criticism Series. Edited by Oliver Freiberger. Oxford University Press, 2006, 179–209.

Crossan, John Dominic. *The Birth of Christianity: Discovering What Happened in the Years Immediately after the execution of Jesus*. San Francisco, CA: HarperSanFrancisco, 1998.

Cruse, Audrey. *Roman Medicine*. Gloucestershire: Tempus Publishing Ltd, 2004.

Cuesta, Janini. *La Antropología y la medicina pastoral de San Gregorio de Nisa*. Madrid: Consejo Superior de Investigaciones Científicas, 1946.

Daley, Brian, S.J. *The Hope of the Early Church: A Handbook of Patristic Eschatology*. Grand Rapids, MI: Baker Academic, 1991.

Daley, Brian E., S.J. "'At the Hour of Our Death': Mary's Dormition and Christian Dying in Late Patristic and Early Byzantine Literature." *Dumbarton Oaks Papers* 55 Byzantine Eschatology: Views on Death and the Last Things, 8th to 15th Centuries (2001): 71–89.

Davies, Jon. *Death, Burial and Rebirth in the Religions of Antiquity*. London: Routledge, 1999.

De Gubernatis, Angelo. *Zoological Mythology: Or, Legends of the Animals*, Vol. II. London: Trübner & Company, 1968.

Decker, Michael. "Frontier Settlement and Economy in the Byzantine East." *Dumbarton Oaks Papers* 61 (2007): 217–67.

Delehaye, Hippolyte. *Les légendes hagiographiques*. Bruxelles, Société des Bollandistes, 1927.

_____. *Mélanges d'hagiographie grecque et latine.* Subsidia Hagiographica 42. Bruxelles: Mélanges Bidez, 1934.

_____. *L'Ancienne hagiographie byzantine: les sources, les premiers modèles, la formation des genres.* Subsidia Hagiographica 73. Brussels: B. Joassart and X. Lequeux, 1991.

Delmas, F. "Remarques sur la Vie de Sainte Marie l'Egyptienne." *Echos d'Orient* 4 (1900–1901): 35–42.

Den Boer, W. *Private Morality in Greece and Rome: Some Historical Aspects.* Leiden: E.J. Brill, 1979.

Déroche, Vincent. *Études Sur Léontios De Néapolis.* Uppsala University Press, 1995.

Desprez, Vincent. *Le Monachisme Primitif: Des origines jusqu'au concile d'Éphèse*, Spiritualité Orientale n° 72. Begrolles-en-Mauges: Abbaye De Bellefontaine, 1998.

Dietz, Maribel. *Wandering Monks, Virgins and Pilgrims: Ascetic Travel in the Mediterranean World, A.D. 300–800.* Pennsylvania State University Press, 2005.

Dodds, E.R. *The Greeks and the Irrational.* University of California Press, 1963.

Douglas, Mary. Implicit Meanings: Essays in Anthropology. London: Routledge & Kegan Paul, 1975.

Downy, Glanville. "Who is my Neighbor? The Greek and Roman Answer," *Anglican Theological Review* 47 (1965): 1–25.

Duffy, John. "Byzantine Medicine in the Sixth and Seventh Centuries, Aspects of Teaching and Practice," *Dumbarton Oaks Papers* 38 Symposium on Byzantine Medicine (1984): 25–7.

_____. "Observations on Sophoronius' Miracles of Cyrus and John," *Journal of Theological Studies* 35, No. 1 (1984): 71–90.

Dunn, Geoffrey D., David Luckensmeyer and Lawrence Cross (eds). *Prayer and Spirituality in the Early Church: Poverty and Riches.* Strathfield, Australia: St Paul's Publications, 2009.

Dunn, Marilyn. *The Emergence of Monasticism: From the Desert Fathers to the Early Middle Ages.* Oxford: Blackwell, 2003.

Durling, Richard J. "Medicine in Plutarch's *Moralia*," *Traditio* 50 (1995), 311–14.

Economist (The). "The Rich are Different from You and Me: They Are More Selfish." http://www.economist.com/node/16690659. July 31, 2010.

Edelstein, Ludwig. "The Relation of Ancient Philosophy to Medicine." *Ancient Medicine: Selected Papers of Ludwig Edelstein.* Edited by Owsei Temkin and C. Lilian Temkin. Baltimore, MD: Johns Hopkins University Press, 1967, 299–316.

Elliott, Dyan. *Spiritual Marriage: Sexual Abstinence in Mediaeval Wedlock.* Princeton University Press, 1993.

Elm, Susanna. *Virgins of God: The Making of Asceticism in Late Antiquity.* Oxford University Press, 1996.

Engelhardt, H. Tristram, Jr. "The Concepts of Health and Disease," in *Concepts of Health and Disease: Interdisciplinary Perspective.* Edited by L. Arthur

Caplan, H. Tristram Engelhardt Jr. and James J. McCartney. Reading, MA: Addison-Wesley, 1981.
Escolan, Philippe. *Monachisme et église: le monachisme syrien du IVe au VIIe siècle: un ministère charismatique*. Paris: Beauchesne, 1999.
Every, George. "Toll Gates on the Air Way," *Eastern Churches Review* 8, No. 2 (1976): 139–51.
Fedwick, Paul. "Death and Dying in Byzantine Liturgical Traditions." *Eastern Churches Review* 8, No. 2 (1976): 151–61.
Ferngren, Gary B. *Medicine & Health Care in Early Christianity*. Baltimore, MD: Johns Hopkins University Press, 2009.
Finn, Richard. *Almsgiving in the Later Roman Empire: Christian Promotion and Practice (313–450)*. Oxford University Press, 2006.
Flusin, Bernard. *Saint Anastase le Perse: et l'histoire de la Palestine au début du VIIe Siècle*, Paris: Editions du Centre National de la Recherche Scientifique.
Follieri, Enrica. "Dove e quando mori Giovanni Mosco?" *Rivista di studi bizantini e neoellenici* 25 (1988): 3–39.
Foss, Clive. "Syria in Transition, A.D. 550–750: An Archaeological Approach." *Dumbarton Oaks Papers* 51 (1997): 189–269.
_____. "The Persians in the Roman near East (602–630 AD)." *Journal of Roman Studies* 13, No. 2 (2003): 149–70.
Foucault, Michel. *The History of Sexuality, Volume I: An Introduction*. Translated by Robert Hurley. New York: Random House, 1980.
_____. *Michel Foucault: Beyond Structuralism and Hermeneutics*. Edited by Hubert L. Dreyfes and Paul Rabinow. University of Chicago Press, 1983.
_____. *The Essential Foucault: Selections from The Essential Works of Foucault 1954–1984*. Edited by Paul Rabinou and Nikolas Rose. New York: The New Press, 2003.
Frank, Richard I. "Augustus' Legislation on Marriage and Children," *California Studies in Classical Antiquity* 8 (1975): 41–52.
Friesen, Steven J. "Injustice or God's Will? Early Christian Explanations of Poverty." *Wealth and Poverty in Early Church and Society*. Edited by Susan R. Holman. Ada, MI: Baker Academic, 2008, 17–36.
Fronimopoulos, J. and J. Lascaratos. "'Eye injuries' by the Byzantine writer Aetios Amidinos," *Documenta ophthalmologica. Advances in ophthalmology* 1–2 (1988): 121–4.
Funkenstein, Amos. "Collective Memory and Historical Consciousness," *History & Memory* 1, No. 1 (1999): 5–26.
Gardner, Jane F. "Aristophanes and Male Anxiety: The Defense of the *Oikos*." *Women in Antiquity*. Greece and Rome Studies 3. Edited by Ian McAuslan and Peter Walcot. Oxford University Press, 1996, 146–57.
Garland, Robert. *The Greek Way of Death*. Cornell University Press, 1985.
Garrison, F.H. *An Introduction to the History of Medicine*. Philadelphia, 1921.
Garrison, Roman. *Redemptive Almsgiving in Early Christianity*. Journal for the Study of the New Testament Supplement. England: Sheffield, 1994.

Geary, Patrick. "Sacred Commodities: the Circulation of Medieval Relics *The Social Life of Things: Commodities in Cultural Perspective.* Edited by Arjun Appadurai. Cambridge University Press, 1986, 169–95.

Géorgios. "Théodore Comme Thaumaturege, Médecin et Directeur D'Ames." *Vie de Théodore de Sykéôn: Traduction, commentaire et appendice.* Translated by André-Jean Festugière. *Subsidia Hagiographica* 48. Bruxelles, Société des Bollandistes, 1970, 145–7.

Giet, Stanislas. *Les idées et l'action sociales de saint Basile.* Paris: Librairie Lecoffre, 1941.

Gleason, Maud. "Visiting and News: Gossip and Reputation-Management in the Desert," *Journal of Early Christian Studies Studies* 6, No. 3 (1998): 501–21.

Goehring, James E. "The Encroaching Desert: Literary Production and Ascetic Space in Early Christian Egypt," *Journal of Early Christian Studies* 1, No. 3 (1993): 281–96.

González, Justo. *Faith and Wealth: A History of Early Christian Ideas on the Origin, Significance, and Use of Money.* Eugene, OR: Wipf and Stock Publishers, 1990.

Goodich, Michael. "Sexuality, Family, and the Supernatural in the Fourteenth Century." *Journal of the History of Sexuality* 4, No. 4 (1994): 493–516.

Goody, Jack. *The Development of the Family and Marriage in Europe.* Cambridge, 1983.

Gould, Graham. "Moving On and Staying Put in the *Apophthegmata Patrum.*" *Studia Patristica* 20 (1989): 231–7.

_____. *The Desert Fathers on Monastic Community.* Oxford: Clarendon Press, 1993.

Grierson, Philip. *Byzantine Coinage.* Washington, DC: Dumbarton Oaks, 1999.

Griffith, Susan Blackburn. "Iatros and Medicus: The Physician in Gregory Nazianzen and Augustine." In F. Young, M. Edwards, P. Parvis (eds), *Studia Patristica,* Vol. 41. Leuven: Peeters, 2006.

Grillmeier, Alois and Heinrich Bacht (eds). *Das Konzil von Chalkedon: Geschichte und Gegenwart,* 3 vols. 1951–4. Würzburg: Echter-Verl., 1979.

Grmek, B. "Les conséquences de la peste de Justinien dans l'Illyricum" *Acta XIII Congressus internationalis archaeologiae christianae* 3 vols. Vaticano: Pontificio Istituto di archeologia christiana; Split: Arheološki muzej, 1998, 2: 787–94.

Grünbart, Michael et al. *Material culture and well-being in Byzantium (400–1453): Proceedings of the International Conference (Cambridge, 8-10 September 2001).* Wien: Verlag der Österreichischen Akademie der Wissenschaften, 2007.

Haldon, J. "The Works of Anastasias of Sinai: A Key Source for the History of Seventh-Century East Mediterranean Society and Belief." *The Byzantine East and Early Islamic Near East I: Problems in the Literary Source Material.* Edited by Averil Cameron and Lawrence I. Conrad. Princeton, NJ: Darwin Press: 1992, 107–47.

Haldon, John. "The Reign of Heraclius. A Context for Change?" *The Reign of Heraclius (610–641): Crisis and Confrontation.* Edited by Gerrit J. Reinik, Bernard H. Stolte. Leuven: Peeters, 2002, 1–16.

Halkin, F. "La vision de Kaioumos et le sort eternal de Philentolos Olympiou." *Analecta Bollandiana* 63 (1945): 56–64.

_____. *Recherches et documents d'hagiographie Byzantine.* Subsidia Hagiographica 51. Brussels, 1971.

Hall, John E. *Guyton and Hall Textbook of Medical Physiology.* Philadelphia: Saunders, 2010.

Hamel, Gildas. *Poverty and charity in Roman Palestine, first three centuries C.E.* Berkeley, CA: University of California Press, 1990.

Hands, A.R. *Charities and Social Aid in Greece and Rome.* Cornell University Press: 1968.

Harlow, Mary and Ray Laurence. *Growing Up and Growing Old in Ancient Rome: A Life Course Approach.* London: Routledge, 2002.

Harmless, William. *Desert Christians: An Introduction to the Literature of Early Monasticism.* Oxford University Press, 2004.

Harvey, Susan Ashbrook. "Physicians and Ascetics in John of Ephesus: An Expedient Alliance." *Dumbarton Oaks Papers* 38 Symposium on Byzantine Medicine (1984): 87–93.

_____. "Women in Early Byzantine Hagiography: Reversing the Story." *That Gentle Strength: Historical Perspectives on Women in Christianity.* Edited by Lynda L. Coon, Katherine J. Haldane and Elisabeth W. Sommer. University Press of Virginia, 1990, 19–35.

Hendy, Michael F. *Studies in Byzantine Monetary Economy, c. 300–1450.* Cambridge University Press, 1985.

Herrin, Judith. "In Search of Byzantine Women: Three Avenues of Approach." *Images of Women in Antiquity.* Edited by Averil Cameron and Amélie Kuhrt. Wayne State University Press, 1983, 167–90.

_____. *The Formation of Christendom.* Princeton University Press, 1987.

Hertz, Robert. "St. Besse: A Study of an Alpine Cult." *Saints and Their Cults: Studies in Religious Sociology, Folklore and History.* Edited by Stephen Wilson. Cambridge University Press, 1983, 55–100.

Hirschfeld, Yizar. "Edible Wild Plants: The Secret Diet of Monks in the Judean Desert," *Israel: Land and Nature* 16 (1990): 25–8.

_____. *The Judean Desert Monasteries in the Byzantine Period.* Yale University Press, 1992.

Holman, Susan R. *The Hungry are Dying: Beggars and Bishops in Roman Cappadocia.* Oxford University Press, 2001.

_____. "Rich and Poor in the *Miracles of Saints Cyrus and John.*" *Wealth and Poverty in Early Church and Society.* Edited by Susan R. Holman. Ada, MI: Baker Academic, 2008, 103–24.

_____. *God Knows There's Need: Christian Responses to Poverty.* Oxford University Press, 2009.

Hopkins, Keith. *Death and Renewal*. Sociological Studies in Roman History 2. Cambridge University Press, 1983.

Horden, Peregrine. "Saints and Doctors in the Early Byzantine Empire: The Case of Theodore of Sykeon." *The Church and Healing: Papers Read at the Twentieth Summer Meeting and the Twenty-First Winter Meeting of the Ecclesiastical History Society*. Edited by W.J. Sheils. Oxford: Basil Blackwell, 1982, 1–13.

——. "The Death of Ascetics: Sickness and Monasticism in the Early Byzantine Middle East." *Monks: Hermits and the Ascetic Tradition: Papers Read at the 1984 Summer Meeting and The 1985 Winter Meeting of the Ecclesiastical History Society*. Edited by W.J. Shiels. Great Britain: Basil Blackwell, 1985, 41–52.

——. "The Earliest Hospitals in Byzantium, Western Europe and Islam." *Journal of Interdisciplinary History* 35, No. 3 (2005): 361–89.

Howard-Johnston, James. *Witnesses to a World Crisis: Historians and Histories of the Middle East in the Seventh Century*. Oxford University Press, 2012.

Ivanov, Sergey A. *Holy Fools in Byzantium and Beyond*. Oxford Studies in Byzantium. Oxford University Press, 2006.

de Jerphanion, Guillaume. *Une Nouvelle Province de L'art Byzantin: Les Eglises Rupestres de Cappadoce*. Paris: P. Geuthner, 1934.

Jotischky, Andrew. *A Hermit's Cookbook: Monks, Food and Fasting in the Middle Ages*. London: Continuum International, 2011.

Judge, E.A. "The Earliest Use of Monachos for 'Monk,' and the Origins of Monasticism." *Jahrbuch für Antike und Christentum* 20 (1977): 80.

Kaegi, Walter E. "Reconceptualizing Byzantium's Eastern Frontiers in the Seventh Century." *Shifting Frontiers in Late Antiquity*. Edited by Ralph W. Mathisen and Hagith S. Sivan. Aldershot, UK: Variorum, Ashgate, 1996, 83–92.

——. *Heraclius, Emperor of Byzantium*. Cambridge University Press, 2007.

Kaldellis, Anthony. "The Literature of Plague and the Anxieties of Piety in Sixth-Century Byzantium." *Piety and Plague: From Byzantium to the Baroque*. Sixteenth Century Essays and Studies. Edited by Franco Mormando and Thomas Worcester. Truman State University Press, 2007, 1–22.

Kazhdan, A. and S. Franklin. *Studies on Byzantine Literature of the Eleventh and Twelfth Centuries*. Paris: Editions de la Maison des sciences de l'homme, 1984.

Kazhdan, A.P. and Ann Wharton Epstein. *Change in Byzantine Culture in the Eleventh and Twelfth Centuries*. Berkeley, CA: University of California Press, 1985.

Keenan, Sister Mary Emily. "St. Gregory of Nazianzus and Early Byzantine Medicine." *Bulletin of the History of Medicine* 9 (1941): 8–30.

Kennedy, Hugh. "From Polis to Medina: Urban Change in Late Antique and Early Islamic Syria." *Past and Present*, 106 (1985) 3–27.

Kerras, R.M. "Holy Harlots: Prostitute Saints in Medieval Legend," *Journal of the History of Sexuality* 1, No. 1 (1990): 3–32.

Klein, Holger A. "Eastern Objects and Western Desires: Relics and Reliquaries between Byzantium and the West." *Dumbarton Oaks Papers* 58 (2004): 283–314.

Kleinman, Arthur. *Patients and Healers in the Context of Culture: an Exploration of the Borderland between Anthropology, Medicine, and Psychiatry*. Berkeley, CA: University of California Press, 1980.

Kondakov, N.P. *An Archeological Journey Through Syria and Palestine*. St Petersburg, 1904.

Kostof, Spiro. *Caves of God: the monastic environment of Byzantine Cappadocia*. Cambridge, MA: MIT Press, 1972.

Krakauer, Jon. "Death of an Innocent: How Christopher McCandless lost his way in the wilds," *Outside Magazine*, January, 1993.

_____. *Into the Wild*. New York: Anchor Books, 1996.

Krakauer, Jon and Sean Penn. *Into the Wild*. Film directed by Sean Penn. Los Angeles, Paramount Vantage, 2007.

Krause, Jens-Uwe. *Spätantike Patronatsformen im Westen des Römischen Reiches*. München: C.H. Beck, 1987.

Krueger, Derek. *Writing and Holiness: The Practice of Authorship in the Early Christian East*. University of Pennsylvania Press, 2004.

_____. "Literary Composition and Monastic Practice in Early Byzantium: On Genre and Discipline," in *Monastères, images, pouvoirs et société à Byzance*. Paris: Publications de la Sorbonne, 2006.

_____. "Early Byzantine Hagiography and Hagiography as Different Modes of Christian Practice," in *Writing 'True Stories': Historians and Hagiographers in the Late Antique and Medieval Near East*. Edited by Arietta Papaconstantinou. Belgium: Brepols, 2010.

_____. *Symeon the Holy Fool: Leontius's Life and the Late Antique City*. Transformation of the Classical Heritage. University of California Press, 1996.

_____. "Writing as Devotion: Hagiographical Composition and the Cult of the Saints in Theodoret of Cyrrhus and Cyril of Scythopolis." *American Society of Church History* 66, No. 4 (1997): 707–19.

_____. "Hagiography as an Ascetic Practice in the Early Christian East." *Journal of Religion* 79, No. 2 (1999): 216–32.

_____. "Between Monks: Tales of Monastic Companionship in Early Byzantium," *Journal of the History of Sexuality* 20, No. 1 (2011): 28–61.

Laiou, Angeliki E. *Mariage, Amour et Parenté à Byzance aux XIe–XIIIe Siècles*. Paris, 1992.

_____. *Gender, Society and Economic Life in Byzantium*. Aldershot, UK: Ashgate, 1992.

_____. "The Church, Economic Thought and Economic Practice." *The Christian East, Its Institutions and Its Thoughts*. Edited by Robert F. Taft, S.J. Pontificio Istituto Orientale, Rome, 1993, 435–64.

_____. "Trade, Profit and Salvation in the Late Patristic and the Byzantine Period." *Wealth and Poverty in Early Church and Society*. Edited by Susan R. Holman. Ada, MI: Baker Academic, 2008, 243–64.

_____ (ed.). *The Economic History of Byzantium: From the Seventh Through the Fifteenth Century*, Vol. 1. Washington, DC: Dumbarton Oaks, 2002.

Lee, A.D. *War in Late Antiquity: A Social History.* Wiley-Blackwell, 2007.

Lee, Karen C. "Fertility Treatments and the Cost of a Healthy Baby," *Nursing for Women's Health* 15, No. 1 (2011): 15–18.

Leonard, Prestige. "Hades in the Greek Fathers: Lexicon of Patristic Greek." *Journal of Theological Studies* 24 (1923): 476–85.

Little, Lester K. "Life and Afterlife of the First Plague Pandemic." *Plague and the End of Antiquity: The Pandemic of 541–750.* Edited by Lester K. Little. Cambridge University Press, 2007, 3–32.

Llewellyn Ihssen, Brenda. "Money in the Meadow: Conversion and Coin in John Moschos' *Pratam spirituale*." Paper presented at the XVI International Conference on Patristic Studies, Oxford, England, August 9, 2011.

_____. "Forewarned is Forearmed: Predetermination in John Moschos' *Pratum spirituale.*" Paper presented at the annual meeting of the North American Patristics Society, Chicago, IL, May 26, 2012.

_____. "God's Servants, Working Together: Liminality and Laity in John Moschos' *Pratumspirituale*." Paper presented at the annual meeting of the Byzantine Studies Association of North America, Brookline, MA, November 2, 2012.

_____. "Curing & Enduring: Medical Care for Monks and Multitudes in Byzantine Beneficial Tales." Paper presented at the annual national meeting of the American Academy of Religion, Chicago, IL, November 17, 2012.

_____. *They Who Give From Evil: The Response of the Eastern Church to Moneylending in the Early Christian Era.* Eugene, OR: Pickwick Publications, 2012.

Longenecker, Bruce W. *Remember the Poor: Paul, Poverty, and the Greco-Roman World.* Grand Rapids, MI: Wm. B. Eerdmans Publishing Company, 2010.

Louth, Andrew. "Did John Moschos Really Die in Constantinople?" *Journal of Theological Studies* 49, No. 1 (1998): 149–54.

_____. *St. John Damascene: Tradition and Originality in Byzantine Theology.* Oxford University Press, 2002.

_____. *Denys the Areopagite.* Westport, CT: Continuum, 2002.

Lowrie, Donald A. *Christian Existentialism: A Berdyaev Anthology.* London, 1965.

MacCoull, Leslie. "Coptic Egypt During the Persian Occupation." *Studi classici e orientali* 36 (1986): 307–13.

Magoulias, Harry J. "The Lives of the Saints as Sources for Byzantine Agrarian Life in the Sixth and Seventh Centuries." *Greek Orthodox Theological Review* 35, No. 1 (1990): 59–70.

Mandell, Gerald L., John E. Bennet and Raphael Dolin. *Principles and Practice of Infectious Diseases.* Philadelphia, PA: Churchill Livingstone, 2004.

Manger, Lois N. *A History of Infectious Diseases and The Microbial World.* Westport, CT: Praeger, 2009.

Mango, Cyril. *Byzantium: The Empire of New Rome.* New York: Charles Scribner's Sons, 1980.
Majno, G. *The Healing Hand: Man and Wound in the Ancient World.* Boston, MA: Harvard University Press, 1975.
McLaughlin, Megan. *Consorting with Saints: Prayer for the Dead in Early Medieval France.* New York: Cornell University Press, 1994.
McGuckin, John. *Saint Greogry of Nazianzus: An Intellectual Biography.* Crestwood, NY: St Vladimir's Seminary Press, 2001.
de Meester, D. Placido. *Liturgia Bizantina,* ii, *Part* vi: *Rituale-Benedizionale Bizantino.* Rome: Leonina, 1929.
Merry, Sally Engle. "Rethinking Gossip and Scandal," in *Towards A General Theory of Social Control, Volume I:Fundamentals.* Edited by Donald Black. Orlando: Academic Press, Inc., 1984.
Meyendorff, John. *Imperial Unity and Christian Division: The Church 460–680 A.D.*, The Church in History, Vol. III. Crestwood, NY: St Vladimir's Seminary Press, 1989.
_____. *Byzantine Theology: Historical Trends and Doctrinal Themes.* New York: Fordham University Press, 1979.
Meyer, Dick. "Wall St. Moral Rot: Spreading To Politics, Main St.?" http://www.npr.org/templates/story/story.php?storyId=95013900. September 25, 2008.
Miller, Patricia Cox. "Desert Asceticism and the 'The Body from Nowhere.'" *Journal of Early Christian Studies* 2, No. 2 (1994): 137–53.
_____. "Strategies of Representation in Collective Biography: Constructing the Subject as Holy." *Greek Biography and Panegyric in Late Antiquity.* The Transformation of the Classical Heritage. Edited by Tomas Hägg, Christian Høgel and Philip Rousseau. University of California Press, 2000, 209–54.
_____. "Is There a Harlot in This Text? Hagiography and the Grotesque." *Journal of Medieval and Early Modern Studies* 33, No. 3 (2003): 419–35.
_____.*The Corporeal Imagination: Signifying the Holy in Late Antique Christianity.* University of Pennsylvania Press, 2009.
Miller, Timothy S. "Byzantine Hospitals," *Dumbarton Oaks Papers* 38 Symposium on Byzantine Medicine (1984): 53–63.
Miller-McLemore, Bonnie J. "Thinking Theologically About Modern Medicine." *Journal of Religion and Health* 30, No. 4 (1991): 287–98.
Mioni, Elpidio. 'Il Pratum Spirituale di Giovanni Mosco: gli episodi inediti del Cod. Marciano greco II.21' *Orientalia Christiana Periodica* (1951): 61–94.
Møller-Christiensen, Vilhelm. "Evidence of Leprosy in Earlier Peoples." *Diseases in Antiquity: A Survey of the Diseases, Injuries, and Surgery of Early Populations.* Edited by Don Brothwell and A.T. Sandison. Springfield, IL: Charles C. Thomas, 1967, 295–306.
Monceaux, P. "Une invocation au Christus medicus sur une pierre de Timgad." *Comptes-rendus des séances de l'Académie des Inscriptions et Belles-Lettres* 68, No. 1 (1924): 75–83.

Monks, George R. "The Church of Alexandria and the City's Economic Life in the Sixth Century Author(s)," *Speculum* 28, No. 2 (1953): 349–62.

Montagne, Renee and Stephen Green. "Bankers Need A Moral Compass." http://www.npr.org/templates/story/story.php?storyId=123897141. February 22, 2010.

Monteserrat, Dominic. "'Carrying On the Work of The Earlier Firm': Doctors, Medicine and Christianity in the *Thaumata* of Sophronios of Jerusalem." *Health in Antiquity*. Edited by Helen King. New York, New York: Routledge, 2005, 230–42.

Morris, Ian. *Death-Ritual And Social Structure in Classical Antiquity*. Cambridge University Press, 1992.

Morrisson, Cécile and Jean-Pierre Sodini. "The Sixth Century Economy." *The Economic History of Byzantium: From the Seventh Through the Fifteenth Century*. Editor-in-Chief, Angeliki A. Laiou. Washington, DC: Dumbarton Oaks, 2007, 171–220.

Munitiz, Joseph A., "The Predetermination of Death: The Contribution of Anastasios of Sinai and Nikephoros Blemmydes to a Perennial Byzantine Problem." *Dumbarton Oaks Papers* 55 Byzantine Eschatology: Views on Death and the Last Things, 8th to 15th Centuries (2001): 9–20.

National Infertility Association, http://www.resolve.org/about/funding-vital-research.html.

National Public Radio. "Human Greed Lies At Root Of Economic Crisis," http://www.npr.org/templates/story/story.php?storyId=94930841&ps=rs. September 23, 2008.

Nunn, John. *Ancient Egyptian Medicine*. University of Oklahoma Press, 2002.

Nutton, Vivian. "Galen to Alexander, Aspects of Medicine and Medical Practice in Late Antiquity," *Dumbarton Oaks Papers* 38 Symposium on Byzantine Medicine (1984): 5–9.

_____. *Ancient Medicine*. Sciences of Antiquity Series. New York: Routledge, 2005.

O'Brien, Kevin J. *An Ethics of Biodiversity: Christianity, Ecology, and the Variety of Life*. Georgetown University Press, 2010.

Olster, David Michael. *The Politics of Usurpation in the Seventh Century: Rhetoric and Revolution in Byzantium*. Amsterdam: Adolf M. Hakkert, 1993.

Palmer, Andrew. *Monk and Mason on the Tigris Frontier: The Early History of Tur 'Abdin*. Cambridge University Press, 1990.

Palmer, José Simón. "Materielle Kultur im Pratum spirituale vom Johannes Moschos." *XVIIth International Congress of Byzantine Studies. Summaries of communications*, Vol. 2. Washington, DC, 1991, 1068–70.

_____. *El monacato oriental en el Pratum spirituale de Juan Mosco*. Madrid, 1993.

_____. "Demonología en el Pratum spirituale de Juan Mosco." *Acta XIII Congressus internationalis archaeologiae christianae. Congreso Español de Estudios Clásicos,* Vol.3. Madrid, 1994, 304–8.

_____. "El monje ye la ciudad en el *Pratum spirituale* de Juan Mosco." *Χαρις Διδασκαλιας, Studia In Honorem Ludovici Aegidii Edendi Curam Paraverunt.* Madrid: Editorial Complutense, 1994., 495–504.

_____. "Juan Mosco y la defensa del dogma de Calcedón," in *La religión en el mundo griego. De la Antigüedad a la Grecia moderna.* Edited by M. Morfakidis and M. Alganza. Granada, 1997.

_____. "John Moschus as a Source for the Lives of St. Symeon and St. Andrew the Fools." *Studia Patristica* 32 (1997): 366–70.

Parkin, Tim G. *Old Age in the Roman World: A Cultural and Social History.* Baltimore, MD: Johns Hopkins University Press, 2003.

Patlagean, Évelyne. "Sur la limitation de la fécondité dans la haute époque Byzantine," *Annales,* (1969): 1353–69.

_____. "Birth Control in the Early Byzantine Empire." *Biology of Man in History: Selections from the Annales Economies, Societies, Civilisations (Vol. 1).* Edited by Robert Forster and Orest Ranum. Baltimore, MD: Johns Hopkins University Press, 1975, 1–22.

_____. "L'histoire de la femme déguisée en moine et l'évolution de la sainteté féminine à Byzance." *Studi Medievali* 3, No. 17 (1976): 597–623.

_____. *Pauvreté économique et pauvreté sociale à Byzance, 4e–7e siècles.* Civilisations et Sociétés 48. Paris, De Gruyter Mouton, 1977.

_____. *Structure sociale, famille, chretiente a Byzance, IVe–XIe siecle.* London: Variorum Reprints, 1981.

_____ (ed.). *Maladie et Société à Byzance.* Spoleto: Centro italiano di studi sull'alto medioevo, cop. 1993.

_____. "Ancient Byzantine Hagiography and Social History." *Saints and Their Cults: Studies in Religious Sociology, Folklore and History.* Edited by Stephen Wilson. University of Cambridge, 1993, 101–22.

Patrich, Joseph. *Sabas, Leader of Palestinian Monasticism: A Comparative Study in Eastern Monasticism, Fourth to Seventh Centuries.* Dumbarton Oaks Studies 32. Washington, DC: Dumbarton Oaks, 1995.

Pattenden, Philip. "The Text of the Pratum Spirituale." *Journal of Theological Studies* 26 (1975): 38–54.

_____. *Prolegomena to a New Edition of the Pratum Spirituale of John Moschus with a Specimen of the Edition.* PhD diss. University of Oxford, 1979.

Pease, Arthur Stanley. "Medical Allusions in the Works of Jerome." *Harvard Studies in Classical Philology* 25 (1914): 73–86.

Peeters, Paul. "Saint Thomas d'Émèse et la Vie de Sainte Marthe." *Analecta Bollandiana* 45 (1927): 262–96.

Perkins, Judith. *The Suffering Self: Pain and Narrative Representation in the Early Christian Era.* London: Routledge, 1995.

Piff, Paul K., Michael W. Kraus and Stéphane Côté et. al. "Having Less, Giving More: The Influence of Social Class on Prosocial Behavior." *Journal of Personality and Social Psychology* 99, No. 5 (2010): 771–84.

Pilch, John J. *Healing in the New Testament: Insights from Medical and Mediterranean Anthropology.* Minneapolis, MN: Fortress Press, 2000.

Porteous, E.N.W. "The Care of the Poor in the Old Testament." *Service to Christ: Essays Presented to Karl Barth on his 80th Birthday.* Edited by J.I. McCord and T.H.L. Parker. Edinburgh, 1950. Reprinted: London/New York: Nelson, 1963, 143–56.

Porterfield, Amanda. *Healing in the History of Christianity.* Oxford University Press, 2005.

Ramsay, Boniface. "Almsgiving in the Latin Church: the Late Fourth and Early Fifth Centuries," *Theological Studies* 43 (1982): 226–59.

Rapp, Claudia. "Ritual Brotherhood in Byzantium." *Traditio* 52 (1997): 285–326.

———. "Storytelling as Spiritual Communication in Early Greek Hagiography: The Use of Diegesis." *Journal of Early Christian Studies* 6, No. 3 (1998): 431–48.

———. *Holy Bishops in Late Antiquity: The Nature of Christian Leadership in an Age of Transition.* Berkeley, CA: University of California Press, 2005.

Rawson, Beryl. "The Roman Family." Pages 1-57 in *The Family in Ancient Rome: New Perspectives.* Edited by Beryl Rawson. Ithaca, NY: Cornell University Press, 1986.

Rebillard, Éric. "Les formes de l'assistance funéraire dans l'Empire romain et leur évolution dans l'Antiquité tardive." *Antiquite tardive* VII (1999): 269–82.

Rodley, Lyn. *Cave Monasteries of Byzantine Cappadocia.* Cambridge University Press, 1985.

Rousseau, Philip. *Ascetics, Authority and the Church: In the Age of Jerome and Cassian.* Oxford University Press, 1978.

———. "The Desert Fathers, Antony and Pachomius." *The Study of Spirituality.* Edited by Cheslyn Jones, Goeffrey Wainwright and Edward Yarnold, SJ. Oxford: Oxford University Press, 1986, 119–30.

———. "Christian Asceticism and the Early Monks." *Early Christianity: Origins and Evolution to A.D. 600.* Edited by Ian Hazlett. London: Abingdon Press, 1991, 112–22.

———. *Basil of Caesarea.* Berkeley, CA: University of California Press, 1994.

———."The Identity of the Ascetic Master in the *Historia Religiosa* of Theodoret of Cyrrhus: A New Paideia?" *Mediterranean Archeology* 11 (1998): 229–44.

———. "The World Engaged: The Social and Economic World," *Ascetics, Society, and The Desert*, Studies in Antiquity and Christianity. Edited by James E. Goehring. Harrisburg, PA: Trinity Press International, 1999.

———. "The Desert Fathers and Their Broader Audience," in *Foundations of Power and Conflicts of Authority in Late-Antique Monasticism: Proceedings of the International Seminar Turin, December 2–4, 2004.* Edited by Alberto Camplani and Giovanni Filoramo. Leuven: Peeters, 2006.

———. *Ascetics, Authority and the Church in the Age of Jerome and Cassian.* University of Notre Dame Press, 2010.

Rush, Alfred. *Death and Burial in Christian Antiquity.* Catholic University of America Press, 1941.
Russell, James. "Transformations in Early Byzantine Urban Life: the Contribution and Limitations of Archaeological Evidence." *17th International Byzantine Congress, Major Papers.* New Rochelle, NY: Aristide d Caratzas, 1986.
Saintyves, Pierre. *Les Saints Successeurs Des Dieux.* Paris: E. Nourry, 1907.
Samellas, Antigone. *Death in the Eastern Mediterranean 50–600 A.D: The Christianization of the East: An Interpretation.* Tübingen: Mohr Siebeck, 2002.
Sandison, A.T. and Calvin Wells. "Diseases of the Reproductive System." *Diseases in Antiquity: A Survey of the Diseases, Injuries and Surgery of Early Populations.* Edited by Don Brothwell and A.T. Sandison. Springfield, IL: Charles C. Thomas, 1967, 498–520.
Scarborough, John (ed.). *Symposium on Byzantine Medicine. Dumbarton Oaks Papers* 38. Washington, DC: Dumbarton Oaks Research Library and Collection, 1984.
Scheff, Thomas J. "Shame and Community: Social Components in Depression." *Psychiatry* 64, No. 3 (2001): 212–24.
Schipperges, H. "Zur Tradition des 'Christus Medicus' im frühen Christentum und in der älteren Heilkunde." *Arzt und Christ* 11 (1965): 12–20.
Scott, James C. *Domination and the Arts of Resistance: Hidden Transcripts.* Yale University Press, 1992.
Sendrail, Marcel. *Histoire Culturelle de la Maladie.* Toulouse: Privat, 1980.
Severson, Eric R. *The Least of These: Selected Readings in Christian History.* Eugene, OR: Cascade Books, 2007.
Singer, Charles and E. Ashworth Underwood. *A Short History of Medicine.* Oxford University Press, 1962.
Sivan, Hagith. *Palestine in Late Antiquity.* Oxford University Press, 2008.
Stager, Lawrence. "Eroticism and Infanticide at Ashkelon." *Biblical Archaeological Review* 17, No. 4 (1991): 35–53.
Stannard, Jerry. "Aspects of Byzantine Materia Medica." *Dumbarton Oaks Papers* 38 Symposium on Byzantine Medicine (1984): 205–11.
Stark, Rodney. *The Rise of Christianity: How the Obscure, Marginal, Jesus Movement Became the Dominant Religious Force in the Western World in a Few Centuries.* San Francisco, CA: Harperone, 1997.
Stathakopolous, Dionysios. "Crime and Punishment: The Plague in the Byzantine Empire, 541–750." *Plague and the End of Antiquity: The Pandemic of 541-750.* Edited by Lester K. Little. Cambridge University Press, 2008, 99–118.
Sterer, Yuval. "A Mixed Litter of Horned and Hornless Horned Vipers: Cerastes Cerastes Cerastes (Ophidia: Viperidae)," *Israel Journal of Zoology* 37 (1992): 247–9.
Sterk, Andrea. *Renouncing the World Yet Leading the Church: The Monk-Bishop in Late Antiquity.* Cambridge, MA: Harvard University Press, 2004.
Stratos, Andreas N. *Byzantium in the Seventh Century, I: 602–634.* Translated by Marc Ogilvie Grant. Amsterdam: Adolf M. Hakkert, 1968.

Synnot, Anthony. "Puzzling Over the Sense: From Plato to Marx." *The Varieties of Sensory Experience: A Sourcebook in the Anthropology of the Sense.* Edited by David Howes. University of Toronto Press, 1991, 61–78.

Talbot, Alice-Mary. "Old Age in Byzantium," *Byzantinische Zeitschrift* 77 (1984): 267–78.

_____. "Pilgrimage to Healing Shrines: The Evidence of Miracle Accounts," *Dumbarton Oaks Papers* 56 (2002): 153–73.

_____ (ed.). *Holy Women of Byzantium: Ten Saints' Lives in English Translation.* Translated by Maria Kouli. Washington, DC: Dumbarton Oaks, 1996, 70–93.

Temkin, Owsei. *Hippocrates in a World of Pagans and Christians.* Baltimore, MD: Johns Hopkins University Press, 1995.

Thompson, Pauline. "The Disease That We Call Cancer." *Health, Disease and Healing in Medieval Culture.* Edited by Sheila Campbell, Bert Hall and David Klausner. New York: St Martin's Press, 1992, 1–11.

Toda, Satoshi. "Pachomian Monasticism and Poverty." *Prayer and Spirituality in the Early Church: Poverty and Riches*, Vol. 5. Edited by Edited by Geoffrey D. Dunn, David Luckensmeyer and Lawrence Cross. Strathfield, Australia: St Paul's Publications, 2009, 191–200.

Toynbee, J.M.C. *Death and Burial in the Roman World.* New York: Cornell University Press, 1971.

Teteriantnikov, Natalia B. "Burial Places in Cappadocian Churches." *Greek Orthodox Theological Review* 29, No. 2 (1984): 141–74.

Treadgold, Warren T. *The Nature of The Bibliotheca of Photius.* Washington, DC: Dumbarton Oaks, 1980.

Trumbower, Jeffrey A. *Rescue For the Dead: The Posthumous Salvation of Non-Christians in Early Christianity.* Oxford University Press, 2001.

United States, Defense Intelligence Agency. *Venomous Snakes of the Middle East: Identification Guide.* Washington, DC: Defense Intelligence Agency, 1991.

Vaile, S. "Jean Mosch." *Echos d'Orient* 5 (1901): 107–16.

Valantasis, Richard. "Constructions of Power in Asceticism." *Journal of the American Academy of Religion* 63, No. 4 (1995): 775–821.

_____. "A Theory of the Social Function of Asceticism." *Asceticism.* Edited by in Vincent L. Wimbush and Richard Valantasis. Oxford: Oxford University Press, 1995, 544–52.

VanDellen, T.R. "Sudden Death ... Premonition of Things to Come." *Illinois Medical Journal* 141, No. 4 (1973): 392.

Vasiliev, Alexander A. "Notes on Some Episodes concerning the Relations between the Arabs and the Byzantine Empire from the Fourth to the Sixth Century." *Dumbarton Oaks Papers* 9/10 (1956): 306–16.

_____. *History of the Byzantine Empire*, Vol. 1. University of Wisconsin Press, 1980.

Veyne, Paul. *Bread and Circuses: Historical Sociology and Political Pluralism.* London: A. Lane, the Penguin Press, 1990.

Vikan, Gary. "Art, Medicine and Magic in Early Byzantium," *Dumbarton Oaks Papers* 38 Symposium on Byzantine Medicine (1984): 65–86.
Vivian, Miriam Raub. "Monastic Mobility and Roman Transformation: The Example of St. Daniel the Stylite." *Studia Patristica* 39. Leuven: Peeters, 2009, 461–2.
Vivian, Tim (ed.). *Witness to Holiness: Abba Daniel of Scetis*. Kalamazoo, MI: Cistercian Publications, 2008.
Von Campenhausen, Hans. *Tradition and Life in The Church; Essays and Lectures in Church History*. Translated by A.V. Littledale. Philadelphia, PA: Fortress Press, 1968.
Vööbus, Arthur. *History of Asceticism in the Syrian Orient: A Contribution to the History of Culture in the Near East*. Vol. I. Louvain: Secrétariat du Corpus. Corpus Scriptorum Christianorum Orientalium, 1958.
_____. *History of Asceticism in the Syrian Orient: A Contribution to the History of Culture in the Near East*. Vol. II. Louvain: Secrétariat du Corpus. Corpus Scriptorum Christianorum Orientalium, 1960.
Walsh, Efthalia Makris. "The Ascetic Mother Mary of Egypt," *Greek Orthodox Theological Review* 34, No. 1 (1989): 59–69.
Ware, Kallistos. "The Way of the Ascetics: Negative or Affirmative?" in *Asceticism*. Edited by Vincent L. Wimbush. Oxford University Press, 1995.
Weber, Max. *The Sociology of Religion*. Translated by Ephraim Fischoff. Boston, MA: Beacon Press, 1963.
Weintraub, Arlene. *Selling the Fountain of Youth: How the Anti-Aging Industry Made a Disease Out of Getting Old-And Made Billions*. New York: Basic Books, 2010.
Whitby. Michael. "Greek Historical Writing After Procopius: Variety and Vitality." *The Byzantine and Early Islamic Near East: Problems in the Literary Source Materials*. Studies in Late Antiquity and Early Islam, No. 1. Edited by Averil Cameron, Lawrence I. Conrad and John Haldon. Princeton, NJ: Darwin Press, 1992, 25–80.
Whittow, Mark. *The Making of Byzantium, 600–1025*. Berkeley, CA: University of California Press, 1996.
Wilson, Stephen. "Introduction," in *Saints and Their Cults: Studies in Religious Sociology, Folklore and History*. Edited by Stephen Wilson. Cambridge University Press, 1983.
Wood, Philip. '*We have no king but Christ': Christian Political Thought in Greater Syria on the Eve of the Arab Conquest*. Oxford University Press, 2010.
Wortley, John. *Spiritually Beneficial Tales of Paul, Bishop of Monembasia*. Kalamazoo, MI: Cistercian Publications, 1996.
_____. "Grazers (ΒΟΣΚΟΙ) in the Judaean Desert." *The Sabaite Heritage In the Orthodox Church from the Fifth Century to the Present*. Edited by Joseph Patrich. Leuven: Peeters, 2001, 37–48.
_____. "Death, Judgment, Heaven, and Hell in Byzantine 'Beneficial Tales.'" *Dumbarton Oaks Papers* 55 Byzantine Eschatology: Views on Death and the Last Things, 8th to 15th Centuries (2001): 53–69.

_____. "Getting Sick and Getting Cured in Late Antiquity." *Washington Academy of Sciences* 90–93 (2004): 91–107.

_____. "The Origins of Christian Veneration of Body Parts." *Revue de l'histoire des religions* 1 (2006): 5–28.

_____. "What the Desert Fathers meant by 'being saved.'" *Zeitschrift für Antikes Christentum* 12, No. 2 (2008): 322–43.

_____. "The Genre of the Spiritually Beneficial Tale." *Scripta & Escripta* 8–9 (2010): 565.

Zias, Joseph. "Was Byzantine Herodium a Leprosarium?" *Biblical Archaeologist* 49, No. 3 (1986): 182–6.

Index

This index covers the main body of text including the Introduction and Conclusion. Greek terms have been transliterated into Latin script and are accompanied by a loose translation, shown in parenthesis. Where there is a difference, American English spellings have been used throughout the index—e.g. edema instead of oedema, humor instead of humour. Where filing positions differ greatly, cross references are used.

abbas *see* elders
Alexandria 3, 52, 78, 132
alms
    indication of social status 63–4
    instrument of forgiveness 63, 68–9
    reflection of God's character 65–6
    sacrifice 64–5
almsgiving 50–52, 62–4, 139
    clothing 54–5
    and punishment 66
    redemptive 63, 68–9
anachōrēsis (withdrawal) 23
anchorites 25–7, 33
Antioch 3, 6, 8, 54, 130
Antony the Great
    as combative subject 117
    on death 105
    on leadership 111
    transformation in death 115
    on wandering 21
    see also Vita of St Antony
apocalyptic theology 134–6
Apophthegmata Patrum 62
Aristotle, on giving 62
ascetic life
    illness as activity within 71, 80–82, 99
    improvement by secular figures 41–2
    solitude 100, 124
    tension within 43–4
    withdrawal 23, 25–7
ascetic practice 32–3
    close to the ground 25, 29, 34–5
    lay participation 38–9
    leading to illness 82–3
asceticism
    autonomy 21–3, 30–31, 34, 116–17, 119–20
    definitions 23–4
    post-mortem tension with monastic community 119–20, 122, 124
    proving 22, 27–8, 29, 30–31, 34
    and travel 21
ascetics
    anonymity in death 122–3
    autonomy 21–3, 30–31, 34, 116–17
    care of others 99–100
    pious withdrawal 30–31
    practices 32–3
    relationships with secular figures 23–4, 41–2
    subversive relationships 27–8
Athanasius
    on anonymity in death 123
    on Antony the Great 81, 105, 115
    on incarnation 48
autonomy 21–3, 30–31, 34, 116–17, 119–20, 141–2

Basil of Caesarea 49, 67, 139
    on divine gift of medicine 79–80, 81–2
    medical knowledge 78
    on renunciation 57
    on starvation 79
Bauckham, Richard, on fish tales 50–51

Baun, Jane, on apocryphal texts 134
Baynes, Norman H, on *Spiritual Meadow* 12–13
beneficial tales 10–12, 72
    on almsgiving 65–6, 68
    on anonymity in death 122–3
    on autonomy in ascetic life 122
    brevity 32, 88, 108, 116
    on burial 114
    on charitable acts 50–52
    of combative corpses 132–3
    of comical corpses 134–5
    compared to hagiography 12, 36
    on compassion 58
    on death 106–7, 110–11, 112–13, 114
    dichotomous 24–5, 31–2
    on discernment 95–6
    of displeased dead 128–9, 130
    of dutiful dead 126–7
    on enduring illness 98–9
    on healing 88–9
    of holy relics 120–21
    humorous 135–6
    on illness 83
    on illness asceticism 80
    on infertility 91
    on lay-monastic boundaries 37–8
    on lending to God 52
    on obedience 37–8, 95–6, 126–7
    on plague 87
    on power over the dead 119–20
    on predetermination 112
    proving ascetic programs 27, 33
    on sacraments 112–13, 114
    on sexual temptation 27, 101–2
    on virtuous conduct 28–9
    on women 28–9, 30–31, 88–9, 93–4
blood poisoning 95–7, 98
Blum, Richard and Eva Maria, on inevitability of death 115
bodily resurrection 126
Booth, Philip, on Moschos' death 4
Brändle, Rudolph, on Chrysostom 49
breast cancers 88–9, 94
Brown, Peter
    on lay-monastic relationships 35
    on privatization of the holy 121
bubonic plague 86–7

burial
    importance of location 118–19
    tales on 114
Byzantine era
    attitudes to death 105–6, 107
    economic issues 45–7
    literature 9–10
    political and military upheaval 5–8
    practice of medicine 71–2, 84
    theological dissention 8–9

Cameron, Averil, on theology texts as historical sources 14
Caner, Daniel, on wealth 47
Cassian, Jean, on religious travel 20
Castelli, Elizabeth, on fertility rates 92–3
Cerastes cerastes (type of venomous snake) 96
Chalcedonian Christians 3, 8–9
Charanis, Peter, on monastic life 43
charitable acts, tales on 50–52
charity 49–52, 139–40
    repentance 58–9
    see also giving
Christ manifest in the poor 52–5
Christian healing 75–7
Christian philanthropy 52–3
    poor to poor 58–9, 139–40
"Christus medicus" 76, 82
Chrysostom, John 49, 139
    on Christ manifest in the poor 55
    on market activity 51–2
    on outcasts in society 79
    on renunciation 57
    on showing mercy 58
Cicero, on liberality 63
Clark, Elizabeth, on theology texts as historical sources 14
Climacus, John, Saint, on predetermination 107
combative subject 117–18, 122, 131–3
compassion 63, 78, 79
    tales on 58
Constantinople 4, 8, 101
Constas, Nicholas, on post-mortem relationship of soul to body 126, 131, 143

Conybeare, Frederick, on theology texts as historical sources 14
corpses, tales of
    combative 131–3
    comical 134–6
    displeased 128–9, 130
    dutiful 126–7
Crislip, Andrew
    on diagnosis 90
    on illness asceticism 81, 141
cures 87–8
    see also doctors; healing; illness

death 143–4
    acquisition of corpses 124
    anonymity of ascetic 122–3
    Byzantine attitudes to 105–6, 107
    consequences of life actions 135
    continued relationship after 128–9
    dignity 133
    preceding rituals 126
    re-integration into community 120–21
    relationship to living 124–5
    remembrance of 130–31
    resistance to 114–15
    tales on 106–7, 110–11, 112–13, 114
Delehaye, H., on beneficial tales 11
Déroche, Vincent
    on economic issues 46
    on "l'économie miraculeuse" 51
Diadocus of Photike, on trust in doctors 82
diagnosis methods 90
dichotomies in tales
    city and desert 31
    good and evil 31
    withdrawal and inhabited world 24–5, 31–2
dietary practices, ascetics 32
Dietz, Maribel, on religious travel 20
dignity in death 133
Dionysius, on predetermination 110
discernment 40–41, 43, 90–91, 96–7, 143
    tales on 95–6
disciples 37, 39
disease
    deterrent of sin 102
    effect on religious behaviour 86
    see also doctors; healing; illness

divine economy 45, 140
    medicine as 71–2, 79–80, 82
    participation in 96
doctors 82–3, 84–5, 143
domestic pressures on women 93–4
Dorotheos of Gaza, on remembrance of death 130–31
Douglas, Mary, on jokes 135
dropsy 98–9, 100

economics and religious life 45–6, 47–9, 50–52
"l'économie miraculeuse" 51–2
Edelstein, Ludwig, on autonomy of patients 141–2
edema 98–9, 100
elders 39
    secular figures 37, 41–4
    women as 138
Elijah, Abba
    proving ascetic program 29, 33–4
    tale of 27–8
endurance of illness 97, 141–2
    soul's salvation 100–101, 103
    tales on 98–9
eschatological theology 125
eschatology 127
Evagrios, philosopher 116
    tale of 52–4
Evagrius Scholasticus, on displeased dead 130

female grazer, tale of 28–9, 30–31
Ferngren, Gary B., on ancient medicine 85
fertility 91–3
fevers 102
fish, wealth appearing in 50–51
Follieri, Enrica, on Moschos' death 4
forgiveness, through almsgiving 63, 68–9
Foucault, Michel
    on dutiful dead 127
    on power over the dead 120
free will, determining salvation 108–10

Galen, on poisons 95
Garrison, Roman, on redemptive almsgiving 63, 68–9

giving 47, 61–2, 139
   and social status 63–4
   see also charity
Gleason, Maud 27
   on monastic gossip 43
gospels 48–9, 56, 74
   on death 105
   on healing 75
grave-robbing 132–3
grazers 25–7, 112–13
   autonomy 34
   female 28–9, 30–31
greed 66–7, 138
Gregory Nazianzus
   on compassion 79
   medical knowledge 78
Gregory of Antioch, on liberality 62
Gregory of Nyssa 47, 48–9, 139
   on illness 79
gyrovagues 20

hagiography 23, 46, 51
   on ascetic healing 83
   compared to beneficial tales 12, 36
   cult following promoted in 83
   lack of humor 135
   study of medicine 72
   women in 14, 31
Halkin, F., on beneficial tales 11
healing 40–41, 140
   of body and soul 76–7, 90–91, 141
   compassion in 78, 79
   curing or enduring 74–5, 87–8, 97–8
   in the gospels 74–6
   Hellenistic philosophies 77–8
   tales on 88–9
   theology of 73–5
   see also doctors; illness
health, indicator of right theology 81
Hellenistic philosophies
   on eschatology 125
   on healing 77–8
Herrin, Judith, on xeniteia 3
Hirschfeld, Yizhar, on *Spiritual Meadow* 13
Holman, Susan R., on poverty 46–7
holy relics, tales of 120–21
honor 60–62

Horden, Peregrine, on endurance of illness 142
hospitals 84
humility 111, 112–13
humor in beneficial tales 135–6

illness
   beneficial tales on 83
   endurance 97, 100–101, 103, 141–2
   equated with holiness 87–8
   treatment 71
   see also doctors; healing
illness asceticism 71, 80–82, 99, 141
incarnational theology, influence on economic issues 47–9
infertility 94
   tales on 91
integrative subject 118

James of Cyrrhestica, anchorite, tale of 80
Jerome, on religious travel 20
Jesus, healing ministry 74–5, 75–6
John 9:1-41 74
John of Damascus, on predetermination 109, 113

Kaegi, Walter, on Moschos' death 4
Krueger, Derek 33
   on authors of asceticism texts 22
   on humor in Christian literature 135
   on Moschos/Sophronios relationship 2

Laiou, Angeliki E.
   on church economic practice 53
   on economic issues 46
laity, partaking in monastic life-style 137–8
lay-monastic action 127–8
lay-monastic boundaries 36–7
lay-monastic relationships 31, 40–44, 137–8
leadership positions 110–11
lending to God 50–51
   tales on 52
Leontios, Abba, tale of 65–6
leprosy 101, 102
liberality 62–3
Life of St Theodore of Sykeon (Georgios, ho Eleusios) 85–6

Louth, Andrew
  on Dionysius 110
  on Moschos' death 4

Macarius the Egyptian, on divine healing 99
magical practices in medicine 97
Magoulian, Harry J., on agrarian life 46
Mary of Egypt 28, 30
Matthew 19:24-25 56
Matthew 25:31-46 48–9
medical language, use in religious literature 77–9
medical management 80
  religious reasoning 71–2
medicine
  magical practices 97
  as part of divine economy 79–80, 82
  practice in Byzantine era 71–2, 84
  see also doctors; healing; illness
Miller, Cox, on authors of asceticism texts 22
monastic community, post-mortem tension with solitary 124
monastic life, autonomy 116–17
monastic movement 19–21
monastic-lay action 127–8
monastic-lay boundaries 36–7
monastic-lay relationships 39, 40–44, 137–8
Monks, George R., on economic issues 46
Monteserrat, Dominic, on healing shrines 143
Moschos, John
  ascetic wanderings 3–4
  asceticism practices 2–3
  biographical detail 1–2
  death, scholarly comment 4–5
  relationship with Sophronios 2
  theology 9
mourners 26

Nicholas, Abba, tale of 37
nudity, in ascetics 32–3

obedience 39, 127
  tales on 37–8, 95–6, 126
oedema *see* edema

oikoumenê (inhabited world) 24
ophthalmia 132, 133
Origen
  on divine healing 99
  on predetermination 109

pain free treatment 89–90
Palladius
  on endurance of illness 100
  on religious travel 20
Palmer, J.S., on *Spiritual Meadow* 13
pandemics 86–7
Paradise 57–8
paternity 91
Patlagean, Évelyne, on economic issues 46
Pattendon, Philip, on *Spiritual Meadow* 13–15
Perkins, Judith, on endurance of illness 142
philanthropy 52–3, 58, 139–40
Photios, Patriarch, medical knowledge 78
Piff, Paul K., on charity amongst poor 139–40
Pilch, John J., on Jesus' healing ministry 74
Plato, on giving 62–3
Pliny the Younger, on liberality 63
Poemon, Abba, tale of 33
poison, treatment of 95–7
Porterfield, Amanda, on spiritual healing 77
poverty 138–40
  in Byzantine era 47
prayer 42–3
predetermination
  as literary device 108
  resistance to 114–15
  tales on 112
  theology of 107–8
proof of ascetic life 28–30
  in relationships 22–4
  telling own tale 34
  use of witnesses 27, 31
providence 39, 109, 110, 112

Rapp, Claudia, on authors of asceticism texts 21–2
reconciliation 113
redemptive almsgiving 63, 68–9

Regulae brevius tractatae (Basil) 65, 67
religious life
    economics and 45–6, 47–9, 50–52
    influence of disease 86
religious travel 19–21
remnouth 20
renunciation
    physical risk 57–8
    practice of 55–7
    sexual activity 27–8, 40–43
repentance and charity 58–9
resurrection of the body 126
Rome 1, 3, 4, 6
Rousseau, Philip, on lay-monastic relationships 35

sacraments, tales on 112–13, 114
salvation
    determined by free will 108–10
    physical risk 57–8
    through poverty 58–60
    through renunciation 55–7
    through wealth 61–2
sarabaites 20
Schonborn, Christoph von, on Moschos' death 4
secular figures
    as elders 37, 41–4
    relationships with ascetics 23–4, 41–2
septicemia 95–7, 98
sexual activity
    consequences 42–3
    renunciation 27–8, 40–43
    temptation 27, 101–3
sight 133
Sisinios, Abba, tale of 58
snake bite 95–7
snakes 95–6
social agency 34–5
social care 52–3, 58–9
    in early church 54–5
social relations, ascetics and secular figures 23–4, 41–2
solitude in ascetic life 100, 116–17, 124
Sophronios, of Jerusalem
    ascetic wanderings 3–4
    itinerant life 20–21
    literary grazer 35
    relationship with Moschos 2
soul
    healing of 97
    salvation through endurance 100–101, 103
spiritual healing 76–7, 90–91, 141
Spiritual Meadow, The 10
    benefit to religious scholarship 12–13
    manuscript tradition 14–15
    social history source 13–14, 16–17
    tales (*see* beneficial tales)
Stark, Rodney, on fertility rates 92
stylite 33

temptation 97, 101–3
Theodore, "non-monastic" monastic, tale of 37–9
Theodoret of Cyrrhus, tale of 80
theology, right and health 81
"threshold monasticism" 38–9

Vailhe, on Moschos' death 4
Valantasis, Richard
    on ascetic relations 124
    on ascetic typologies 117–18
    on asceticism 23–4, 31–2
virtuous conduct, tales on 28–9
Vita of St Antony 38, 81
    see also Antony the Great
voskoi (grazers) 25–7
    see also grazers

Ware, Kallistos, on anachōrēsis 23
wealth 47, 138
    redistribution through alms 68
    retention vs distribution 66–7
    salvation 61–2
wilderness living 19–20, 25–7, 29, 30–32
women
    domestic pressures 93–4
    elders 138
    grazers 28–9, 30–31
    in hagiography 14
    independence 103
    lack of voice 89–90, 140–41, 143
Wortley, John
    on beneficial tales 12, 26–7

on Byzantine theology of death 106
on humility 111
on illness asceticism 83
on lay-monastic relationships 35
on monastic movement 19–20
on Moschos' death 4

on salvation 43
on *Spiritual Meadow* 13–14

xeniteia 2–3

Zeno, Emperor, tale of 68

Printed in Great Britain
by Amazon